THE
COMPLETE
BOOK OF
MIXED
DRINKS

ALSO BY ANTHONY DIAS BLUE

American Wine

Thanksgiving Dinner (WITH KATHRYN K. BLUE)

Buyer's Guide to American Wines

ANTHONY DIAS BLUE

THE
COMPLETE
BOOK OF
MIXED
DRINKS

More Than 1,000 Alcoholic and
Nonalcoholic Cocktails

Harper Perennial
A Division of HarperCollins*Publishers*

Much of the text of this book has appeared in *Bon Appétit* magazine in slightly different form.

HarperCollins books may be purchased for educational, business, or sales promotional use. For information please write: Special Markets Department, HarperCollins Publishers, Inc., 10 East 53rd Street, New York, NY 10022.

Designed by Dorothy S. Baker
Line drawings of glasses by Jennifer Harper
Line drawings by Frank Ronan

Library of Congress Cataloging-in-Publication Data
Dias Blue, Anthony.
    The complete book of mixed drinks : More than 1,000 alcoholic and nonalcoholic cocktails / Anthony Dias Blue. — 1st ed.
      p.   cm.
    Includes index.
    ISBN 0-06-095007-2
    1. Cocktails.   I. Title.
TX951.D48   1993
641.8′74—dc20   92-54840

97 CC/HC 10 9 8 7 6 5

To the spirit of conviviality and friendship

Contents

Acknowledgments

Writing this book has been enlightening, entertaining, and delicious. It was, however, much more work than I anticipated when my editor, Susan Friedland, suggested the project. (It also took a little more time than Susan expected.)

I never could have done it without the help of four bright, talented and devoted young women—Sally Horchow, Elizabeth Weinreb, Lindsay Moran, and Lisa Giannini. They have each left an indelible mark on the manuscript.

This book would have been impossible without the support of *Bon Appétit* magazine. Editor-in-chief Bill Garry was kind enough to allow us to use several of my articles from the magazine for the book. I am grateful to Bill as well as to Barbara Fairchild and the entire *Bon Appétit* staff.

Thanks also to my staff, especially Jack Weiner and Carol Siebert, who covered for me when I was busy shaking and stirring; and to my wife, Kathy, and my children, Caitlin, Toby, Jessica, and Amanda, whose patience is legendary.

Introduction: The Return of the Cocktail

Americans are fickle. We have evolved from cocktails to beer to white wine to bottled water and back to cocktails in a very short time. Or maybe it's just that there are so many people in this country that every interest, no matter how obtuse, seems like a trend.

Anyway, the interest in mixed drinks is greater now than it has been in years. The martini is back and a new generation has discovered the soothing medicinal qualities of a social drink or two at the end of the day. As a result, there are a slew of new cocktails with names that would make your Aunt Millie blush.

There are also a whole bunch of new ingredients that weren't available to our forefathers as they took the first halting steps toward stocking their bars. They never had the benefit of peppermint schnapps or Irish cream to make their cocktails.

The world of mixed drinks has taken on a texture and a complexity that were missing in the Roaring Twenties or the bland fifties. Today's cocktails are lively, inventive, exciting, and delicious. But first, a little history.

The national taste in drink was fixed on rum during the nation's early days. But after the abolition of the slave trade in 1808, rum was harder to get and the whiskey being made in Kentucky became more attractive to the populace. In a complete reversal of tastes, the American drink of choice became good country bourbon with a splash of "branch water."

Then, with the advent of Prohibition, the cocktail jumped to the forefront. The reason for this was quite simple: Most of the illegal liquor available at that time was undrinkable on its own. Much of what was obtainable was rough, raw, and homemade. To render these beastly spirits palatable, it was necessary to bury them with juices, syrups, and other flavorings.

The "noble experiment" ended in 1933, but even after decent, commercially prepared liquor was once again available, Americans maintained their fondness for cocktails. In the 1930s and 1940s, at all the best places, the cocktail was king. Every bartender worth his swizzle stick could speedily create a sidecar, a Rob Roy, or a gin fizz without ever looking at a recipe book. And, above all others, martinis and manhattans held sway.

Things changed drastically at the end of the 1960s. The trend toward healthiness and lightness brought a dramatic transformation to the bar business. Suddenly, two-fisted whiskey drinkers were bellying up to the bar and ordering "White wine, please" or, even more surprising, "Perrier and lime." Bartenders spent most of their time pouring Chardonnay, while the old cocktail mixing tools gathered dust.

The 1970s and most of the 1980s were dreary times for the cocktail. Most active bars offered a "wine by the glass" program, and cocktails were ordered rarely, usually by people who remembered the 1920s.

But tastes are cyclical and they were not about to lock in at this extreme. The pendulum has begun to swing again. Wine and Perrier are still popular, but among younger people the cocktail is making a strong comeback.

However the cocktail is not staging its comeback in the same fashion everywhere in the country. Margaritas are hot in some places, martinis in others. In some upscale bars, champagne-based drinks are all the rage, whereas, in other, more casual places, shooters may be the rule. Everywhere you look there are trends, and they all seem to be sending different messages.

One small but significant trend is the growth of serious nonalcoholic cocktails. Although it probably began as a way for the designated driver to join in the fun without having to drink a milkshake, this category has taken on a life of its own. Many bars and restaurants now offer their own list of nonalcoholic cocktails for designated drivers, teetotalers, or people who are just taking a night off.

The modern world of mixed drinks is a very different place than it has ever been before. The purpose of this book is to bring you up to date and—even more important—enhance your enjoyment. Cheers!

STOCKING THE BAR

Like cooking, mixing drinks requires a full complement of good equipment. It's difficult to make a beurre blanc on a hot plate, and making a pineapple daiquiri is virtually impossible without a blender. The best ingredients and the right equipment are necessary to get the full benefits of this book.

Throughout the book, I have tried to use generic ingredient names, not brand names. There are too many good choices available within each category to recommend specific brands. I must point out, however, that cut-rate bargain brands are usually no bargain. Quality ingredients are essential to most of the recipes in this book.

About the Bar

BASIC EQUIPMENT

The following devices are part of the complete bar. Except for the blender, these are all simple and inexpensive tools.

BLENDER   A powerful, heavy-duty blender is needed to grind the ice for frozen drinks. The basic kitchen blender may not be strong enough to do the job. Look for the powerful stainless steel commercial versions.

BOTTLE OPENER   A standard lever-type of bottle opener is essential, the simpler the better.

CAN OPENER   A "church key," or standard kitchen opener, is best for opening juice cans.

CHAMPAGNE STOPPER   A good champagne stopper will preserve the carbonation in champagne and sparkling wine for at least 24 hours. The best type has a spring mechanism and two metal pieces that hook under the lip of a typical champagne bottle.

CORKSCREW   The classic wine opener is the waiter's corkscrew, a basic lever. There are many versions of this simple tool and they vary widely in quality. My favorite corkscrew is the Screwpull, a remarkably well designed device full of space-age technology. If you have to open large numbers of bottles, the best corkscrew is the Leverpull, made by the same company. Many California wine folk use the Ah-So, the opener with the two prongs. This device can push the cork into the wine if you're not careful, but its best feature is the fact that it doesn't puncture the cork. This is quite helpful to people who want to recork wine bottles for future use. My least favorite opener is the wing-type, mainly because the corkscrew is usually too tightly wound. All the best corkscrews have an open spiral with a channel down the middle.

GLASS PITCHER   A glass pitcher is always handy, as it is a very attractive way to serve drinks for more than two guests. It is also useful for pouring water and juices.

ICE BUCKET   The ice bucket is the most practical and attractive way to keep ice at your bar. Use tongs to dispense the ice.

JIGGER   A jigger provides ounce measurements and is absolutely essential. The best jigger is the double-headed, stainless steel variety that marks 1-ounce and 1½-ounce measurements.

MEASURING CUP   A small Pyrex glass 1-cup measure is perfect for recipes that call for amounts greater than 2 ounces.

MEASURING SPOONS   A standard kitchen set works perfectly.

MIXING GLASS   Any tall 16-ounce glass will work.

MIXING SPOON   A long stainless steel spoon with a thin twisted handle that is used for mixing, stirring, and occasionally muddling. Sometimes a glass stirrer is used.

MUDDLER   This term refers to squeezing the juice from herbs or fruit and blending it with dry ingredients. A mortar and pestle is usually used for muddling, but you can also use a mixing spoon.

PARING KNIFE A paring knife is needed for cutting fruit wedges and twists. It will also help to make your garnishes attractive.

SHAKER There are two popular types of shakers: the Boston and the standard. The Boston shaker has two pieces, a glass receptacle and a stainless steel container of comparable but slightly larger size. When shaking, the glass is capped by the metal top and the liquid is transferred back and forth from one receptable to the other.

The standard shaker has three pieces: a stainless steel strainer, a lid, and a receptacle. The top often has a small capped spout.

Shakers are used to combine ingredients that need more homogenizing than stirring can provide. Carbonated beverages are never put in a shaker; they lose their bubbles.

STRAINER The Hawthorn strainer is usually used. It has an attached spring that holds it in the top of a standard mixing glass or shaker.

Also necessary are these assorted accessories: cocktail napkins, straws, coasters, and toothpicks.

GLASSWARE

ALL-PURPOSE BALLOON GLASS A popular 10- to 14-ounce stemmed glass with a large bowl. It is often used when a recipe calls for a large wineglass. It is used for margaritas and other stylish cocktails.

COCKTAIL GLASS A stemmed glass, with sloping sides and a wide mouth that will hold 3 to 6 ounces.

COLLINS GLASS A straight-sided glass that is similar to the highball, but the collins will hold 10 to 14 ounces.

DELMONICO GLASS Another name for the sour glass.

FLUTE A tall, graceful, stemmed glass used for champagne and sparkling wine.

HIGHBALL GLASS An 8- to 10-ounce glass with straight sides. Highballs, fizzes, eggnogs, and swizzles are often served in this glass.

HURRICANE GLASS A tall glass shaped like a hurricane lamp with a pinched-in center. Usually used for tropical drinks.

IRISH COFFEE

HURRICANE

HIGHBALL

COLLINS

POUSSE-CAFÉ

OLD-FASHIONED

SHOT

PARFAIT

PILSNER

IRISH COFFEE GLASS   A short-stemmed glass that widens at the top and often has a handle.

LARGE WINEGLASS   See definition for all-purpose balloon glass.

MARGARITA GLASS   See definition for all-purpose balloon glass.

OLD-FASHIONED GLASS   A short, squat, straight-sided glass that will hold from 8 to 10 ounces. A double old-fashioned glass will hold 14 to 16 ounces.

PARFAIT GLASS   A tall glass with a pinched center. Similar to a hurricane glass but smaller. Often used for drinks containing fruit or ice cream, it holds 7½ ounces.

PILSNER GLASS   A tall, slope-sided beer glass that can hold 10 to 12 ounces.

COCKTAIL

CHAMPAGNE

CORDIAL

BRANDY

BEER

WHISKEY

SHERRY

RED WINE

WHITE WINE

TULIP
CHAMPAGNE

PONY GLASS   A stemmed glass that will hold up to 2 ounces. Liqueurs and brandies are often served in the pony glass.

SHOT GLASS   A shot glass can come in all shapes and sizes, but it doesn't hold more than 2 ounces.

SOUR GLASS   A stemmed, short, flute-style glass that is used to serve all types of sours. It holds 5 to 6 ounces.

SNIFTER   A short-stemmed glass with a large bowl used to serve brandy, Cognac, and liqueurs. The larger the bowl the better, as it is easier to sniff the spirit's aroma.

TULIP GLASS   A tall-stemmed glass that widens at the top to make a tulip shape. It is used to serve champagne and sparkling wine.

UP GLASS   Also known as a cocktail glass or martini glass.

Directions/Definitions

ALEMBIC POT STILLS   The stills used in the distillation of Cognac. Made of copper, the stills are impervious to most acids and are good conductors of heat. Experiments with steel and glass stills have proved only that copper is the best material. Alembic stills process the distillate one lot at a time; column stills, used in big commercial distilleries, are continuous.

BLEND   Blending requires a powerful electric blender in order to purée ice and other solid ingredients to a smooth consistency. Do not blend for more than 4 to 5 minutes.

CHAI   An aging warehouse used to store barrels of wine or Cognac. This term is most prevalent in Bordeaux.

CHILL   The best way to chill glasses is in a refrigerator for about 30 minutes, or in a freezer for 10 minutes. If you don't have access to either, place ice cubes in the glass while preparing the drink in a shaker. When you are finished mixing, the glass will be chilled. Pour out the ice cubes before adding the fresh mixture.

CRUSHED ICE   Also called "cracked" ice, these are ice cubes that have been pulverized with a mallet or other heavy object. In the book I have used "scoop" as a unit of measure. This corresponds to 6 ounces of well-packed crushed ice.

FLOAT   The last direction in a recipe may call for a float of rum or other spirit. Follow this direction by slowly pouring the liquid over the back of a spoon so that the liquid floats on top of the drink in a layer. Do not stir before serving.

FUSEL OILS   The high-proof alcohols that are a by-product of the distillation process. These oils are found in all spirits, but too much of them can cause hangovers.

MIX   Mixing thoroughly combines ingredients and is usually done in a mixing glass. The purpose is to chill the alcohols quickly without diluting them. Mix with a glass stirring rod or bar spoon and several ice cubes.

MUDDLE   Muddling requires the use of a mortar and pestle or a mixing spoon to grind fresh herbs or fruit with sugar.

POMACE   The remnants of the winemaking process. This includes pits, stems, leaves, and skins.

SHAKE   First combine the ingredients and ice in a shaker. Then shake the canister vigorously to chill the mixture quickly without diluting it.

SIMPLE SYRUP OR SUGAR SYRUP   Stir 4 ounces of sugar and 4 ounces of water together in a small pan. Bring to a boil and simmer for 3 to 5 minutes, until the mixture becomes a pale yellow syrup. Cool. (Makes enough for several drinks. This recipe may be increased to any size that can be comfortably accommodated in a saucepan. It will keep for several months tightly capped in the refrigerator.)

STRAIN   A Hawthorn strainer will fit over either a mixing glass or shaker. The purpose is to separate ice and other solids from the mixture before serving.

Drink Terminology

APÉRITIF   A drink traditionally served before a meal to whet the appetite. It is usually a flavored bitters or vermouth.

CHASER   A mixer, beer, or nonalcoholic drink that is swallowed soon after a straight shot of whiskey, bourbon, tequila, or other spirit.

COBBLER   A tall drink usually served in a collins glass filled with crushed ice and garnished with fresh fruit and mint sprigs. The original cobbler was made of sherry, pineapple syrup, and fresh fruit garnishes.

COLLINS   A tall drink of ice, sugar, citrus juice, and a spirit, topped off with club soda or ice water. The famous Tom Collins is made with gin.

COOLER   The cooler is a tall iced drink served in a collins glass. The basic formula includes a wine or spirit, a carbonated beverage, and a citrus rind for garnish. The citrus garnish is usually one continuous spiral that hooks over the rim of the glass.

CRUSTA   A drink served in a wineglass or a short glass, with the optional sugar-coated rim. The inside of the glass is lined with a strip of citrus rind. The recipe usually includes brandy, maraschino liqueur, bitters, lemon juice, and crushed ice.

DAISY   The daisy is an oversize cocktail, usually with more alcohol than a normal cocktail. Made with rum or gin, the daisy is often sweetened with a fruit syrup and served over crushed ice. The margarita is an example of a daisy.

EGGNOG   A traditional Christmas holiday punch that is served cold in tall glasses or in punch cups with grated nutmeg on top. It is a creamy concoction made with sugar, milk, egg yolks, and brandy, rum, or bourbon.

FALERNUM SYRUP   A sweet syrup made in Barbados for the Sazerac Company of New Orleans, it consists of mixed fruits, spices, sugar cane, and a little bit of alcohol. It is used frequently in tropical drinks. If you can't find Falernum, simple syrup (page 7) is an acceptable substitute.

FIX   A small cobbler, sour-type drink made with sugar, lemon juice, alcohol, and crushed ice. It also can be made with pineapple syrup.

FIZZ   A drink traditionally served in the late morning. The basic recipe includes sugar, citrus juice, club soda or sparkling wine, and traditionally, gin. The name comes from the fizz of bubbles created when the drink was topped off with soda from the old siphon bottles. Famous fizzes include the gin fizz, the Ramos gin fizz, and the sloe gin fizz.

FLIP   Originally, flips were served hot by plunging a red-hot flip iron into the drink. Now they are served as a cold, creamy drink made with eggs, sugar, alcohol, and citrus juice.

GROG   Originally, grog was a mixture of rum and water issued to sailors of the Royal Navy (see page 51). Now a grog is any rum-based drink made with fruit and sugar.

JULEP   The julep is made of bourbon, sugar, and mint leaves. It originated in Kentucky and is usually made with Kentucky bourbon.

KÜMMEL   A liqueur made from several herbs, with caraway seeds predominant. Records show that the first caraway liqueurs were made in Amsterdam in 1575.

LEMON WHEEL   A thinly sliced piece of lemon cut from the wide part of the lemon.

MIST   Any drink when the spirit is poured into a glass over crushed ice.

NEAT   The term for serving a spirit straight, without mixers or ice.

ON-THE-ROCKS   Poured over ice cubes.

ORGEAT   An almond-flavored sweet syrup.

PUFF   A traditional afternoon drink of equal parts spirit and milk, topped off with club soda. Served over ice.

PUNCH   A drink mixture prepared in large quantities. Originally a blend of five ingredients including fruit juice, now the mixture can include any combination of spirits, sweeteners, juices, wine, flavorings, and fruit garnishes.

SHOOTER   A mixed drink, served straight up in a shot glass, to be swallowed in one gulp. The shooter is different from neat because it calls for mixers.

SLING   A tall drink made with lemon juice, sugar, and spirits, topped off with club soda.

SMASH   A short julep, served in an old-fashioned glass.

SOUR   Usually served in a sour glass or an old-fashioned glass, a sour is made of lime or lemon juice, sugar, and spirits.

SWIZZLE   Originally, the swizzle was a tall rum drink made with crushed ice and stirred with long twigs until the glass was frosty. Today, any tall drink made with a spirit and crushed ice can be called a "swizzle" if it is stirred with a glass rod until frosty.

TODDY   The toddy was originally a hot drink. It was a mixture of sweetener, spirit, spices, and hot water. Now a toddy may be served cold, and is distinguished from a sling by using plain water instead of club soda.

TONIC   A tall drink with ice, spirit, and tonic water.

Mixology Tips

• Try to chill all ingredients before using.

• Don't overfill shakers and mixers. Mix drinks in half portions to avoid this.

• Never chill the glass and mix the drink with the same ice.

• Always shake vigorously.

• If you live in an area where the water is too hard or unpleasant tasting, make ice with bottled water.

• Be organized. Assemble all ingredients before beginning to mix a drink.

• Don't make cocktails in advance; serve them as soon as they are prepared.

• Use quality ingredients as well as fresh fruit and herbs whenever possible.

• Most servings are for one, unless otherwise noted. The recipes can be doubled or tripled for more people, but it is best to start from scratch each time.

• When brandy is called for, any good quality brandy is acceptable including American, Spanish, Italian, or French bottlings. If you want to add extra complexity and depth to brandy drinks, use Cognac or Armagnac.

Warning: In some parts of the United States there have been incidents of salmonella poisoning from eggs. A number of the recipes in this book call for raw eggs to be used. Be very cautious and make sure that you are getting your eggs from a reliable source.

MEASUREMENTS

1 quart	=	32 ounces	=	2 pints	=	4 cups
1 pint	=	16 ounces	=	2 cups		
1 cup	=	8 ounces	=	½ pint		
1 jigger	=	1½ ounces				
1 wineglass	=	6 ounces				
1 teaspoonful	=	⅛ ounce				
1 dash	=	⅙ teaspoon				
1 tablespoon	=	3 teaspoons				
1 tablespoon	=	⅜ ounce	=	½ ounce		
4 tablespoons	=	¼ cup	=	2 ounces		
8 tablespoons	=	½ cup	=	4 ounces		
16 cups	=	4 quarts	=	1 fluid gallon		
1 scoop	=	1 cup				

SPIRIT BOTTLE MEASURES

METRIC (BOTTLE SIZE)	FLUID (OUNCES)	BOTTLES (PER CASE)
50 ml.	1.7	120
200 ml.	6.8	48
500 ml.	16.9	24
750 ml.	25.4	12
1 liter	33.8	12
1.5 liters	50.8	6

BAR-SUPPLY CHECKLIST

MIXERS:

Essential
   Club soda
   Cola
   Cranberry juice
   Ginger ale
   Grenadine syrup
   Lemon juice
   Orange juice
   Pineapple juice
   Rose's lime juice
   Simple sugar syrup
   Tabasco
   Tonic water
   V-8 juice
   Worcestershire sauce

Occasionally called for
   Coconut cream
   Orgeat
   7-UP
   Sweet 'n' sour mix

GARNISHES:

   Black olives
   Cherries
   Cocktail onions
   Fresh lemons
   Fresh limes
   Green olives
   Lemon spirals
   Lemon twists
   Nutmeg
   Orange wedges
   Salt
   Sugar

ALCOHOLIC BEVERAGES:

Essential
   Beer
   Blended whiskey
   Bourbon
   Brandy
   Dry red wine
   Dry sparkling wine
   Dry vermouth
   Dry white wine
   Gin
   Rum, light
   Rum, dark
   Scotch whisky
   Sweet vermouth
   Tequila
   Triple Sec
   Vodka

Occasionally called for
   Campari
   Coffee liqueur
   Irish cream liqueur
   Orange-brandy liqueur
      (Grand Marnier)
   Schnapps, various flavors

Nice to have but not essential
   Amaretto
   Applejack or Calvados
   Aquavit
   Chartreuse
   Crème de cacao
   Crème de menthe
   Grappa
   Jagermeister

Madeira
Mandarin Napoleon
Pernod
Pimm's Cup

Port
Sherry, dry
Sherry, medium
Sherry, cream

CALORIE CHART
(*Calories Per Ounce*)

ALCOHOLIC BEVERAGES:		MIXERS:	
Ale	18	Club soda	0
Beer (imported)	16	Cola	17
Beer (U.S.)	14	Cream (heavy)	106
Bourbon	86	Diet soda	0
Brandy	72	Ginger ale	9
Canadian whiskey	86	Tonic water	9
Gin	75	Lemon juice	8
Irish whiskey	84	Lime juice	8
Liqueurs	75–175	Orange juice	14
Port	40	Pineapple juice	17
Rums	97		
Rye whiskey	92		
Scotch whisky	78		
Sherry	37		
Tequila	95		
Vermouth (dry)	28		
Vermouth (sweet)	42		
Vodka	87		
Wine (dry)	25		
Wine (sweet)	50		

WHITE GOODS

Vodka

The incredible success of vodka in the American market has its roots, surprisingly enough, in the Russian revolution. Before 1917 this clear, fiery spirit was essentially a regional drink, confined to Russia and Poland. It was first produced in the fourteenth century and was originally known as *zhizennia voda* ("water of life.") The name was eventually shortened to "vodka," a diminutive of the word for water. The new name meant, literally, "dear little water."

("Water of life" seems to have been the accepted sobriquet for distilled spirits throughout Europe. In the north countries, "aquavit" was derived from this title; in Ireland, the Celtic word for "water of life" was *uisgebaugh,* which was eventually shortened to "whiskey.")

For one hundred years before the revolution, the Smirnoff family had been Russia's leading distillers. They became extremely wealthy and developed a close relationship with the czar and the rest of the royal household, but the violent upheaval of 1917 changed all that. Only one of Peter Smirnoff's three sons managed to escape Russia. His name was Vladimir and, after fleeing through Turkey and Poland, he eventually settled in Paris where, with the help of other Russian émigrés, he started a small distillery.

Vodka certainly didn't take the world by storm at that point, but it sold steadily in modest quantities in various markets. Soon after Prohibition ended in the United States in 1933, a Smirnoff distillery was established in Connecticut. But until the end of World War II, sales languished at about 6,000 cases a year.

Today, vodka sits perched atop the spirits world with no challenger in sight. U.S. sales in the 1980s have reached beyond the 40 million case mark and show no sign of abating. Seven brands, headed by Smirnoff, account for nearly 50 percent of American vodka sales, but there are an additional 300 brands jostling for position in this lucrative market.

An important sub-market that has developed over the past ten years or so is the imported vodka business. Vodkas from traditional sources such as Russia, Finland, Sweden, Norway, and Poland have been joined by distillates from Holland, Canada, England, and Japan. The import segment of the vodka business is certainly small, but it is getting bigger all the time, growing much faster than the domestic vodka market. Presently, imports account for around 2 million case sales per year.

Many of the vodka imports are distinctively flavored and are less likely to be used in mixed drinks. They are popular with people who drink them straight or on the rocks and treat them with the same respect one might lavish on fine brandy or single-malt Scotch whisky. Incidentally, these excellent products are even smoother and more appealing when they are served directly from the freezer.

Here are the most popular vodka imports, listed by country of origin:

RUSSIA

Vodka making has been going on for more than a thousand years in Russia, where it is most certainly the unofficial national drink. Many people will tell you that Russian vodka is made from potatoes, which just isn't true. Stolichnaya, Russia's finest vodka, is made from wheat (unlike domestic versions that are usually made from corn or rye).

Stolichnaya is made with the soft glacial waters of Lake Ladoga, an icy body of water north of St. Petersburg and close to the Finnish border. Before bottling, the vodka is filtered through both quartz and activated charcoal.

The result of this process is a vodka that has a rich but elegant nose, a slightly thick texture, and clean, soft, gentle flavors.

"Stoli" comes in both 80 proof and 100 proof. It also is sold in three flavored versions, Limonnaya (lemon), Okhotnichya and Pertsovka (pepper), and a special deluxe bottling called Cristall.

Limonnaya is an 80-proof vodka that has a smooth, soft, candied lemon flavor. It is lovely on the rocks and appropriate for mixed drinks that use citrus flavors.

Okhotnichya ("hunter's vodka") is a 90-proof spirit flavored with ginger, tormentil, ash woodroots, cloves, pepper, juniper, coffee beans, anise, white port, sugar, and orange peel, among other things. This liqueur-like drink is spicy and herbal with a strong licorice flavor undertone. It is particularly attractive on the rocks as an after-dinner drink.

Pertsovka is the most popular of the flavored Russian vodkas. It is dark amber and has been infused with red, white, and black peppers. A 70-proof spirit, Pertsovka is aged for some months in wood. The result is a spicy, rich, hot vodka that is excellent on the rocks or as an ingredient in a fiery Bloody Mary.

Cristall is a super-premium vodka, introduced into the U.S. market in 1990. It is a limited production spirit made by a secret process that is based on fine winter wheat. It is elegant and dense with creamy texture and exquisite flavor—surely the Château Lafite of vodkas.

Introduced into the U.S. market in 1989, Tarkhuna is a Russian spirit that has been flavored with tarkhuna grass, a fragrant herb that grows wild in the Soviet Georgian countryside. The spirit (it can't be called vodka on its label because Stolichnaya has the exclusive right to use that word on a spirit imported from Russia) is light green in color, gentle and herbal, with a flavor that is quite reminiscent of tarragon.

POLAND

The Polish are insistent that their country, not mother Russia, was the birthplace of vodka. There is evidence to corroborate the claims of both nations. In any case, there is a long history of vodka production in Poland.

Wodka Wyborowa, a vodka made from rye, has been an important part of the Polish lifestyle since 1489. It is a soft and elegant spirit with lush, smooth texture. This fine vodka comes in both 80 proof and 100 proof. It is delicious on the rocks or in a snifter.

Although most vodkas today are made from grain, there are still some that follow the ancient practice of using potatoes as a base. Luksusowa is an attractive and very smooth spirit that is triple distilled from potatoes. This vodka is good for most people who are allergic to grain.

Another famous Polish vodka, Zubrowka, is no longer allowed to be imported into the United States. The blade of buffalo grass contained in this vodka has been found to contain coumarin, a diuretic drug that has not been approved, in this form, by the FDA.

FINLAND

Finland's vodka tradition dates to the sixteenth century. Finnish soldiers, returning from wars in other parts of Europe, brought home with them the technology of distillation. At the end of the last century, several small distilleries were constructed. One of these, at Rajamaki, is where Finlandia is manufactured today. Made from high-quality Finnish grain, Finlandia is produced in 80-proof and 100-proof versions. This vodka is crisp, fresh, and very clean. It has a lovely smooth texture and comes in a handsome modern bottle designed by Finnish sculptor Tapio Wirkala. It is an excellent mixer as well as being quite attractive on its own.

SWEDEN

Sweden has produced vodka for centuries, but Absolut is a product that was created in the mid-1970s with the American market in mind. This nicely packaged, clean-flavored vodka has been the fastest growing imported vodka on the market for the past few years, and in 1985, thanks in part to a first-rate advertising and marketing effort, it actually became the best-selling of all imports. Absolut is lovely in mixed drinks and also quite delicious on the rocks.

Absolut is made in 80 proof and 100 proof. A completely clear, flavored version, Absolut Peppar, which is infused with jalapeño pepper and paprika, is available, as is Absolut Citron, a lively lemon-flavored product.

NORWAY

Heublein, the producer of Smirnoff domestically and the importer of Finlandia, has recently introduced Vikin Fjord into the U.S. market. This congenial, smooth 80-proof vodka is distilled from potatoes. Made from "pure glacial waters," Vikin Fjord is a fine mixer.

DENMARK

Introduced in the U.S. market in 1991, Denaka is an 80-proof smooth vodka from Denmark that comes in a handsome, clear, triangular bottle. It has a creamy soft texture and a flavor that has tones of vanilla and caramel. The finish is soft and lush. Denaka 101 proof, which is packaged in a black bottle, is obviously stronger but still retains this brand's characteristic smoothness.

HOLLAND

Krimskaya is another of the recently arrived imports. It is being brought in by one of the Heineken group of companies. This clean and aromatic vodka is charmingly smooth with a subtle hint of herbs on the finish. Krimskaya is 80 proof and it is at its best when served on the rocks, or chilled and straight up.

ENGLAND

James Burrough, the maker of Beefeater London dry gin since 1820, also distills a lovely vodka that is just as painstakingly produced as the company's gin. Made from choice English corn and barley and filtered through charcoal made from Sussex oak trees, Burrough's English Vodka is a spicy and distinctively rich product that is excellent when served on the rocks or neat.

One of the newest super-premiums on the market is Tanqueray Sterling, a vodka that has been double distilled and filtered over granite. Packaged in a frosted bottle with the same shape as the famous Tanqueray gin bottle, the vodka is soft and lush, velvety, complex, and quite elegant.

ICELAND

Another new entry in the super-premium vodka sweepstakes is Icy, a distillate from Iceland. This silky 80-proof vodka is bottled in a clear flask with a silver top. It is soft and clean with a dry, crisp finish and a silky texture.

CANADA

Not to be outdone, giant Seagram has introduced a spicy, assertive 80-proof vodka called Seagram's Imported Vodka. This product has clean, intense flavors and an attractive selling price. It is a delicious mixer and quite acceptable on its own.

JAPAN

The Suntory Company was started in 1899 by Shinjiro Torii and its first product was Akadama sweet wine. Today this giant, $3-billion corporation produces wine, beer, whiskey, soft drinks, soup, and pharmaceuticals, among other things.

Suntory makes a crisp and very clean vodka that is packaged in a beautiful, squared-off bottle decorated with Japanese calligraphy and a handsome drawing of trees. The 80-proof version is elegant and smooth with a dry, refreshing finish. The 100-proof version is fiery and intense, but still retains a fresh, clean quality. These vodkas are excellent in mixed drinks and charming on the rocks.

UNITED STATES

Not to be outdone, American distillers are belatedly getting into the super-premium vodka market. Attakiska, an 80-proof entry from Alaska, is made in Anchorage from glacier water. The vodka is crisp and dry with a soft vanilla nose and a long, spicy finish.

Smirnoff Silver Private Reserve is a 90.4-proof American-made entry in the super-premium field. Packaged in a handsome squat bottle with squared-off corners, the vodka has a soft and creamy nose and a silky texture. The flavor is smooth, dry, and rich with a snappy bite on the finish.

CLASSICS

Black Russian

1½ ounces vodka
¾ ounce coffee liqueur
1 scoop crushed ice

Combine all the ingredients in a shaker or blender. Mix well and pour into a chilled old-fashioned glass.

Bloody Bull

2 ounces vodka
3 ounces V-8 juice
3 ounces beef bouillon, beef
   broth, or beef consommé
½ ounce lemon juice
Dash of Tabasco
Dash of Worcestershire sauce
Pinch of white pepper
1 scoop crushed ice

Combine all the ingredients in a mixing glass. Mix well and pour into a chilled old-fashioned glass.

Bloody Mary

2 ounces vodka
4 to 6 ounces tomato juice
1 teaspoon lemon juice
¼ teaspoon Worcestershire sauce
Several dashes of Tabasco
Pinch of white pepper
Several pinches of celery salt,
   or to taste
½ teaspoon chopped dill
   (fresh or dried)

In a shaker or blender, mix all the ingredients with ice. Strain the mixture into a chilled collins glass. Add additional ice cubes, if necessary.

Bombay Mary

1½ ounces vodka
4 ounces tomato juice
½ teaspoon curry powder,
   or to taste
Pinch of ground coriander
Pinch of celery seed or celery salt
Dash of soy sauce, or to taste
Dash of Worcestershire sauce
Dash of Tabasco
Dash of lemon juice
1 scoop crushed ice

Stir together all the ingredients in a 14-ounce double old-fashioned glass.

Cajun Martini

1½ to 3 ounces vodka
1 thin garlic slice
Several slices of pickled jalapeño
  pepper
Several pickled cocktail onions
Dash of dry vermouth

Let the vodka steep, for about an
hour, with garlic, pepper, and onions in a sealed container in the refrigerator or freezer. Combine the
steeped vodka and vermouth in a
mixing glass with ice. Strain into a
chilled cocktail glass. Garnish with
a pepper slice or onions, blotted to
remove vinegar taste.

Moscow Mule

2 to 3 ounces vodka
1 teaspoon lime juice
Ginger beer
Lime slice or wedge

Pour the vodka and lime juice into a
chilled highball glass with several ice
cubes. Stir. Top off with the ginger
beer and garnish with the lime.

Kamikaze

1½ ounces vodka
Splash of lime juice
Splash of Triple Sec
Lime wedge

Mix the vodka, lime juice, and Triple
Sec in a shaker with crushed ice.
Strain the mixture into a martini
glass and garnish with the lime
wedge.

Salty Dog

Pinch of salt
Pinch of granulated sugar
Lime wedge
2 ounces vodka
Grapefruit juice

On a sheet of wax paper, mix together the salt and sugar. With the
lime wedge, moisten the rim of an
old-fashioned glass. Press the rim of
the glass onto the wax paper until it
is evenly coated with the salt-sugar
mixture. Fill the glass with several ice
cubes, the vodka, and the grapefruit
juice. Stir well and serve.

Sea Breeze

2 ounces vodka
3 ounces grapefruit juice
3 ounces cranberry juice
1 scoop crushed ice

Mix all the ingredients, except the crushed ice, in a shaker. Pour the mixture into a chilled highball glass filled with the crushed ice.

Vodka Gimlet I

2 ounces vodka
½ ounce Rose's lime juice

Combine all the ingredients in a mixing glass with several ice cubes. Stir and strain into a chilled cocktail glass.

Vodka Gimlet II

1½ ounces vodka
1 ounce fresh lime juice
½ ounce sugar syrup

Mix all the ingredients in a shaker with ice. Strain the mixture into a chilled cocktail glass.

Vodka Screwdriver

1½ ounces vodka
4 ounces orange juice
Orange slice

Pour the vodka and the orange juice into a chilled double old-fashioned glass filled with ice cubes. Stir and garnish with the orange slice.

Vodka Sour

1½ to 2 ounces vodka
¾ ounce lemon juice
1 teaspoon sugar syrup
Lemon slice
1 maraschino cherry

Mix the vodka, lemon juice, and sugar syrup in a shaker with ice. Strain the mixture into a chilled whiskey sour glass. Garnish with the lemon slice and the cherry.

White Russian

1½ ounces vodka
1 ounce white crème de cacao
¾ ounce heavy cream
1 scoop crushed ice

Mix all the ingredients in a shaker. Strain into a chilled cocktail glass.

CREATIVE CONCOCTIONS

Belmont Stakes

1½ ounces vodka
½ ounce gold rum
½ ounce strawberry liqueur
½ ounce lime juice
½ teaspoon grenadine
1 scoop crushed ice
Orange slice

Mix all the ingredients, except the orange slice, in a shaker. Strain the mixture into a chilled cocktail glass and garnish with the orange slice.

Bloodhound

1½ ounces vodka
½ ounce dry sherry
4 ounces tomato juice
Dash of lemon juice
Pinch of salt
Pinch of white pepper
Lime slice

In a collins glass with ice, combine all the ingredients, except the lime slice. Mix well and garnish with the lime slice.

Big Yellow Banana

1½ ounces vodka
½ ounce banana liqueur
1 teaspoon lime juice
1 scoop crushed ice
Cold club soda
Mint sprigs

Mix the vodka, banana liqueur, lime juice, and crushed ice in a shaker. Pour this mixture into a chilled highball glass. Top off the glass with the club soda and stir gently. Garnish with the mint sprigs.

Bloody Brew

1½ ounces vodka
3 ounces beer
4 ounces tomato juice
Pinch of salt
Dill pickle spear

Mix all the ingredients, except the pickle, in a highball glass with ice. Garnish with the pickle and serve.

Bloody Joke

Makes 2 servings

4 ounces vodka
8 ounces tomato juice
1 ounce lemon juice
Pinch of celery salt
1 egg white
Several dashes of oyster sauce
Several fresh celery tops or leaves
1 scoop crushed ice

Combine all the ingredients in a blender. Blend until smooth. Pour this blend into chilled highball glasses.

Bloody Marie

1½ to 2 ounces vodka
4 ounces tomato juice
¼ ounce lemon juice
½ teaspoon Pernod
Several dashes of Worcestershire sauce
Several dashes of Tabasco
Salt
Freshly ground white pepper

Mix all the ingredients, except the salt and pepper, with ice in a mixing glass. Strain the mixture into a chilled double old-fashioned glass. Add salt and pepper to taste.

Bolshoi Ballet

1 ounce vodka
½ ounce light rum
½ ounce strawberry liqueur
1 teaspoon lime juice
Dash of grenadine
1 scoop crushed ice
Brut champagne
1 fresh strawberry

In a shaker, mix together all the ingredients, except the champagne and strawberry. Pour this mixture into a large, chilled wineglass. Top off the glass with the champagne and garnish with the strawberry.

Bullshot

1½ to 2 ounces vodka
4 ounces beef consommé or beef bouillon
1 teaspoon lemon juice
Several dashes of Worcestershire sauce
Several dashes of Tabasco
½ teaspoon prepared horseradish
Pinch of celery salt or celery seed

In a mixing glass, combine all the ingredients with several ice cubes. Mix well and pour into a chilled double old-fashioned glass.

Cape Codder

1½ ounces vodka
Dash of lime juice
4 ounces cranberry juice
1 teaspoon sugar syrup, or to taste
1 scoop crushed ice

Combine all the ingredients in a shaker. Mix well and strain into a chilled double old-fashioned glass.

Catalina Cocktail

1½ ounces vodka
1½ ounces white port
1 teaspoon Campari
Dash of grenadine

Stir all the ingredients in a mixing glass with ice. Pour the mixture into a chilled cocktail glass.

Chiquita

1½ ounces vodka
½ ounce banana liqueur
¼ cup sliced bananas
½ ounce lime juice
1 teaspoon orgeat or sugar syrup
1 scoop crushed ice

In a shaker, mix all the ingredients until smooth. Pour the mixture into a chilled deep-saucer champagne glass.

Clam Digger

2 ounces vodka
4 ounces V-8 juice
2 ounces clam juice
2 teaspoons lemon juice
Several dashes of Tabasco
Dash of Worcestershire sauce
Pinch of freshly ground white pepper
1 scoop crushed ice

Mix all the ingredients in a mixing glass. Pour the mixture into a chilled highball glass.

Cock 'n' Bull Shot

1½ ounces vodka
2 ounces chicken consommé
2 ounces beef bouillon, beef consommé, or beef broth
½ ounce lemon juice
Dash of Tabasco
Dash of Worcestershire sauce
Pinch of freshly ground white pepper
Pinch of celery salt
1 scoop crushed ice

Mix all the ingredients in a mixing glass. Stir well and pour into a chilled old-fashioned glass.

Coffee Cooler

1½ ounces vodka
1 ounce coffee liqueur
1 ounce heavy cream
4 ounces iced coffee
1 scoop crushed ice
1 scoop coffee ice cream

In a shaker, mix all the ingredients, except ice cream. Pour the mixture into a chilled double old-fashioned glass. Top off the drink with the coffee ice cream.

Cossack Charge

1½ ounces vodka
½ ounce Cognac
½ ounce cherry brandy
1 scoop crushed ice

Mix all the ingredients in a shaker. Pour the mixture into a chilled cocktail glass.

Count Stroganoff

1½ ounces vodka
¾ ounce white crème de cacao
½ ounce lemon juice

Mix all the ingredients in a shaker with ice. Strain the mixture into a chilled cocktail glass.

Creamy Screwdriver

2 to 3 ounces vodka
1 egg yolk
6 ounces orange juice
2 teaspoons sugar
1 scoop crushed ice

Mix all the ingredients in a shaker. Pour the mixture into a chilled collins glass.

Creole Martini

1½ to 2 ounces vodka
Dash of dry vermouth, or to taste
Large jalapeño pepper

Mix the vodka and vermouth in a shaker with ice. Strain the drink into a chilled cocktail glass. Garnish with the pepper.

Doctor G.

1 ounce vodka
1 ounce Swedish punsch liqueur
1 ounce orange juice
1 ounce lemon juice

Mix all the ingredients in a shaker with ice cubes. Strain the mixture into an old-fashioned glass with fresh ice cubes.

Egghead

1½ ounces vodka
4 ounces orange juice
1 egg
1 scoop crushed ice

Mix all the ingredients in a blender and blend until smooth. Pour the blend into a chilled old-fashioned glass.

Eiffel Tower

1 ounce vodka
1 ounce Cognac
½ ounce anisette
½ ounce Triple Sec

Mix all the ingredients in a shaker with ice. Strain the mixture into a chilled cocktail glass.

Emerald Bay

1½ ounces vodka
3 ounces pineapple juice
Juice of 1 lime
½ teaspoon sugar syrup
1 scoop crushed ice
½ ounce green crème de menthe
Pineapple spear

Mix all the ingredients, except crème de menthe and pineapple, in a shaker. Pour the mixture into a chilled hurricane glass. Top off the drink with a float of the crème de menthe and garnish with the pineapple spear.

Georgia Peach

1½ ounces vodka
¾ ounce peach-flavored brandy
1 teaspoon peach preserves
1 teaspoon lemon juice
1 slice canned or peeled fresh
  peach, chopped
1 scoop crushed ice

Combine all the ingredients in a blender. Blend until smooth. Pour the blend into a chilled double old-fashioned glass.

Gingersnap

3 ounces vodka
1 ounce ginger wine
Club soda

Combine the vodka and ginger wine in a double old-fashioned glass. Add several ice cubes and top off with the soda. Stir gently.

Ginza Mary

1½ ounces vodka
1½ ounces tomato juice cocktail
1½ ounces sake
½ ounce lemon juice
Several dashes of Tabasco
Dash of soy sauce
Pinch of freshly ground white
   pepper

Mix all the ingredients with ice in a
mixing glass. Pour the mixture into
a chilled old-fashioned glass.

Green Fly

1½ ounces vodka
½ ounce green crème de menthe
½ ounce white crème de menthe
1 scoop crushed ice

Mix all the ingredients in a shaker.
Pour the mixture into a chilled collins glass.

Green Spider

1½ ounces vodka
½ ounce green crème de menthe

Pour both ingredients into an old-
fashioned glass over ice.

Hot Vodka

1½ ounces pepper vodka
3 ounces tomato juice

In a shaker with crushed ice, mix
both ingredients. Strain the mixture
into an old-fashioned glass with
fresh ice cubes.

Ice Pick

1½ ounces vodka
6 ounces sweetened iced tea
Lemon wedge

Fill a highball or collins glass with
several ice cubes. Add the vodka to
the glass, then top it off with the
iced tea. Squeeze the lemon over the
drink and drop it in.

Iceberg

1 ounce peppermint schnapps
1 ounce vodka
1 scoop crushed ice

In a mixing glass, stir together the
schnapps, the vodka, and several ice
cubes. Strain the mixture into a
brandy snifter over crushed ice.

Jessica's Blue

2 ounces vodka
1 ounce blue curaçao
Several dashes of kirsch
1 scoop crushed ice

Mix all the ingredients in a shaker. Strain the mixture into a chilled cocktail glass.

Jungle Joe

1 ounce vodka
1 ounce crème de banane
1 ounce milk
1 scoop crushed ice

In a shaker, mix all the ingredients. Pour the mixture into a chilled old-fashioned glass.

Kangaroo

1½ ounces vodka
¾ ounce dry vermouth
Lemon peel twist

Stir the vodka and vermouth in a mixing glass with ice. Strain the mixture into a cocktail glass, or over ice in an old-fashioned glass. Garnish with the lemon twist.

Kempinsky Fizz

1½ ounces vodka
½ ounce crème de cassis
1 teaspoon lemon juice
Cold ginger ale, bitter lemon soda, or club soda

Pour the vodka, crème de cassis, and lemon juice into a chilled highball glass with ice. Top off with the soda and stir gently.

The Kremlin

1 ounce coffee liqueur
1 ounce vodka
1 ounce half-and-half
1 scoop crushed ice

In a blender, combine all the ingredients. Blend until smooth. Pour the blend into a chilled cocktail glass.

La Banane

1 ounce vodka
1 ounce crème de banane
1 ounce half-and-half

Mix all the ingredients in a shaker with ice. Strain the mixture into a chilled cocktail glass.

Lieutenant Bill

1 ounce vodka
1 ounce apricot liqueur
1 ounce orange juice

Mix all the ingredients in a shaker with ice. Strain the mixture into a chilled cocktail glass.

Loose Lips Lemon Drop

1½ ounces vodka
1 lemon wedge
Sugar

Pour the vodka into a shot glass. Saturate a wedge of lemon with granulated sugar by pressing the wedge into a bowl of sugar. Bite into the sugar-coated wedge, but do not swallow. With the pulp still in your mouth, quickly drink down the shot glass of vodka.

Madame de Melrose

1 ounce vodka
½ ounce white crème de cacao
½ ounce curaçao
1 ounce heavy cream
1 scoop crushed ice

In a shaker, mix all the ingredients. Pour the mixture into a chilled cocktail glass.

Moscow Milk Toddy

1½ ounces vodka
½ ounce grenadine
4 ounces milk
1 scoop crushed ice
Ground cinnamon

In a shaker, mix all the ingredients, except the cinnamon. Pour the mixture into a chilled old-fashioned glass. Sprinkle the cinnamon on top before serving.

Olympic Circle

1 ounce vodka
1 ounce curaçao
½ ounce lime juice
½ ounce lemon juice
4 ounces orange juice
1 scoop crushed ice
Orange slice

Mix all the ingredients, except the orange slice, in a shaker. Pour this mixture into a chilled old-fashioned glass. Garnish with the orange slice.

Polynesian Pepper Pot

1½ ounces vodka
¾ ounce gold rum
4 ounces pineapple juice
½ ounce orgeat or sugar syrup
½ teaspoon lemon juice
1 tablespoon cream
Several dashes of Tabasco
¼ teaspoon cayenne
1 scoop crushed ice
Curry powder

Mix all the ingredients, except the curry powder, in a shaker. Pour the mixture into a chilled double old-fashioned glass. Sprinkle lightly with the curry powder.

Red Snapper

2 dashes of salt
2 dashes of black pepper
2 dashes of cayenne
3 dashes of Worcestershire sauce
Dash of lemon juice
1½ ounces vodka
2 ounces tomato juice
1 celery rib

Combine the salt, pepper, cayenne, Worcestershire sauce, and lemon juice in a shaker glass. Add ice, vodka, and tomato juice. Shake and pour the drink into a highball glass. Garnish with the celery.

Rich Babe

1 ounce vodka
1 ounce crème de cacao
½ ounce lemon juice
½ teaspoon grenadine

In a shaker, mix all the ingredients with ice. Strain the mixture into a chilled cocktail glass.

Rudolf Nureyev

1 ounce vodka
1 ounce apricot liqueur
½ ounce lemon juice
4 ounces orange juice
1 scoop crushed ice
Orange slice

In a shaker, mix all the ingredients, except the orange slice. Pour the mixture into a chilled wineglass. Garnish with the orange slice.

Russian Bear

1 ounce vodka
1 ounce dark crème de cacao
1 ounce heavy cream
1 scoop crushed ice

Mix all the ingredients in a shaker. Strain the mixture into a chilled cocktail glass.

Russian Cocktail

1 ounce vodka
1 ounce gin
1 ounce white crème de cacao

Mix all the ingredients in a shaker with ice. Strain the mixture into a chilled cocktail glass.

Russian Coffee

½ ounce vodka
1½ ounces coffee liqueur
1 ounce heavy cream
1 scoop crushed ice

Mix all the ingredients in a blender. Pour the blend into a chilled brandy snifter.

Russian Rose

2 ounces vodka
½ ounce grenadine
Dash of orange bitters

Combine all the ingredients in a mixing glass with ice. Stir well and strain into a chilled cocktail glass.

Smokin' Mary

1½ ounces vodka
4 ounces tomato juice
½ ounce lemon juice
½ ounce barbeque sauce
Dash of Tabasco
Dash of Worcestershire sauce
1 scoop crushed ice
Lemon slice

Mix all the ingredients, except the lemon slice, in a double old-fashioned glass. Garnish with the lemon slice.

St. Lawrence Cooler

1½ ounces vodka
3 ounces grapefruit juice
½ ounce crème de cassis
1 scoop crushed ice
Cold ginger ale
Mint sprig
Orange slice

In a shaker, mix the vodka, grapefruit juice, crème de cassis, and ice. Pour the mixture into a chilled collins glass. Top off with the ginger ale. Garnish with the mint sprig and orange slice.

St. Petersburg

2 ounces vodka
¼ teaspoon orange bitters
1 orange wedge

Combine the vodka and bitters in a mixing glass with several ice cubes. Stir and pour into a chilled old-fashioned glass. Garnish with the orange wedge.

Unified Team

1½ ounces vodka
½ ounce light rum
½ ounce curaçao
¼ ounce lime juice
1 teaspoon sugar syrup, or to taste

Mix all the ingredients with ice in a shaker. Strain this mixture into a chilled cocktail glass.

Vodka Cooler

1½ ounces vodka
½ ounce sweet vermouth
½ ounce lemon juice
½ ounce sugar syrup
1 scoop crushed ice
Cold club soda

Mix all the ingredients, except the club soda, in a shaker. Pour the mixture into a chilled collins glass and top off with the club soda.

Vodka Grand Marnier

1½ ounces vodka
½ ounce Grand Marnier
½ ounce lime juice
1 scoop crushed ice
Orange slice

Mix all the ingredients, except the orange slice, in a shaker. Pour this mixture into a chilled cocktail glass. Garnish with the orange slice.

Vodka Grasshopper

½ ounce vodka
¾ ounce green crème de menthe
¾ ounce white crème de cacao

Mix all the ingredients in a shaker with ice. Strain into a chilled cocktail glass.

Vodka Stinger

1½ ounces vodka
1 ounce white crème de menthe

In a mixing glass, stir the vodka and crème de menthe with ice cubes. Strain into a chilled cocktail glass.

Vulgar Boatman

1½ ounces vodka
¾ ounce cherry liqueur
¼ ounce dry vermouth
½ ounce lemon juice
¼ teaspoon kirsch
Dash of orange bitters
1 scoop crushed ice

Mix all the ingredients in a shaker. Strain the mixture into a chilled cocktail glass.

Warsaw

1½ ounces vodka
½ ounce blackberry liqueur
½ ounce dry vermouth
1 teaspoon lemon juice
Crushed ice
Lemon peel

Mix all the ingredients, except the lemon peel, in a shaker. Strain the mixture into a chilled cocktail glass. Twist the lemon peel over the drink and drop it in.

West Coast Samba

½ cup fresh fruit (bananas, strawberries, oranges, pineapple as desired)
Root beer
1½ ounces vodka
1 scoop orange sherbet

Place the fruit on the bottom of a very tall glass. Fill the glass three quarters full with root beer. Add the vodka to the glass and stir. Finally, add the orange sherbet and garnish with more fresh fruit.

White Wim

1½ ounces vodka
1½ ounces lemon juice
1 ounce pineapple juice
Cold club soda

Mix the vodka, lemon juice, and pineapple juice in a shaker. Pour the mixture into a collins glass and top off with the soda. Stir gently.

Yorsh

1½ ounces vodka
12-ounce mug of beer

Drink the shot of vodka and follow it with a mug of beer, or add the vodka to the mug of beer and drink them together.

SIGNATURE DRINKS

Alaskan Martini

ASTA, SAN FRANCISCO

1½ ounces Alaskan vodka
3 drops crème de menthe
1 small candy cane

Pour the vodka and crème de menthe into a shaker with ice. Stir with a bar spoon for about 10 seconds. Strain the mixture into a chilled cocktail glass. Serve with the candy cane hooked on the side of the glass.

Algonquin Bloody Mary

THE BLUE BAR, ALGONQUIN HOTEL, NEW YORK CITY

1½ ounces vodka
4 ounces tomato juice
Salt and freshly ground black
  pepper to taste
Juice of half a lime
1 teaspoon Worcestershire sauce
4 to 6 dashes of Tabasco
1 lime wedge

Combine all the ingredients, except the lime wedge, in a shaker filled with ice. Using the glass and metal container, shake quickly, nine or ten times. Strain into a fresh glass and drop in the lime wedge.

Bix Bloody Mary

BIX, SAN FRANCISCO

1½ ounces vodka
Tomato juice
Juice of 1 whole lemon
Dash of Worcestershire sauce
Dash of salt and pepper
1 thinly sliced lemon wheel

Fill a shaker with ice and add all the ingredients, except the lemon wheel. Shake vigorously and strain into a stemmed 6- to 8-ounce glass. Garnish with the lemon wheel.

Note: No Tabasco, no ice in drink, no celery, no gimmicks.

Bolshoi Punch

RUSSIAN TEA ROOM, NEW YORK CITY

1 ounce vodka
¼ ounce light rum
¼ ounce crème de cassis
Juice of 1 lemon
1 to 2 teaspoons sugar syrup,
  to taste
1 scoop crushed ice

Combine all the ingredients in a shaker. Mix well and strain into a chilled cocktail glass.

Bravo

BRAVO, DALLAS

4 ounces pink lemonade
1 ounce vodka
1 ounce Triple Sec
Splash of lime juice
4 ounces grapefruit juice
1 scoop crushed ice

Blend all the ingredients until frothy. Pour this blend into a large wineglass.

Cary Grant Cocktail

"21" CLUB, NEW YORK CITY

2 ounces vodka
½ ounce dry sherry
½ ounce lime juice
Lime twist

Combine all the ingredients, except the lime twist, in a mixing glass. Stir well and pour into a champagne flute. Garnish with the lime twist.

Cement Mixer

THE BALBOA CAFE, SAN FRANCISCO

1 ounce vodka
½ ounce cranberry juice
½ ounce Irish cream

Pour the vodka and cranberry juice into a shot glass. Float the Irish cream on top. The Irish cream will cause the drink to congeal and thicken. By the time it reaches your throat, it feels like cottage cheese.

Cosmopolitan

JULIE'S SUPPER CLUB, SAN FRANCISCO

1¼ ounces vodka
¼ ounce Triple Sec
¼ ounce lime juice
Splash of cranberry juice
Lime wedge

Pour all the ingredients, except the lime wedge, over ice in a large mixing glass. Stir and strain into a chilled martini glass. Squeeze and garnish with the lime.

Cosmotron

JULIE'S SUPPER CLUB, SAN FRANCISCO

1¼ ounces citron vodka
¼ ounce Triple Sec
¼ ounce Rose's lime juice
Splash of cranberry juice
Lemon wedge

Pour all the ingredients, except the lemon wedge, over ice into a large mixing glass. Stir and strain into a chilled martini glass. Squeeze and garnish with the lemon wedge.

Eccentric Martini

THE ECCENTRIC, CHICAGO

2 ounces vodka
Splash of vermouth
Olive

In a shaker, mix the vodka and vermouth with ice. Strain the mixture into a 3-ounce beaker. Pour the mixture into a chilled martini glass and garnish with the olive.

Essex Lemonbreeze

GRISWOLD INN, ESSEX, CONNECTICUT

1½ ounces lemon-flavored vodka
6 ounces lemonade
Splash of cranberry juice

Pour the vodka, lemonade, and cranberry juice into a tall collins glass filled with ice.

Fuzzy Navel

PAT O'SHEA'S MAD HATTER, SAN FRANCISCO

1 ounce vodka
½ ounce peach schnapps
6 ounces orange juice
1 scoop crushed ice
Orange slice

Combine all the ingredients, except the orange slice, in a shaker. Shake well and pour into a chilled collins glass. Garnish with the orange slice.

Gazpacho Fizz

THE WESTIN ST. FRANCIS, SAN FRANCISCO

1½ ounces vodka
2 ounces Bloody Mary mix
2 fresh tomato slices
1 scoop crushed ice
Cold club soda
Salt and freshly ground pepper
½ celery rib
½ scallion
Cherry tomato

Blend the vodka, Bloody Mary mix, tomato, and ice. Pour the blend into an all-purpose tulip glass. Top off with the soda. Season to taste. Garnish with the celery, scallion, and cherry tomato.

Green Eye-Opener

THE SIGN OF THE DOVE, NEW YORK CITY

1 ounce vodka
2 ounces fresh lime juice
3 ounces orange juice
5 to 6 drops blue curaçao
½ ounce Triple Sec
1 celery rib

In a shaker, mix all the ingredients, except the celery rib, with ice. Pour into a tall glass. This drink is green because, as you remember from art class, that is what you get when you mix blue and yellow. Garnish with the celery.

Hawaiian Vacation

LENT HOWARD, BALBOA CAFE,
SAN FRANCISCO

½ ounce vodka
½ ounce amaretto
½ ounce Southern Comfort
1 ounce orange juice
1 ounce pineapple juice
Splash of lime juice

Pour all the ingredients into a shaker
with crushed ice. Mix well and strain
into an old-fashioned glass.

Hot Sand

CHEF ALLEN'S, MIAMI

1 ounce hazelnut liqueur
4 ounces heavy cream
1 ounce vodka
Fresh ginger

Combine all the ingredients, except
the ginger, in a shaker. Add ice to
the mixture and shake until frothy.
Strain into a rocks glass and top with
a slice of the ginger.

The Kiss

GRAND HYATT HOTEL, NEW YORK CITY

1½ ounces vodka
¾ ounce chocolate-cherry liqueur
¾ ounce heavy cream
½ fresh strawberry

Mix all the ingredients, except the
strawberry, in a shaker with ice.
Strain into a chilled cocktail glass
and garnish with the strawberry.

Lemon Lambada

CHEF ALLEN'S, MIAMI

Juice of 1 fresh lemon
1½ ounces vodka
2 ounces sour mix
3 ounces 7-Up
1 lemon wheel
1 scoop crushed ice

Fill a tall 10-ounce glass three quarters full with crushed ice. Pour the
lemon juice into the glass. Top with
the vodka, sour mix, and 7-Up. Stir
well and garnish with the lemon
wheel.

Long Island Iced Tea

THE BALBOA CAFE, SAN FRANCISCO

½ ounce vodka
½ ounce gin
½ ounce tequila
½ ounce white rum
½ ounce Triple Sec
1 ounce sweet 'n' sour mix
Cola

Pour all the ingredients into a tall
collins glass filled with ice cubes. Stir
well before serving.

Magnolia Mist

FOUR SEASONS HOTEL, BOSTON

1 ounce lemon vodka
1 ounce blackberry liqueur
Dash of grenadine
1 scoop crushed ice
Orange twist

Mix all the ingredients, except the orange twist, in a blender. Pour the mixture into a martini glass and garnish with the orange twist.

Melon Breeze

MICKEY'S PLACE, BALDWIN, NEW YORK

1 ounce vodka
3/4 ounce melon liqueur
1 1/2 ounces pineapple juice
1 1/2 ounces cranberry juice
Pineapple wedge
Watermelon wedge

Mix the vodka and melon liqueur over ice in a highball glass. Add the juices. Garnish with the fruit wedges on a stick.

Miami Mango

CHEF ALLEN'S, MIAMI

1 scoop crushed ice
1 1/2 ounces fresh mango juice
2 1/2 ounces freshly squeezed
   orange juice

1/2 ounce orange liqueur
1 1/2 ounces vodka
1 slice fresh mango or orange

Fill a large margarita glass three quarters full with crushed ice. Top off the glass with the remaining ingredients, except fruit slice. Garnish with the fresh mango or orange slice.

Nuts and Berries

THE BALBOA CAFE, SAN FRANCISCO

1/2 ounce vodka
1/2 ounce Irish cream
1/2 ounce hazelnut liqueur
1/2 ounce blackberry liqueur

Mix all the ingredients in a shaker with crushed ice. Strain the mixture into a shot glass.

Parisian

THE ECCENTRIC, CHICAGO

1 1/2 ounces vodka
1/4 ounce white vermouth
1/4 ounce blackberry liqueur
Champagne or sparkling wine
1 raspberry

Shake the vodka, vermouth, and liqueur with ice and strain into a martini glass. Top off with the champagne and garnish with the raspberry.

Peppered Bloody Mary

REDWOOD ROOM, THE CLIFT HOTEL,
SAN FRANCISCO

1¼ ounces pepper-flavored vodka
3 ounces Bloody Mary mix or
   Sangrita mix (page 149)
1 lime wedge
1 celery rib

Pour the vodka and then Bloody
Mary mix over ice into a highball
glass. Garnish with the lime wedge
and the celery rib.

Pink Lemonade

CHIP PYRON, SAM'S ANCHOR CAFE,
SAN FRANCISCO

1½ ounces lemon-flavored vodka
1 ounce 7-Up
1 ounce sweet 'n' sour mix
½ ounce fresh lemon juice
1½ ounces cranberry juice
Lemon peel twist

In a tall glass filled with ice, pour in
the ingredients in the order listed.
Do not stir before serving. Garnish
with the lemon twist.

The Pink Thing

CYPRESS CLUB, SAN FRANCISCO

1¼ ounces vodka
1 teaspoon orange juice
1 teaspoon cranberry juice
½ ounce blueberry schnapps

Combine all the ingredients in a
shaker with crushed ice. Mix well
and strain into a shot glass.

Prickly Pear Paradise

WESTCOURT IN THE BUTTES,
TEMPE, ARIZONA

2 ounces vodka
8 to 10 each of fresh raspberries,
   blueberries, and blackberries
2 medium scoops raspberry sorbet
1 tablespoon prickly pear
   marmalade
1 ounce cranberry juice
1 ounce sweet 'n' sour mix
2 tablespoons sugar
Splash of 7-Up
1 scoop crushed ice
Pear wedge

In a mixer, blend all the ingredients,
except the pear wedge, until the
consistency is thick and frothy. Pour
this blend into an 8-ounce wineglass
and garnish with the pear wedge.

Pterodactyl

JULIE'S SUPPER CLUB, SAN FRANCISCO

1¼ ounces lemon-flavored vodka
¼ ounce Triple Sec
Splash of sweet 'n' sour mix
Splash of pineapple juice
Lemon twist

Pour all the ingredients, except the lemon twist, over ice into a large mixing glass. Stir and strain into a chilled martini glass. Garnish with the lemon twist.

Pump Martini

THE PUMP ROOM, CHICAGO

Olives, lemon twist, or onions
B&B
1½ ounces vodka
Splash of dry vermouth

In one mixing glass, marinate the olives, a lemon twist, or onions in B&B. In a second mixing glass, combine vodka, vermouth, and several ice cubes. Stir and strain into a chilled martini glass. Garnish with the marinated olives, lemon twist, or onions.

Purple Hooter

THE BALBOA CAFE, SAN FRANCISCO

¾ ounce vodka
¾ ounce sweet 'n' sour mix
½ ounce blackberry liqueur
Splash of 7-Up

In a shaker with crushed ice, mix all the ingredients, except the 7-Up. Strain the mixture into a shot glass and add a splash of 7-Up.

Red Rock Canyon

CAESAR'S PALACE, LAS VEGAS

1½ ounces vodka
¼ ounce crème de cassis
¼ ounce peach brandy
¼ ounce Triple Sec
Several splashes of Campari
1 maraschino cherry
Orange slice

Mix the vodka, crème de cassis, brandy, and Triple Sec in a blender with ice. Pour into a chilled collins glass. Top with a Campari float. Garnish with the cherry and orange slice.

Russian Apple

THE BALBOA CAFE, SAN FRANCISCO

1 ounce vodka
½ ounce cranberry juice
½ ounce pineapple juice

Mix all the ingredients in a shaker with crushed ice. Strain the mixture into a shot glass.

Russian Quaalude

THE BALBOA CAFE, SAN FRANCISCO

½ ounce vodka
½ ounce Irish cream
½ ounce coffee liqueur
½ ounce half-and-half

Mix all the ingredients in a shaker with crushed ice. Strain the mixture into a shot glass.

San Francisco Blues

THE WESTIN ST. FRANCIS,
SAN FRANCISCO

1 ounce vodka
¼ ounce blue curaçao
6 ounces pineapple juice
Splash of soda
Pineapple wedge

Pour all the ingredients, except the pineapple wedge, over ice into a mixing glass. Stir and strain into an all-purpose tulip glass. Garnish with the pineapple wedge.

Sex on the Beach

THE BALBOA CAFE, SAN FRANCISCO

¾ ounce vodka
¾ ounce peach schnapps
1 ounce pineapple juice
1 ounce cranberry juice
Splash of blackberry liqueur

This drink can be served as a shot or as a cocktail. As a shot, add all the ingredients to a shaker with crushed ice. Mix and strain into an old-fashioned glass. As a cocktail, pour all the ingredients directly into a cocktail glass with several ice cubes.

Sir John's Folly

FOX AND HOUNDS PUB, ST. LOUIS

½ ounce vodka
½ ounce rum
1 ounce sweet 'n' sour mix
2 ounces orange juice
¼ ounce blue curaçao
1 scoop crushed ice
Orange slice

In a shaker, mix all the ingredients, except ice and orange slice. Serve in a snifter over crushed ice. Garnish with the orange slice.

Southampton Stinger

FOX AND HOUNDS PUB, ST. LOUIS

1 ounce vodka
½ ounce Galliano
½ ounce apricot brandy
1 scoop crushed ice

Mix all the ingredients in a blender with crushed ice. Strain over ice in a brandy snifter.

Southside

"21" CLUB, NEW YORK CITY

6 fresh mint sprigs
2 ounces vodka
Juice of ½ lemon
1½ teaspoons confectioners' sugar

Put aside 2 mint sprigs. Combine the rest of the ingredients in a shaker with ice. Strain into a cocktail glass. Garnish with the 2 fresh mint sprigs.

Stars Russian

STARS, SAN FRANCISCO

2 ounces frozen vodka
1 ounce Moka liqueur

Pour the vodka into a frosted stem glass. Add the liqueur and stir gently.

Summer Aid

THE PUMP ROOM, CHICAGO

1½ ounces vodka
Juice of 2 oranges, 1 lemon, and 1 lime
Splash of cranberry juice
Sugar syrup to taste
1 scoop crushed ice

Mix all the ingredients in a shaker. Strain into a chilled highball glass.

Tahoe Julius

HARRAH'S HOTEL AND CASINO, LAKE TAHOE, NEVADA

1½ ounces vodka
3 ounces orange juice
1 ounce cream
1 egg
1 teaspoon sugar syrup
1 cup ice cubes

Combine all the ingredients in a blender and blend until smooth. Pour into a chilled wineglass.

Visitor

JASPER'S, BOSTON

1½ ounces vodka
½ ounce Triple Sec
¼ ounce Grand Marnier
½ ounce orange juice
1 teaspoon crème de banane

Combine all the ingredients in a shaker with crushed ice. Mix well and pour into a martini glass or wineglass.

Watermelon Shooter

THE BALBOA CAFE, SAN FRANCISCO

½ ounce vodka
½ ounce sloe gin
½ ounce melon liqueur
1 ounce pineapple juice
1 scoop crushed ice

Combine all the ingredients in a shaker. Mix well and strain into an old-fashioned glass.

Woo Woo

JULIE'S SUPPER CLUB, SAN FRANCISCO

1¼ ounces vodka
½ ounce peach schnapps
Splash of cranberry juice

Pour all the ingredients over ice into a large mixing glass. Stir and strain into a chilled martini glass.

TROPICAL DRINKS

Chi-Chi

1½ ounces vodka
2 ounces pineapple juice
1 ounce coconut cream
1 cup ice

Combine all the ingredients in a blender. Blend until smooth and pour into a saucer-shaped champagne glass.

Tropical Moc-Olada

Makes 4 servings

4 ounces vodka
¼ cup lemon-flavored instant tea mix, sweetened
1 cup cold water
1 cup light cream or half-and-half
1 (8-ounce) can crushed pineapple in natural juice
2 teaspoons coconut extract
1½ teaspoons lime juice
½ medium banana

Combine all the ingredients in a blender. Slowly add 2 cups of ice cubes while blending at high speed. Blend until frothy and serve in wineglasses.

Volcano

1 ounce vodka
½ ounce crème de almond
2 ounces coconut cream
1 scoop vanilla ice cream

Combine all the ingredients in a blender and blend until smooth. Pour the blend into a chilled parfait glass.

Waikiki Comber

1½ ounces vodka
6 ounces guava juice
½ ounce fresh lime juice
1 scoop crushed ice
½ ounce black raspberry liqueur

Mix all the ingredients, except the liqueur, in a shaker. Pour the mixture into a chilled collins glass. Over the back of a spoon, float the raspberry liqueur.

Rum

In 1492 Christopher Columbus concluded that "the Indies" he had discovered would be ideal for the cultivation of sugarcane. As a result, on his second voyage to the New World, he brought along some sugar experts and several hundred cane shoots from the Canary Islands. Commercial plantations were developed on what are now Haiti, Puerto Rico, Cuba, and Jamaica—islands that all became important sources of rum.

Puerto Rico is, today, the biggest rum producer in the world and the booming business contributes millions of dollars to the Puerto Rican economy. But this is nothing new for this Caribbean island. Rum production in Puerto Rico goes back to well before the island was handed over to the United States by Spain in 1898, at the end of the Spanish-American War. The locals produced a crude distillate called *aguardiente* that achieved considerable popularity throughout the Spanish colonial empire.

But the true foundation was laid at the beginning of the nineteenth century. At that time a Spaniard named Don Sebastian Serralles emigrated from Catalonia to settle in Puerto Rico and work on a sugar plantation. After his death, his son, Juan, expanded the family estate his father had established and built a sugar factory. In 1865 he bought a French pot still and began making Puerto Rico's first commercial rum.

He named it "Don Q," after his favorite figure in Spanish literature, Cervantes's Don Quixote. (Today, more than 135 years later, Don Q is still the best-selling rum in Puerto Rico.)

In late 1940—after World War II had seriously curtailed the American yen for rum—it looked as if the Puerto Rican distillery industry was on the verge of extinction. But the government took bold measures to improve the production of rum in order to save the island's most valuable product. First a strict "Mature Spirits Act" was passed that mandated that rum be aged for at least one year. The act went on to specify that, after aging, all export rums must be blended to give them a smoother, more complex flavor.

The most important government decision, however, was the establishment of a Rum Pilot Plant as a branch of the University of Puerto Rico. Placed in charge of this project was Dr. Victor Rodriguez-Benitez, who immediately set to work defining the standards of what Puerto Rican rum should be.

Until that point the rum of Puerto Rico had been syrupy, dark, and sweet. Dr. Rodriguez-Benitez and his staff determined that the American market wanted a lighter, drier rum. They also insisted that Puerto Rican rum be a pure product, free of harsh-tasting fusel oils and aldehydes that could cause hangovers and upset stomachs.

Over the nineteen years of Dr. Rodriguez-Benitez's stewardship, every aspect of rum production was studied and important guidelines were given, free of charge, to any rum producers in the world who were interested. Many took advantage of this generosity and the quality of rum improved everywhere it was made.

* * *

There are basically four different kinds of rum: white or light; gold or amber; dark; and spiced or aromatic.

White or light rums are clear in color and have a very light and dry molasses flavor. They must be aged a minimum of one year, and are aged in glass or stainless steel containers or uncharred barrels.

Gold or amber rum is darker and has a stronger flavor than light rum. The darker color is caused by the addition of caramel coloring or by being aged in charred barrels. Gold or amber rums are aged in barrels for a minimum of three years. These rums are often labeled "anejo."

White and gold rums are both considered light-bodied rums. These light-bodied rums are usually produced in Cuba, the Dominican Republic, Haiti, Puerto Rico, and the Virgin Islands.

Full-bodied rums, or dark rums, are produced in Barbados, Jamaica, Martinique, Trinidad, and Guyana, where Demerara rum is made. A special fermentation process gives the dark rums a pronounced flavor of vanillin, butter, and molasses. These rums are aged from five to seven years in oak barrels, and when ready for bottling, caramel is added to darken the color.

Spiced rums are becoming popular in mixed drinks. These are light or amber rums that have been flavored with peppers and other tropical spices. Aromatic rums are made on the island of Java in Indonesia. Dried Javanese rice cakes are added during fermentation. Aromatic rums are aged for three to four years in Java, then shipped to the Netherlands for more aging.

Most rums are shipped at 80 proof, with a few checking in at 85 or 86 proof. A few producers also ship a high-proof version that is sometimes useful in mixed drinks and punches. These fiery rums are generally bottled at a potent 151 proof.

*   *   *

Centuries before advanced technology was developed in Puerto Rico, crude rum was produced wherever sugarcane was grown. The process that converts cane juice into sugar yields thick, sweet syrup as a by-product. After a period when this syrup was put to such undignified uses as fertilizer and cattle feed, one of Columbus's observant settlers noticed that the brown, sticky fluid—called molasses by the English—fermented when it was left out in the sun. A coarse, very sweet drink resulted.

It wasn't until the seventeenth century, however, that enterprising colonists used the process of distillation, newly fashionable in Europe, to make a spirit drink from the molasses. This libation quickly became so popular that some growers had to be firmly reminded by the government that their primary purpose was to produce sugar, not inebriants. Mr. W. Hughes wrote after a visit in 1672: "They make a sort of strong water they call Rumbullion, stronger than spirit of wine."* The name, a product of English country slang, was eventually shortened to "rum."

Rum Yesterday and Today by Hugh Barty-King & Anton Massel (London: Heinemann, 1983), p. 12.

In 1655 the Royal Navy, after failing to capture the Spanish-held island of San Domingo, turned its attention to Jamaica rather than returning to England empty-handed. The attack was successful, Jamaica was annexed to the expanding British empire, and the sailors were rewarded with a ration of rum found on the island. Prior to this conquest, British navy men on long sea voyages had depended on water or beer for refreshment. But these liquids had a tendency to deteriorate over time; the water would become brackish and the beer would turn flat and sour. Rum, on the other hand, remained stable for months.

It became customary to give each British seaman a ration of a half pint of rum each day, a substantial amount by today's standards. Unfortunately, many sailors adopted the practice of bolting the whole half pint all at once, a routine that, as you might imagine, caused them to be a little unsteady on their feet.

The admiralty was at a loss to deal with this problem. Discontinuing the rum ration might lead to a mutiny; there had to be a more moderate solution. The answer eluded the Royal Navy until it was solved dramatically by Admiral Vernon, a dapper and intelligent fellow who always wore a heavy waterproof boat-cloak made of a coarse fabric woven from silk, mohair, and wool. This material was called grogram and it earned Vernon the nickname "Old Grogram."

Vernon's solution to the rum problem was to issue a decree in 1740 that ordered all ships' captains to mix each sailor's daily rum ration with a quart of water. He also suggested the use of sugar and limes to make the mixture "more palatable to them."*

Almost immediately a name was coined by sailors for this concoction. In honor of Old Grogram, the new rum ration was called "grog." Later, after Lord Admiral Nelson's death at Trafalgar in 1805, the drink was also known as "Nelson's blood."

In putting forth his ingenious recipe, Admiral Vernon had not only saved the Royal Navy, he had inadvertently invented the rum cocktail. From that time on, rum was often blended with other ingredients, most frequently with fruit juices.

Throughout the eighteenth century, the modish drink was "punch,"

---

*349 Order to Captains, August 21, 1740. See *Nelson's Blood* by James Pack (Havant, Hampshire: K. Mason, 1982), p. 22.

a mixture that took many forms but that often contained rum. The name was an anglicization of the Hindustani "panch," meaning "five." The classic punch was a combination of five ingredients: spirit, sugar, lime juice, spice, and water.

In 1896 one of the most dramatic inventions in the history of rum took place outside Santiago in Cuba. An American named Jennings Cox, who was working in copper mines not far from a village called Daiquiri, combined light rum and lime juice in a cocktail to honor some visiting friends. He called it the daiquiri. The rest is history.

* * *

The greatest rum drink inventor was born in San Francisco six years after the daiquiri was born. The charismatic Vic Bergeron opened his first restaurant in Oakland in 1934. Three years later he changed the name of the place from Hinky Dinks to Trader Vic's and adopted the world-famous "tropical paradise" theme.

One night in 1944, Vic was in the service bar of his Oakland restaurant thinking about creating a new drink. He took down a bottle of 17-year-old Jamaican rum. "The flavor of this great rum wasn't meant to be overpowered with heavy additions of fruit juices and flavorings," Vic wrote in 1970. "I took a fresh lime, added some orange curaçao from Holland, a dash of rock candy syrup, and a dollop of French orgeat, for its subtle almond flavor. A generous amount of shaved ice and vigorous shaking by hand produced the marriage I was after."*

Trader Vic garnished the new drink with a sprig of mint and gave a glass to a Tahitian friend who happened to be in the restaurant that night. She took one sip and said, "Mai tai—roa ae," which means "out of this world—the best" in Tahitian.*

Many other great rum drinks have been invented over the centuries. Planter's punch, swizzle, piña colada, scorpion, bacardi, Cuba libre, and the zombie are just a few of the best known. And we have Christopher Columbus to thank.

**Let's Get the Record Straight on the Mai Tai!* by Victor J. Bergeron (San Francisco: Trader Vic's, 1970).

CLASSICS

Bacardi Cocktail

Makes 1 or 2 servings

3 ounces light rum
Juice of ½ lime
2 dashes of grenadine syrup
1 scoop crushed ice

In a shaker, combine all the ingredients and shake until frothy. Pour the mixture into a cocktail glass.

Between the Sheets

¾ ounce light rum
¾ ounce brandy
¾ ounce Triple Sec
¾ ounce lemon juice

Combine all the ingredients in a shaker with ice cubes. Shake well and pour into a chilled cocktail glass.

Cuba Libre

1¾ ounces light rum
Cola to taste
¼ lime

Mix the rum and cola in a highball glass with a few ice cubes. Add the lime, after giving it a light squeeze over the drink, and stir well.

Daiquiri, Frozen

1¾ ounces light rum
Juice of ½ lime
2 teaspoons sugar
1 scoop crushed ice

Combine all the ingredients in a blender. Blend well. Pour the mixture into a cocktail glass or champagne flute.

Note: Various fruits can be added to the mixture, such as strawberries, raspberries, peaches, watermelon, or mango.

Daiquiri, Strawberry

1¾ ounces light rum
5 large strawberries
Juice of ¼ lime
1 to 2 teaspoons sugar
1 scoop crushed ice

Mix all the ingredients, except 1 strawberry, thoroughly in a blender. Pour the blend into a large cocktail glass or champagne flute. Garnish with the extra strawberry.

Louisiana Planter's Punch

1½ ounces gold rum
¾ ounce bourbon
¾ ounce Cognac
½ ounce sugar syrup
1 ounce lemon juice
Several dashes of bitters
Several dashes of Pernod
1 scoop crushed ice
Club soda
1 lemon slice, seeded
1 orange slice, seeded

Mix all the ingredients, except the soda and fruit slices, in a shaker or blender. Pour the mixture into a chilled highball glass and top with cold club soda. Garnish with the fruit slices.

Mai Tai

1 ounce Jamaican rum, preferably well aged
1 ounce Martinique rum
½ ounce curaçao
¼ ounce rock candy syrup
¼ ounce orgeat
1 scoop crushed ice
Lime peel
Mint sprig
Strip of fresh pineapple

Mix all the ingredients, except the lime peel, mint, and pineapple, in a shaker or blender. Pour the mixture into a chilled double old-fashioned glass. Garnish with the lime peel, mint sprig, and fresh pineapple.

Navy Grog

1 ounce light rum
1 ounce dark rum
1 ounce 86-proof Demerara rum
½ ounce orange juice
½ ounce guava juice
½ ounce lime juice
½ ounce pineapple juice
½ ounce orgeat, or to taste
1 scoop crushed ice
1 lime slice, seeded
1 mint sprig

Mix all the ingredients, except the lime slice and mint sprig, in a shaker or blender. Pour the mixture into a chilled double old-fashioned glass. Garnish with the lime slice and mint sprig.

Piña Colada I

Makes 6 servings

⅔ cup light or dark rum
½ cup coconut cream
1 cup pineapple juice, chilled
2 cups crushed ice
Thin slices of ripe pineapple, each speared to a maraschino cherry with a toothpick

Thoroughly chill 6 cocktail glasses. In an electric blender, combine all the ingredients, except the fruit garnish. Blend at high speed for 30 seconds. Pour the blend into the chilled glasses and garnish with the pineapple and cherry spears.

Piña Colada II

1½ ounces light rum
2 ounces pineapple juice
1 ounce coconut cream
1 scoop crushed ice

Combine and mix all the ingredients in a blender until smooth. Pour the blend into a chilled cocktail glass.

Plantation Punch

1½ ounces dark rum
¾ ounce Southern Comfort
1 teaspoon brown sugar,
    or to taste
1 ounce lemon juice
1 scoop crushed ice
Club soda
1 teaspoon port
Orange slice, seeded
Lemon slice, seeded

Mix the rum, Southern Comfort, sugar, lemon juice, and ice thoroughly in a shaker or blender. Pour the mixture into a tall collins glass and fill with cold club soda. Top off with a float of port and the fruit garnish.

Planter's Punch I

1½ ounces light rum
1½ ounces dark rum
3 ounces fresh orange juice
¾ ounce fresh lime juice
Simple syrup, to taste
Crushed ice
1 unpeeled orange slice, a peeled
    strip of ripe pineapple, and a
    maraschino cherry, all speared
    together with a toothpick

Combine all the ingredients, except the fruit spear, in a shaker. Shake well and pour into a tall, chilled collins glass. Garnish with the fruit spear and serve with straws.

Planter's Punch II

2 ounces dark rum
2¾ ounces orange juice
¾ ounce lemon juice
¼ to ½ ounce grenadine
1 maraschino cherry
1 orange slice, seeded

Mix the rum, juices, and grenadine in a shaker. Pour the mixture into a highball glass with ice. Garnish with the cherry and the orange slice.

Planter's Punch III

2 ounces dark rum
1½ ounces pineapple juice
1½ ounces orange juice
¾ ounce lemon juice
¼ to ½ ounce grenadine
1 maraschino cherry
1 strip fresh pineapple, peeled

Mix the rum, juices, and grenadine in a shaker. Pour the mixture into a highball glass with ice. Garnish with the cherry and the pineapple strip.

Planter's Punch IV

1½ to 2 ounces dark rum
3 ounces orange juice
Juice of ½ lemon or lime
1 teaspoon superfine sugar
Dash of grenadine
1 scoop crushed ice
1 orange slice, seeded
1 maraschino cherry

Mix all the ingredients, except the orange slice and cherry, in a shaker or blender. Pour the mixture into a tall, chilled collins glass. Garnish with the orange slice and cherry.

Planter's Punch V

2 ounces light rum
1 ounce dark rum
½ ounce sugar syrup, to taste
1 ounce lime juice
Several dashes of bitters
1 scoop crushed ice
Club soda
Orange slice
Lemon slice

Mix all the ingredients, except the soda and fruit slices, in a shaker. Pour the mixture into a chilled collins glass and top off with cold club soda. Garnish with the orange and lemon slices.

Rum Collins

1½ ounces light rum
1 ounce fresh lime juice
1 ounce sugar syrup
1 scoop crushed ice
Carbonated soda water
1 maraschino cherry speared with a toothpick to a slice of unpeeled, seeded orange

In a cocktail shaker, combine all the ingredients, except the soda and cherry garnish. Shake vigorously and strain into a tall collins glass. Add additional ice, if desired. Top off with soda water and garnish with the fruit spear.

Variations: For each drink add to taste: fresh orange juice, canned grapefruit juice, tamarind nectar, guava nectar, apple cider, or mango nectar.

Rum Highball

1¾ ounces light or dark rum
Ginger ale, soda water, or
    lemon-lime soda, to taste
Twist of lemon

Combine the rum and choice of soda in a highball glass with ice cubes. Stir well. Garnish with the lemon twist.

Rum Old-Fashioned

1¾ ounces light rum
1 sugar cube, laced with 2 to 3
    splashes of bitters
Maraschino cherry
Wedge of lemon and/or orange
Ice water or soda water, to taste

Mix together the rum and sugar cube in an old-fashioned glass with a few ice cubes. Add the cherry, wedge of lemon, and orange as desired. Top off with ice water or soda water.

Rum Swizzle

1 ounce light rum
½ ounce fresh lime juice
¼ ounce sugar syrup
1 dash of bitters
1 scoop crushed ice
Carbonated soda water
Maraschino cherry (optional)

In a cocktail shaker, combine all the ingredients, except soda and cherry. Shake until frothy, then immediately pour into a highball glass. Top off the glass with chilled soda water. If desired, garnish with the maraschino cherry.

Scorpion

1½ ounces dark rum
¾ ounce light rum
¾ ounce brandy
¼ ounce Triple Sec
1½ ounces orange juice
Juice of ½ lemon or lime
1 scoop crushed ice
Maraschino cherry

Mix all the ingredients, except the cherry, in a shaker. Strain the mixture into a highball glass half filled with fresh crushed ice. Garnish with the maraschino cherry.

Screwdriver

1 to 2 ounces white rum
4 to 6 ounces orange juice
1 scoop crushed ice
Orange slice

Put all the ingredients, except orange slice, in a tall highball glass. Stir well and garnish with the orange slice.

Tom and Jerry

1 egg, separated
1 teaspoon confectioners' sugar
½ ounce brandy
½ ounce rum
Splash of hot milk
Nutmeg

Beat the white and the yolk of the egg separately. Blend them together in a fresh glass. Add the confectioners' sugar to the blend and beat again. Pour in the brandy and the rum. While stirring gently, top with a splash of hot milk and sprinkle with nutmeg.

Zombie

2 ounces light rum
1 ounce dark rum
½ ounce 151-proof Demerara rum
1 ounce curaçao
1 teaspoon Pernod
1 ounce lemon juice
1 ounce orange juice
1 ounce pineapple juice
½ ounce papaya or guava juice (optional)
¼ ounce grenadine
½ ounce orgeat or sugar syrup, to taste
1 scoop crushed ice
Mint sprig
1 strip fresh pineapple

Mix all the ingredients, except the mint and pineapple strip, in a blender. Pour the mixture into a tall, chilled collins or hurricane glass. Garnish with the mint sprig and pineapple strip.

CREATIVE CONCOCTIONS

Admiral Vernon

1½ ounces light rum
½ ounce Grand Marnier
½ ounce lime juice
1 teaspoon orgeat
1 scoop crushed ice

Combine all the ingredients in a shaker. Shake well and strain into a chilled cocktail glass.

Andalusia

¾ ounce light rum
¾ ounce brandy
¾ ounce dry sherry
Several dashes of bitters

Combine all the ingredients in a mixing glass with several ice cubes. Stir well and strain into a chilled cocktail glass.

Angry Bull

1½ ounces light or white rum
Dash of Pickapeppa or
   Worcestershire sauce
Dash of liquid hot pepper sauce
   (optional)
1 scoop crushed ice
Chilled beef bouillon or
   consommé

Put all the ingredients, except the bouillon, in a cocktail glass. Top off the glass with the beef bouillon or consommé. Stir well before serving.

Ankle Breaker

1½ ounces 151-proof rum
1 ounce cherry brandy
1 ounce lemon or lime juice
1 teaspoon sugar syrup, to taste
1 scoop crushed ice

Combine all the ingredients in a shaker. Shake well and pour into a chilled old-fashioned glass.

Apricot Pie

1½ ounces light rum
½ ounce sweet vermouth
1 ounce apricot brandy
1 teaspoon lemon juice
Dash of grenadine
1 scoop crushed ice

Combine all the ingredients in a shaker. Mix well and pour into a chilled cocktail glass.

Apricot Queen

Makes 2 servings

3 ounces light rum
2 ounces apricot-flavored brandy
  or apricot liqueur
1 ounce curaçao
1 ounce lime juice
1 egg white
Crushed ice
Orange slices

Mix all the ingredients, except the orange slices, in a blender. Blend at low speed for 15 seconds. Pour the mixture into chilled old-fashioned glasses and garnish with the orange slices.

Aunt Mary

2 ounces white rum
3 ounces tomato juice
Pickapeppa or Worcestershire
  sauce, to taste
Salt and black pepper, to taste
Dash or two of Tabasco or hot
  pepper sauce (optional)
Wedge of fresh, seeded lime

Place ice cubes in a glass. Add all the ingredients, except the lime wedge. Stir gently and garnish with the lime on the rim of the glass.

Banana Rum

½ ounce light rum
½ ounce banana liqueur
½ ounce orange juice
1 scoop crushed ice

Combine all the ingredients in a shaker. Mix well and strain into a chilled cocktail glass.

Barracuda Bite

1½ ounces light rum
½ ounce Falernum syrup
1 ounce lemon juice
Crushed ice
Club soda
Orange slice

Mix all the ingredients, except the soda and orange slice, in a shaker. Pour mix into a chilled old-fashioned glass and top off with club soda. Garnish with the orange slice.

Bartman

¾ ounce applejack
¾ ounce light rum
½ ounce orange juice
½ ounce lemon juice
¼ ounce grenadine
1 scoop crushed ice
Orange slice

Mix all the ingredients, except the orange slice, in a shaker. Pour the mixture into a chilled old-fashioned glass. Garnish with the orange slice.

Bee's Kiss

1½ ounces light rum
1 teaspoon honey
1 teaspoon heavy cream
1 scoop crushed ice

Mix all the ingredients in a shaker. Strain the mixture into a chilled cocktail glass.

Bee's Knees

1½ ounces gold rum
½ ounce orange juice
½ ounce lime juice
1 teaspoon sugar syrup, or to taste
Several dashes curaçao
1 scoop crushed ice
Orange peel twist

Combine the all ingredients, except the orange peel, in a shaker. Mix thoroughly. Strain the mixture into a chilled cocktail glass and garnish with the orange peel.

Bermuda Cocktail

1½ ounces gold rum
¾ ounce apricot brandy
½ ounce lime juice
½ ounce orgeat or sugar syrup,
    to taste
Dash of grenadine

Combine all the ingredients in a shaker. Mix well and strain into a chilled cocktail glass.

Black Marie

¾ ounce dark rum
¾ ounce brandy
¼ ounce coffee liqueur
1 cup cold strong coffee
1 to 2 teaspoons sugar
2 scoops crushed ice

Combine the rum, brandy, liqueur, coffee, 1 teaspoon of the sugar, and 1 scoop of ice in a shaker. Shake vigorously. Strain the mixture into a highball glass and fill with fresh crushed ice. Add more sugar if desired.

Bolero

1½ ounces light rum
¾ ounce apple brandy or applejack
Several dashes of sweet vermouth
Twist of lemon peel

Combine all the ingredients, except the lemon peel, in a mixing glass with ice. Stir thoroughly and strain into a chilled cocktail glass. Garnish with the lemon peel.

Buccaneer Cocktail

1¾ ounces dark rum
1¾ ounces light rum
1¾ ounces Kahlúa or other coffee
  liqueur
6 ounces pineapple juice
1 scoop crushed ice
2 tablespoons heavy cream
Nutmeg

Combine both rums, the Kahlúa, and pineapple juice in a blender. Pour the mixture into a large wine goblet over crushed ice. Top with the heavy cream and sprinkle with freshly grated nutmeg.

Calypso Cocktail

1½ ounces gold rum
1 ounce pineapple juice
½ ounce lemon juice
1 teaspoon Falernum or sugar
  syrup, to taste
Dash of bitters
1 scoop crushed ice
Pinch of grated nutmeg

Combine all the ingredients, except the nutmeg, in a shaker. Mix well and strain into a chilled cocktail glass. Sprinkle the nutmeg on top.

Captain Bill's Regatta Drink

2½ ounces Jamaican rum
4½ ounces tonic water
4 ice cubes
1 lime wedge

Pour the rum and tonic over ice cubes into a chilled cocktail glass. Twist the lime wedge over the drink and drop it in.

Cardinal

2 ounces light rum
½ ounce amaretto
½ ounce Triple Sec
1 ounce lime juice (fresh or
  bottled)
½ teaspoon grenadine
Lime slice

Mix all the ingredients, except the lime slice, in a shaker with ice. Pour the mixture into a chilled old-fashioned glass and garnish with the lime slice.

Centenario

1½ ounces gold rum
¾ ounce aged white rum
¼ ounce Triple Sec
¼ ounce coffee liqueur
¼ ounce grenadine
Juice of 1 lime
1 scoop crushed ice
Fresh mint sprig

Combine all the ingredients, except the mint, in a highball glass. Stir well. Garnish with the mint sprig.

Coffee Hummer

1 ounce coffee liqueur
1 ounce light rum
½ cup vanilla ice cream

Combine all the ingredients in a blender. Blend until smooth. Pour the blend into a chilled parfait glass.

Conditioner

1 ounce Puerto Rican rum
1 egg yolk
1 ounce curaçao
1 ounce Pernod or Herbsaint

Combine all the ingredients in a shaker with ice. Mix well and strain into a tall collins glass filled with ice.

Creole

1¾ ounces light rum
3½ ounces beef bouillon
2 splashes of lemon juice
Pepper, salt, Tabasco,
    Worcestershire sauce, to taste

Mix the rum, bouillon, and lemon juice in a highball glass with several ice cubes. Flavor to taste with combined seasonings.

Cuban Manhattan (dry)

1½ ounces light rum
¾ ounce dry vermouth
Dash of bitters
Twist of lemon

Mix all the ingredients, except the lemon twist, in a mixing glass with ice cubes. Strain the mixture into a chilled cocktail glass and garnish with the lemon twist.

Cuban Manhattan (sweet)

1½ ounces light rum
Dash of bitters
¾ ounce sweet vermouth
Maraschino cherry

Mix the rum, bitters, and vermouth in a mixing glass with ice cubes.

Strain the mixture into a chilled cocktail glass and garnish with the maraschino cherry.

Curaçao Cooler

1 ounce dark rum
1 ounce curaçao
1 ounce lime juice
1 scoop crushed ice
Club soda
1 orange slice, seeded

Mix the rum, curaçao, lime juice, and ice in a shaker. Pour the mixture into a chilled highball glass and top off with cold club soda. Garnish with the orange slice.

Davis Cocktail

1½ ounces dark rum
¾ ounce dry vermouth
2 dashes of raspberry syrup
Juice of ½ lime
1 scoop crushed ice

Mix all the ingredients in a shaker. Strain the mixture into a cocktail glass.

Derby Special

1½ ounces light rum
½ ounce Triple Sec
1 ounce orange juice
½ ounce lime juice
1 scoop crushed ice

Mix all the ingredients in a blender until almost slushy. Pour the mixture into a chilled cocktail glass.

Devil's Tail

1½ ounces gold rum
½ ounce vodka
½ ounce apricot liqueur
½ ounce lime juice
½ teaspoon grenadine
1 scoop crushed ice
Lime peel, for garnish

Mix all the ingredients, except the lime peel, thoroughly in a blender. Pour the mixture into a chilled cocktail glass. Twist the lime peel over the drink and drop it in.

Doctor Bird Cocktail

1½ ounces light rum
1 teaspoon honey
1 teaspoon heavy cream
Dash or two of grenadine
1 scoop crushed ice
Fresh flower for garnish

Combine all the ingredients, except the flower, in a shaker and shake vigorously. Strain the mixture into a chilled champagne glass and garnish with a rinsed bougainvillea or other fresh flower.

Ernest Hemingway Special

1½ ounces light rum
Juice of ½ lime
¼ ounce grapefruit juice
¼ ounce maraschino liqueur
1 scoop crushed ice

Mix all the ingredients thoroughly in a shaker. Pour the mixture into a chilled cocktail glass.

Gilligan's Island

1½ ounces light rum
Juice of ½ lime
¼ ounce grapefruit juice
¼ ounce maraschino liqueur
1 scoop crushed ice

Mix all the ingredients thoroughly in a shaker. Pour the mixture into a chilled cocktail glass.

Goldie's Rum Fizz

3 ounces light rum
1 egg yolk
1 tablespoon confectioners' sugar
1½ ounces (or more) fresh lime juice
Dash of bitters
Crushed ice
Chilled soda water

Combine all the ingredients, except the soda water, in a shaker. Mix well and strain into a tall highball glass. Top off the glass with chilled soda water.

Happy Apple

1½ ounces gold rum
3 ounces sweet apple cider
½ ounce lemon juice
1 scoop crushed ice
Twist of lime peel

Combine the rum, cider, lemon juice, and ice in a shaker or blender. Mix well. Pour the mixture into a chilled old-fashioned glass and garnish with the lime peel.

Harbour Street Cocktail

1½ to 2 ounces light rum
¾ ounce lime juice
Twist of lime peel

Pour the rum and lime juice into an old-fashioned glass with ice cubes. Stir gently and garnish with the lime peel.

Hawaii Five-O

1 ounce dark rum
1 ounce gin
1 ounce dry red wine
1 ounce orange juice
1 scoop crushed ice
1 lime slice

Combine all the ingredients, except the lime, in a shaker or blender. Mix briefly, just to combine. Pour the mixture into a chilled old-fashioned glass and garnish with the lime slice.

Heavyweight Sailor

1½ ounces 151-proof dark rum
1½ ounces dark rum
¾ ounce light rum
¼ ounce coffee liqueur
1½ ounces lime juice
Juice of ½ lime or lemon
Wedge of lime, seeded

Mix all the ingredients, except the lime wedge, in a shaker with crushed ice. Pour the mixture into a highball glass. Garnish with the lime wedge.

Isle of Pines

1½ ounces light rum
2 ounces grapefruit juice

Pour the rum and juice into a chilled highball glass. Add a few ice cubes and stir well.

Jamaica Blue

2 ounces light rum
½ ounce Triple Sec
½ ounce lemon juice
1 teaspoon blueberry syrup
1 scoop crushed ice
Club soda
Fresh blueberries (optional, for garnish)
Lemon wedge, seeded

Mix all the ingredients, except the soda, blueberries, and lime, in a shaker. Pour the mixture into a chilled collins glass and top off with club soda. Garnish with a few blueberries and the lemon wedge.

Jamaica Cream

1½ ounces light rum
1 ounce gin
1 ounce light cream
1 teaspoon lemon juice
1 teaspoon sugar syrup, or to taste
1 scoop crushed ice
Club soda, chilled

Mix all the ingredients, except the soda, in a blender until thoroughly combined. Pour the mixture into a chilled highball glass and top off with club soda.

Jamaican Martini

2 ounces light rum
¼ to ½ ounce dry sherry
1 scoop crushed ice
Lime peel or green olive

In a mixing glass, stir together the rum, sherry, and ice. Stir until well chilled, but do not allow the mixture to become diluted. Strain the mixture into a chilled martini glass. Garnish with the lime peel or green olive.

Journalist

1½ ounces light rum
Juice of ½ lime
1 teaspoon sugar
2 splashes of apricot brandy
2 splashes of Triple Sec
1 scoop crushed ice
Lime twist

Mix all the ingredients, except the lime twist, in a shaker. Pour the mixture into a cocktail glass and garnish with the lime twist.

Lallah Rookh

1½ ounces light rum
¾ ounce Cognac
½ ounce crème de vanille or vanilla extract
1 teaspoon sugar syrup, or to taste
1 scoop crushed ice
1 generous tablespoon whipped cream

Mix all the ingredients, except the whipped cream, in a shaker or blender. Pour the mixture into a chilled wineglass and top off with a dollop of the whipped cream.

Liberty Cocktail

1½ ounces light rum
¾ ounce applejack
Juice of ½ lime
1 scoop crushed ice
1 teaspoon superfine sugar
1 lime wedge, seeded (optional)

Combine all the ingredients, except the lime wedge, in a shaker, adding the sugar last. Blend thoroughly. Pour the mixture into a chilled cocktail glass. Garnish with the lime, if desired.

Lightweight Sailor

1 ounce dark rum
¾ ounce light rum
¼ ounce sugar syrup
¾ ounce lime juice
Juice of ½ lime or lemon
1 scoop crushed ice
1 lime wedge, seeded

Combine all the ingredients, except the lime wedge, in a shaker and shake vigorously. Strain the mixture into an old-fashioned glass half filled with fresh crushed ice. Garnish with the lime wedge.

Little Flower

1½ ounces orange curaçao
1½ ounces white rum
1½ ounces grapefruit juice
Orange peel

Mix the curaçao, rum, and juice with ice in a shaker. Strain the mixture into a cocktail glass, and garnish with the orange peel.

Mary Pickford

1½ ounces light rum
1½ ounces pineapple juice
Splash of grenadine
1 scoop crushed ice
1 maraschino cherry

Combine all the ingredients, except the cherry, in a shaker. Mix well and pour into a chilled cocktail glass. Garnish with the cherry.

Maude's Downfall

1 scoop crushed ice
2 ounces light rum
Canned or fresh grapefruit juice, well chilled
Salt

In a tall highball glass filled with crushed ice, combine the rum and grapefruit juice. Add salt to taste. Serve with a swizzle stick.

Mojito

Juice of ½ lime
1 teaspoon superfine sugar
Mint leaves, to taste
1 scoop crushed ice
2 ounces light rum
Soda water
Sprig of mint for garnish (optional)

Place lime juice and sugar in a highball glass; stir until sugar is dissolved. Add a few mint leaves, pressing them to the inside of the glass. Fill the glass with crushed ice and pour in the rum, stirring gently. Top off with soda water and garnish with a sprig of mint.

Montego Tea

1 scoop crushed ice
¾ ounce light rum
¾ ounce dark rum
¾ ounce brandy
¾ ounce Triple Sec
¾ ounce orange juice
Juice of ½ lime
Cola to taste

Fill a tall drink glass with the ice. Pour in both rums, the brandy, Triple Sec, and orange juice. Stir well. Add the lime juice and top off with cola.

Myrtle Bank Punch

1½ ounces 151-proof Demerara rum
Juice of ½ lime
1 teaspoon grenadine
1 teaspoon sugar syrup, or to taste
1 scoop crushed ice
½ ounce maraschino liqueur

Combine all the ingredients, except the maraschino, in a shaker or blender. Mix well and pour into a chilled highball glass. Top off with a maraschino float.

Naked Lady Cocktail

Makes 3 servings

4½ ounces light rum
3 ounces sweet vermouth
4 dashes of apricot brandy
2 dashes of grenadine
4 dashes of fresh lime or lemon juice
1 scoop crushed ice

Combine all the ingredients in a shaker. Shake well and strain into 3 chilled cocktail glasses.

Pancho Villa

1 ounce light rum
1 ounce gin
1 ounce apricot liqueur or apricot brandy
1 teaspoon cherry brandy
1 teaspoon pineapple juice
1 scoop crushed ice

Combine and mix all the ingredients in a shaker. Pour the mixture into a chilled cocktail glass.

Pancho's Rum Fizz

Makes 2 servings

1½ ounces light rum
1½ ounces dark rum
1½ ounces apricot brandy
1½ ounces fresh lime juice
1 tablespoon (or more) granulated
  sugar
2 tablespoons heavy cream
1 scoop crushed ice
Chilled soda water

Combine all the ingredients, except the soda, in a shaker. Mix until well blended. Strain the mixture into 2 chilled highball glasses and top off with the soda water.

Pirate's Julep

6 mint leaves
1 teaspoon sugar syrup
Several dashes of bitters
1 scoop crushed ice
2 to 3 ounces gold rum
1 teaspoon curaçao
Mint sprig
Confectioners' sugar

Muddle the mint leaves with sugar syrup in a chilled old-fashioned glass. Add the bitters and fill the glass with crushed ice. Pour in the rum and swizzle mixture until the glass frosts, adding more ice if necessary. Top with curaçao and garnish with a mint sprig dusted with powdered sugar.

Platinum Blonde Cocktail

1½ ounces light rum
1½ ounces Triple Sec
½ ounce cream
1 scoop crushed ice
Green maraschino cherry
  (optional)

Combine all the ingredients, except the cherry, in a shaker. Shake well and strain into a cocktail glass. Garnish with the green maraschino cherry on a cocktail stick, if desired.

Presidente Seco

1½ ounces light rum
¾ ounce dry vermouth
Splash of red curaçao
1 lemon twist

Mix the rum, vermouth, and curaçao in a mixing glass with 6 to 8 ice cubes. Pour the mixture into a chilled cocktail glass and garnish with the lemon twist.

Quaker's Cocktail

¾ ounce light rum
¾ ounce brandy
2 splashes of raspberry syrup
Juice of ½ lime
1 scoop crushed ice

Mix all the ingredients thoroughly in shaker. Strain the mixture into a chilled cocktail glass.

Rampart Street Parade

1 ounce light rum
¾ ounce crème de banane
½ ounce Southern Comfort
1 ounce lime juice
1 scoop crushed ice

Mix all the ingredients in a shaker or blender. Strain the mixture into a chilled cocktail glass.

Riptide

1 ounce dark rum
1 ounce light rum
1 ounce 151-proof rum
1 ounce grapefruit juice
1 ounce orange juice
Several dashes of orange curaçao
Several dashes of Pernod
1 orange slice, seeded
1 maraschino cherry

Mix all the ingredients, except the orange slice and cherry, in a shaker with ice. Pour the mixture into a chilled double old-fashioned glass and garnish with the fruit.

Rum Alexander

1½ ounces light rum
¾ ounce brown crème de cacao
1 ounce cream
Freshly grated nutmeg

Combine all the ingredients, except the nutmeg, in a shaker with a few ice cubes. Mix well and strain into a cocktail glass. Sprinkle the grated nutmeg on top.

Rum Apple

1½ ounces light rum
¾ ounce sweet vermouth
½ ounce Calvados or applejack
1 teaspoon lemon juice
Dash of grenadine
Dash of apricot brandy
1 scoop crushed ice

Combine all the ingredients in a shaker and mix thoroughly. Strain the mixture into a chilled cocktail glass.

Rum Beguine

1½ ounces Martinique or Haitian rum
2 ounces Sauternes, chilled
2 ounces pineapple juice
1 ounce lemon juice
½ ounce Falernum or sugar syrup, to taste
Several dashes of bitters
1 scoop crushed ice
1 fresh pineapple slice

Mix all the ingredients, except the pineapple slice, in a shaker. Pour the mixture into a chilled collins glass. Garnish with the pineapple.

Rum Martini

1¾ ounces light rum
¼ ounce dry vermouth
1 black olive

Mix the rum and vermouth in a stir-ring glass with 6 to 8 ice cubes. Strain the mixture into a chilled mar-tini glass or a chilled small cocktail glass. Garnish with the olive.

Rum Sour

1½ ounces light rum
¼ ounce gold rum
¾ ounce fresh lemon juice
¾ ounce sugar syrup
1 maraschino cherry

Combine all the ingredients, except the cherry, in a shaker with ice cubes. Shake until frothy. Strain the mixture into a chilled sour glass and garnish with the cherry.

Rum and Tonic

1 scoop crushed ice
1½ ounces light rum
Quinine water or tonic water
Wedge of lime, seeded

In a tall highball glass filled with crushed ice, combine the light rum with quinine water or tonic to taste. Garnish with the lime wedge on the rim of the glass.

Salome Cocktail

3 ounces dark rum
1½ ounces crème de banane
¾ ounce fresh lime juice
4 tablespoons simple sugar syrup
1 scoop crushed ice
Thick ripe banana slice speared
     with a toothpick to a
     maraschino cherry

Combine all the ingredients, except the banana garnish, in a shaker. Shake vigorously and strain into a chilled champagne glass. Decorate with the banana garnish.

September Sunrise

2 to 3 ounces light rum
½ ounce lime juice
1 teaspoon grenadine
1 egg white
1 scoop crushed ice

Mix all the ingredients in a shaker until almost frothy. Strain the mix-ture into a chilled cocktail glass.

Sir Walter Cocktail

1 ounce gold rum
¾ ounce brandy
¼ ounce Triple Sec
Splash of grenadine
Juice of ½ lime
1 scoop crushed ice

Mix all the ingredients thoroughly in a shaker with crushed ice. Pour the mixture into a chilled cocktail glass and serve.

Sledgehammer

¾ ounce gold rum
¾ ounce brandy
¾ ounce Calvados or applejack
Dash of Pernod
1 scoop crushed ice

Mix all the ingredients in a shaker. Strain the mixture into a chilled cocktail glass.

Spanish Main Cocktail

2 ounces rum
½ ounce dry vermouth
½ ounce sweet vermouth
Dash of bitters
Maraschino cherry

Put the rum, vermouths, and bitters in an old-fashioned glass filled with ice cubes. Stir well and garnish with the cherry speared onto a cocktail stick.

Sunsplash

1½ ounces light rum
½ ounce dry vermouth
½ ounce sweet vermouth

Combine all the ingredients in a mixing glass with ice cubes and stir well. Strain the mixture into a chilled cocktail glass.

Sweet Gold

1 ounce light rum
1 ounce Triple Sec
1 ounce heavy cream
1 scoop crushed ice

Mix all the ingredients thoroughly in a blender. Strain the mixture into a chilled cocktail glass.

Tobago Cays

1½ ounces gold rum
½ ounce lime juice
½ ounce sugar syrup
½ teaspoon maraschino liqueur
1 scoop crushed ice
½ teaspoon Pernod

Mix all the ingredients, except Pernod, in a blender until smooth. Pour the mixture into a chilled wineglass. Top with a float of Pernod.

Top Gun

1½ ounces light rum
½ ounce guava nectar
½ ounce orange juice
½ ounce lemon juice
1 scoop crushed ice

Combine all the ingredients in a blender. Mix until smooth and uniform in color. Pour the mixture into a chilled deep-saucer champagne glass.

Trade Winds

2 ounces gold rum
½ ounce slivovitz or other plum
   brandy
½ ounce lime juice
½ ounce orgeat or Falernum
1 scoop crushed ice

Combine all the ingredients in a blender and mix until smooth. Pour the mixture into a chilled cocktail glass.

Watermelon Cooler

2 ounces light rum
½ ounce melon liqueur
½ ounce lime juice
½ ounce sugar syrup, or to taste
1 cup seeded and diced
   watermelon
1 scoop crushed ice
1 lime slice, seeded

Mix all the ingredients, except the lime slice, in a blender at low speed for 15 seconds. Pour the mixture into a chilled double old-fashioned glass. Garnish with the lime slice.

Windy City

Makes 2 servings

2 ounces gold rum
2 ounces port
1 ounce lemon juice
1 ounce sugar syrup, or to taste
1 egg white
Crushed ice
Cold club soda

Mix everything except the soda in a shaker. Strain the mixture into chilled collins glasses and top off with the club soda.

SIGNATURE DRINKS

Añejo Highball

DALE DEGROFF, THE RAINBOW ROOM,
NEW YORK CITY

1¾ ounces aged rum
¾ ounce orange curaçao
¾ ounce fresh lime juice
Dash of bitters
Ginger beer
Club soda
Thin wheel of fresh lime
Slice of fresh orange, cut in half

Pour the rum, curaçao, lime juice,
and bitters into a highball glass with
ice. Top off with a splash of ginger
beer and a splash of soda. Garnish
with the lime and orange slices.

Barbados Cocktail

ASTA, SAN FRANCISCO

1½ ounces Barbados rum
½ ounce Triple Sec
Juice from 3 lime wedges
Lime slice

Fill a shaker with ice. Add all the
ingredients, except the lime slice,
and shake with long sweeping shakes
three times. Strain the mixture into a
chilled cocktail glass and garnish
with the lime slice.

Barbancourt Rum Cosmopolitan

CYPRESS CLUB, SAN FRANCISCO

1¼ ounces Barbancourt 15-year
     rum
½ ounce cranberry juice
½ teaspoon lime juice
½ teaspoon Cointreau or
     Triple Sec

Mix all the ingredients in a shaker
with crushed ice. Strain the mixture
into a chilled martini glass.

Bongo Cola

VARIOUS WEST COAST BARS

1½ ounces gold rum
1 ounce coffee liqueur
2 ounces pineapple juice
Dash of kirsch
Dash of lemon juice
1 scoop crushed ice
Cola
Maraschino cherry

Mix all the ingredients, except cola
and cherry, in a shaker. Pour the
mixture into a tall, chilled collins
glass with fresh ice cubes. Top off
the glass with cold cola and stir
gently. Garnish with the cherry.

Captain Cosmo

JULIE'S SUPPER CLUB, SAN FRANCISCO

1¼ ounces spiced rum
¼ ounce Triple Sec
¼ ounce lime juice
Splash of cranberry juice
Lime wedge

Pour all the ingredients, except the lime wedge, into a large mixing glass filled with ice cubes. Stir well and strain into a chilled martini glass. Gently squeeze the lime wedge over the drink, then use it as garnish.

Chapultepec

HOTEL PRESIDENTE, MEXICO CITY

1¼ ounces gold rum
½ ounce brandy
¼ ounce sweet vermouth
¼ ounce tequila
1 teaspoon sugar syrup, or to taste
1 scoop crushed ice

Combine all the ingredients in a shaker or blender. Mix well and pour the mixture into a chilled whisky sour glass.

Caribe Piña Colada

CARIBE HILTON, SAN JUAN, PUERTO RICO

Makes 4 servings

2 ounces dark rum
8 ounces light rum
2 ounces heavy cream
5 ounces coconut cream
10 ounces pineapple juice
2 to 3 scoops crushed ice
4 strips fresh pineapple

Mix all the ingredients, except the pineapple strips, in a blender for 10 seconds. Pour the mixture into chilled hurricane or poco grande glasses. Garnish with the pineapple strips.

Dirty Banana

THE CAFE AT THE SIGN OF THE DOVE, NEW YORK CITY

Makes 8 servings

8 ounces light rum
16 ounces sweet lemon mix*
8 ounces banana liqueur
4 overripe bananas
2 bananas, sliced for garnish

Blend all the ingredients, except the banana garnish, until well mixed. Pour the blend into old-fashioned glasses with ice cubes and garnish with the banana slices.

To make sweet lemon mix: Blend juice from 8 lemons with ¼ cup sugar and 1 egg white until well mixed. Yield: 16 ounces

Dr. Pepper

THE BALBOA CAFE, SAN FRANCISCO

½ ounce 151-proof rum
½ ounce amaretto
½ pint beer

Pour the rum and the amaretto into a small shot glass. Light the liquor in the shot glass. Drop the flaming glass into a half-pint glass of beer.

Foreign Affair

THE ECCENTRIC, CHICAGO

1¼ ounces light rum
¼ ounce coffee liqueur
1 scoop (2 to 3 ounces) vanilla ice cream
Splash of milk
1 pirouette cookie (optional)

Combine all the ingredients, except the cookie, in a blender and mix to a creamy consistency—do not overmix. Pour the blend into a martini glass and garnish with the cookie.

French Stinger

STARS, SAN FRANCISCO

3 ounces light rum
1 ounce green Chartreuse

Stir the rum and Chartreuse in a mixing glass with plenty of ice. Pour the mixture into a frozen stem glass.

Golden Gloves

LA FLORIDA BAR, HAVANA, CUBA

2 ounces rum
1 teaspoon Cointreau or
   Triple Sec
1 teaspoon sugar
Juice of ½ lemon
1 scoop crushed ice
Orange peel

In an electric blender, blend together all the ingredients except the orange peel. Squeeze the peel into a chilled cocktail glass and rub it around the inside of the glass. Pour the mixture into the prepared glass.

Green Eyes

"21" CLUB, NEW YORK CITY

1 ounce dark rum
¼ ounce melon liqueur
½ ounce lime juice
½ ounce coconut cream
1½ ounces pineapple juice

Pour all the ingredients into an old-fashioned glass containing several ice cubes. Stir gently.

Green Lizard

THE BALBOA CAFE, SAN FRANCISCO

¾ ounce 151-proof light rum
¾ ounce green Chartreuse

Pour both ingredients into a shot glass.

Griswold Inn Hot Buttered Rum

GRISWOLD INN, ESSEX, CONNECTICUT

Cinnamon stick
Lemon slice
Dash of ground cloves
Dash of bitters
Dash of superfine sugar
1½ ounces rum
Hot apple cider

Put all the ingredients, except the rum and cider, in a small mug. Add the rum to the mug, then top off with hot cider.

Harpoon

MOORS RESTAURANT, PROVINCETOWN, MASSACHUSETTS

2 ounces rum
4 ounces cranberry juice
½ cling peach
½ ounce grenadine
1 scoop crushed ice
Orange slice
Cherry

In a blender, combine the rum, cranberry juice, cling peach, grenadine, and ice. Blend until frozen. Pour the mixture into a wineglass. Garnish with the orange slice and cherry.

Havana Beach

LA FLORIDA BAR, HAVANA, CUBA

1 ounce light rum
1 ounce pineapple juice
1 teaspoon sugar
1 scoop crushed ice

Combine all the ingredients in a shaker. Mix well and strain into a large chilled cocktail glass.

Henry Morgan Cocktail

"21" CLUB, NEW YORK CITY

2 ounces light rum
3 ounces orange juice
Dash of grenadine
Cold soda

Pour the rum, orange juice, and grenadine over ice into a collins glass. Stir gently. Top off the glass with soda.

Jamaican Dust

DORIAN'S RED HAND, NEW YORK CITY

Makes 3 shots

1 ounce coffee liqueur
2 ounces dark rum
4 ounces pineapple juice
1 scoop crushed ice

Combine all the ingredients in a shaker. Mix well and strain into 3 shot glasses.

Kohala Sunset

MAUNA LANI BAY HOTEL, BIG ISLAND, HAWAII

2 ounces light rum
Dash of orange liqueur
Dash of grenadine
2 ounces orange juice
1 ounce freshly squeezed lemon juice
1 scoop crushed ice
¼ lime
1 maraschino cherry
1 pineapple wedge

Mix the rum, liqueur, grenadine, and juices in a blender with ½ scoop crushed ice. Place the rest of the crushed ice in a 14-ounce punch glass. Squeeze the lime and leave the shell in the glass. Fill the glass with the blended mixture. Garnish with the cherry and pineapple wedge.

Kona

TRADER VIC'S, SAN FRANCISCO

½ lime
¼ ounce maraschino liqueur
1½ ounces light rum
½ ounce lemon juice

Squeeze the lime into a mixing glass with several ice cubes. Drop in the shell and add liqueur, rum, and lemon juice. Stir well and strain into a chilled cocktail glass.

Martian Tweetie

WESTIN PEACHTREE PLAZA, ATLANTA

½ ounce dark rum
½ ounce light rum
½ ounce passion fruit syrup
½ ounce mai tai mix
⅓ ounce or 1 teaspoon honey
2 teaspoons coconut cream

Combine all the ingredients in a blender with ice. Blend well. Pour the mixture over fresh ice cubes in a chilled collins glass.

Prairie Fire

THE BALBOA CAFE, SAN FRANCISCO

1½ ounces 151-proof light rum
3 squirts of Tabasco

Put both ingredients in a shot glass. Carefully ignite the shot with a match. Blow out the flame before drinking!

Rum Punch Happy Jack

DOUG BIEDERBECK, BIX, SAN FRANCISCO

2 ounces light rum
Juice of 1 lime
2 dashes of bitters
Splash of guava juice
1 scant teaspoon superfine sugar
Splash of grenadine
Freshly grated nutmeg

Combine all the ingredients, except the nutmeg, in a shaker with ice and mix thoroughly. Pour the mixture into a 10-ounce highball glass. Garnish with a small amount of the nutmeg.

Shark's Tooth

TRADER VIC'S, SAN FRANCISCO

1 ounce 151-proof rum
Juice of ½ lime (save shell)
½ ounce lemon juice
Dash of grenadine
Dash of sugar syrup
1 scoop crushed ice
Club soda

Combine all the ingredients, except the club soda, in a shaker. Pour the mixture into a large pilsner glass and top off with cold soda. Add the lime shell for garnish. Stir gently.

Sharkbite

THE BALBOA CAFE, SAN FRANCISCO

1 ounce dark rum
1 ounce orange juice
Splash of grenadine

In a shaker with crushed ice, mix together the rum and orange juice. Strain the mixture into a shot glass and top with a splash of grenadine.

T.A.T.'s Mon Dude

T.A.T.'S, PALM BEACH, FLORIDA

½ ounce dark rum
½ ounce light rum
¼ ounce banana liqueur
¼ ounce Galliano
3 ounces orange juice
1 ounce piña colada mix
1 ounce pineapple juice
1 scoop crushed ice
1 slice fresh orange
1 maraschino cherry

In a shaker, mix all the ingredients, except the orange slice and cherry, until smooth. Pour the mixture into a chilled collins glass and garnish with the orange and cherry skewered on a toothpick.

Tahiti Bikini

DORIAN'S RED HAND, NEW YORK CITY

1 ounce rum
1 ounce vodka
1 ounce rum liqueur
1 ounce peach schnapps
1 ounce Triple Sec
1 ounce pineapple juice
1 ounce orange juice
1 thin slice mango or tropical fruit
   (optional)

Pour all the ingredients, except the mango, into a collins glass containing several ice cubes. Stir thoroughly. Garnish with the mango or other tropical fruit.

Tahitian Honey Bee

TRADER VIC'S, SAN FRANCISCO

1 teaspoon honey
½ ounce lemon juice
1½ ounces rum
1 scoop crushed ice
Lemon peel twist

In a shaker, mix together the honey and lemon juice. Add the rum and crushed ice to the shaker. Shake well and strain into a chilled cocktail glass. Garnish with the lemon peel.

Tamarind Treat

CHEF ALLEN'S, NORTH MIAMI, FLORIDA

2 ounces rum
4 ounces tamarind juice
1 slice starfruit (carambola)

Combine the rum and tamarind juice in a highball glass with ice. Stir and garnish with the starfruit.

The Last Resort

EAST COAST GRILL, CAMBRIDGE, MASSACHUSETTS

Makes 10 servings

20 ounces gold rum
1 splash dark rum per drink
1 slice mango or papaya per drink

Last Resort Mixture:
12 ounces papaya juice
12 ounces guava juice
1¼ cups pineapple juice
1¼ cups orange juice
1 cup coconut cream
½ cup grenadine

Combine all the ingredients for the Last Resort mixture in a large container and mix well. Fill a 16-ounce glass with ice and add 2 ounces of the gold rum. Fill the glass to the top of the ice level with the Last Resort mixture. Pour the contents of the glass into a blender. Blend until completely combined, about 1 minute. Pour the mixture into a large wineglass and float a splash of dark rum on top. Garnish with the fruit slice. Repeat for each serving.

Tonga

TRADER VIC'S, SAN FRANCISCO

Makes 25 servings

2 (750 ml) bottles light rum
12 ounces brandy
12 ounces curaçao
12 ounces Passionola or passion
  fruit nectar
1 quart lemon juice
1½ pints orange juice
6 ounces grenadine

Chill all the ingredients beforehand.
After mixing well, pour over a block
of ice in a large punch bowl.

Waikoloa Fizz

VARIOUS WAIKIKI BARS

1½ ounces Barbados rum
½ ounce Jamaica rum
3 ounces pineapple juice
½ ounce passion fruit juice
1 teaspoon coconut syrup
1 scoop crushed ice
Lemon-lime soda
Slice of fresh lime

Mix all the ingredients, except the
soda and lime, in a shaker. Pour the
mixture into a chilled collins glass
and fill with lemon-lime soda. Stir
gently and garnish with the lime
slice.

West Indies Punch

TRADER VIC'S, SAN FRANCISCO

Makes 12 servings

2 cups superfine sugar
1 pint green tea infusion
12 large limes
1 cup guava marmalade
2 cups boiling water
½ bottle (375 ml) dark rum
½ bottle (375 ml) light rum
1 pint Cognac
1 bottle (750 ml) Madeira

Dissolve the sugar in the tea. Halve
the limes, squeeze, and add their
juice and shells to the tea mixture. In
a saucepan, dissolve the guava marmalade in the boiling water. Combine the guava mixture with the lime
juice and tea mixture. Add rum, Cognac, and Madeira and let stand
overnight. The next day, remove the
lime shells and pour the punch over
a large piece of ice in a punch bowl.
Let chill thoroughly before serving.

TROPICAL DRINKS

Acapulco

1¾ ounces light rum
¼ ounce Triple Sec
1 egg white
1 teaspoon sugar, or 2 splashes
    of sugar syrup
Juice of ½ lime
1 scoop crushed ice
1 lime wedge, seeded

Mix all the ingredients, except the lime wedge, in a shaker until well blended. Pour the mixture into a chilled cocktail glass and garnish with the lime wedge.

Note: Ice cubes may be used in place of crushed ice; the drink will no longer have a slushy consistency, but it will still be delicious.

Amanda's Mango Masterpiece

Make 10 servings

1 cup peeled fresh mango
1 cup light rum
¼ cup strained fresh lime juice
¼ cup water
Sugar syrup to taste
1 scoop crushed ice

Have all the ingredients well chilled prior to assembling this recipe. Purée the mango in a blender until

smooth. Add the other ingredients and blend until smooth and very cold. Serve small portions in chilled stemmed cocktail glasses.

Angostura Scorpion

3 tablespoons light rum
2 tablespoons sugar syrup
2 tablespoons strained fresh lime
    juice
Dash of bitters
1 scoop crushed ice

Combine all the ingredients in a shaker. Mix well and strain into a chilled cocktail glass.

Banana Bliss

1½ ounces white rum
1½ ounces crème de banane
1 ounce orange juice
Dash of bitters
1½ ounces heavy cream
2 dashes grenadine
3 banana wheels

In a shaker, mix all the ingredients, except the grenadine and bananas, with ice. Strain the mixture into an old-fashioned glass. Decorate with grenadine and banana wheels.

Banana Colada

1½ ounces rum
2 ounces coconut cream
1 banana, peeled and sliced
1 teaspoon lemon juice
1 cup ice

Combine all the ingredients in a blender and blend until smooth. Pour the mixture into a chilled parfait glass.

Bananarama

1½ ounces gold rum
1 ounce crème de banane
½ ounce 151-proof rum
4 ounces pineapple juice
1 ounce orange juice
½ ounce orgeat
½ ripe banana, peeled and sliced
1 scoop crushed ice
Lime slice

Mix all the ingredients, except the lime slice, in a blender. Blend until smooth. Pour the mixture into a chilled collins glass and garnish with the lime slice.

Barbados Planter's Punch

3 ounces gold rum
Juice of 1 lime
1 teaspoon sugar syrup
Dash of bitters
Club soda or water
1 scoop crushed ice
Ripe banana slice
Orange slices
Maraschino cherry
Pinch of grated nutmeg

Combine all the ingredients, except the fruit and nutmeg, in a shaker. Shake vigorously. Pour the mixture into a chilled large collins glass. Garnish with the banana slice, orange slice, cherry, and a sprinkle of the grated nutmeg.

Batida de Piña

2 to 3 ounces light rum
⅔ cup crushed pineapple
(fresh or canned)
1 teaspoon sugar syrup
Mint sprig (optional)

Mix all the ingredients, except the mint, in a blender with a few ice cubes. Blend until smooth. Pour the mixture into a chilled double old-fashioned glass and garnish with the mint sprig.

Beachcomber

1½ ounces light rum
½ ounce Triple Sec
½ ounce lime juice
Several dashes of maraschino
    liqueur
1 scoop crushed ice

Mix all the ingredients in a blender
until smooth. Strain the mixture into
a chilled cocktail glass.

Cantaloupe Cup

1½ ounces light rum
⅓ cup diced ripe cantaloupe
½ ounce lime juice
½ ounce orange juice
½ teaspoon sugar syrup
1 scoop crushed ice
1 thin slice of cantaloupe

Mix all the ingredients, except the
cantaloupe slice, in a blender until
smooth. Pour the mixture into a
chilled old-fashioned glass and garnish with the cantaloupe slice.

Chocolada

1½ ounces white rum
¼ ounce coffee liqueur
¼ ounce dark rum
¾ ounce chocolate syrup
¾ ounce coconut cream
1 scoop crushed ice
Chocolate shavings

Mix all the ingredients, except the
chocolate shavings, in a blender.
Pour the mixture into a highball
glass and sprinkle chocolate shavings
on top.

Coladascope

1½ ounces white rum
¾ ounce Triple Sec
2 ounces pineapple juice
¼ ounce lime syrup
¾ ounce coconut cream
1 scoop crushed ice

Combine all the ingredients in a
shaker. Shake well. Strain the mixture into a chilled highball glass.

Daiquiri, Apple

1½ ounces light rum
½ ounce Calvados or applejack
½ ounce lemon juice
1 teaspoon sugar syrup,
    or to taste
2 teaspoons apple juice
1 scoop crushed ice
Apple wedge

Mix all the ingredients, except the
apple wedge, in a shaker. Strain the
mixture into a chilled cocktail glass.
Garnish with the apple wedge.

Daiquiri, Banana

1¾ ounces white rum
½ banana
Juice of ¼ lime
1 teaspoon sugar
1 scoop crushed ice

Combine all the ingredients in a blender. Blend until frothy. Pour the mixture into a large, chilled wineglass.

Daiquiri, Coconut

1¼ ounces rum
4 ounces coconut cream
1½ ounces lime juice
1½ cups ice

Combine all the ingredients in a blender and blend until smooth. Pour the mixture into a chilled parfait glass.

Daiquiri, Cool Lime

1½ ounces light rum
¾ ounce dark rum
¾ ounces Triple Sec
Juice of 1 lime
2 teaspoons sugar
1 scoop crushed ice
Lime twist

Mix all the ingredients, except the lime twist, in a shaker. Pour the mixture into a large cocktail glass and garnish with the lime twist.

Daiquiri, Derby Orange

1¾ ounces rum
Juice of 1 orange
Juice of ¼ lime
1 teaspoon sugar
1 scoop crushed ice

Mix all the ingredients thoroughly in a blender. Pour the mixture into a large cocktail glass or champagne flute.

Daiquiri, Florida

1¾ ounces light rum
Juice of ½ lime
2 teaspoons sugar
¼ ounce grapefruit juice
¼ ounce maraschino liqueur
1 scoop crushed ice

Mix all the ingredients thoroughly in a shaker. Pour the mixture into a cocktail glass or champagne flute.

Daiquiri, Frozen Guava

1½ ounces light rum
1 ounce guava nectar
½ ounce lime juice
1 teaspoon crème de banane
    (optional)
1 scoop crushed ice

Mix all the ingredients in a blender until almost slushy. Pour the mixture into a chilled deep-saucer champagne glass.

Daiquiri, Mint

1¾ ounces white rum
1 scoop crushed ice
3 or 4 mint leaves
Juice of ½ lime
2 teaspoons sugar
2 splashes of Cointreau or
    Triple Sec

Combine all the ingredients in a blender. Blend until smooth, letting the blender run a few extra seconds. Pour the mixture into a large cocktail glass or champagne flute.

Daiquiri, Frozen Peach

1½ ounces light rum
½ ounce lime juice (fresh or
    bottled)
1 heaping teaspoon fresh, canned,
    or frozen diced peaches
½ ounce syrup from canned or
    frozen peaches or sugar syrup
1 to 2 scoops crushed ice

Mix all the ingredients in a blender until slushy; the peaches should be well incorporated into the mixture. Pour the mixture into a chilled deep-saucer champagne glass.

Daiquiri, Peach

1¾ ounces light rum
½ peeled ripe peach
Juice of ¼ lime
1 teaspoon sugar
1 scoop crushed ice

Mix all the ingredients thoroughly in a blender. Pour the mixture into a large cocktail glass or champagne flute.

Daiquiri, Pineapple I

Makes 2 servings

4 ounces gold rum
1 ounce 151-proof rum
6 ounces pineapple, finely chopped
1 ounce lemon juice
1 ounce pineapple juice
1 ounce orgeat or sugar syrup to taste
1 egg white
Crushed ice
Club soda
Lime slices, seeded

Mix all the ingredients, except the club soda and lime slices, in a blender until smooth. Pour the mixture into chilled highball glasses. Top off with club soda and garnish with the lime slices.

Daiquiri, Pineapple II

1¾ ounces light rum
1 pineapple slice
Juice of ¼ lime
1 teaspoon sugar
1 scoop crushed ice

Combine all the ingredients in a blender. Blend until smooth. Pour the mixture into a large cocktail glass or champagne flute.

Daiquiri, Pink

1¾ ounces white rum
2 splashes of grenadine
1 teaspoon sugar
Juice of ½ lime
1 scoop crushed ice

Combine all the ingredients in a shaker. Shake well and strain into a cocktail glass.

Deep Sea Diver

2 ounces high-proof dark rum
2 ounces dark rum
¾ ounce light rum
¾ ounce Triple Sec
1 to 2 teaspoons sugar
¼ ounce lime syrup
Juice of 1 lime or lemon

Combine all the ingredients in a shaker with crushed ice. Shake vigorously. Pour the mixture into a tall drink glass.

Don Juan

1 ounce dark rum
1 ounce white tequila
2 ounces pineapple juice
1 ounce grapefruit juice
1 scoop crushed ice
1 orange slice, seeded

Mix all the ingredients, except the orange slice, in a shaker. Strain the mixture into a chilled cocktail glass and garnish with the orange slice.

Eye-Opener

1½ ounces light rum
1 teaspoon Triple Sec
1 teaspoon white crème de cacao
1 teaspoon sugar syrup
½ teaspoon Pernod
1 egg yolk
1 scoop crushed ice

Mix all the ingredients in a shaker until smooth and almost frothy. Strain the mixture into a chilled cocktail glass.

Fiesta Cocktail

¾ ounce light rum
¾ ounce Calvados
¾ ounce dry vermouth
Splash of grenadine
Splash of lime juice
1 scoop crushed ice

Mix all the ingredients thoroughly in a shaker or stirring glass. Pour the mixture into a chilled cocktail glass.

Fiji Fizz

1½ ounces dark rum
½ ounce bourbon
1 teaspoon cherry Marnier
Several dashes of orange bitters
4 ounces cold cola
Lime peel, for garnish

Mix all the ingredients, except the cola and lime peel, in a shaker with ice. Pour the mixture into a chilled collins glass. Top off with cold cola and garnish with the lime peel.

Flamingo

1½ ounces light rum
Juice of ¼ lime
1 ounce pineapple juice
A few splashes of grenadine
1 scoop crushed ice
Wedge of lime, seeded (optional)

Add all the ingredients, except the lime wedge, to a shaker. Mix until almost frothy. Pour the mixture into a cocktail glass and garnish with the lime wedge.

Florida Gator

1½ ounces gold rum
¼ ounce Triple Sec
¾ ounce orange juice
¼ ounce maraschino liqueur
1 scoop crushed ice

Combine all the ingredients in a shaker. Mix well and strain into a chilled cocktail glass.

Flying Kangaroo

1 ounce light rum
1 ounce vodka
¼ ounce Galliano
¾ ounce orange juice
1½ ounces pineapple juice
¾ ounce coconut cream
¼ ounce heavy cream
1 scoop crushed ice

Combine all the ingredients in a shaker. Shake well and pour into a highball glass.

Forbidden Jungle

1½ ounces rum
½ ounce peach schnapps
1 ounce coconut cream
1½ ounces pineapple juice
¼ ounce freshly squeezed lime
    juice
Dash of grenadine
1 scoop crushed ice

Combine all the ingredients in a blender and blend until smooth. Pour the mixture into a chilled par-fait glass.

French Colada

1½ ounces light rum
¾ ounce Cognac
Splash of cassis
1½ ounces pineapple juice
¾ ounce coconut cream
¾ ounce heavy cream
1 scoop crushed ice

Combine all the ingredients in a shaker. Mix well and pour into a chilled collins glass.

Friday

¾ ounce light rum
Fruit of 1 mango
Juice of ¼ lime
1 scoop crushed ice
Wedge of lime, seeded

Mix all the ingredients, except the lime wedge, in a blender. Blend until smooth. Pour the mixture into a highball glass and fill with fresh crushed ice. Garnish with the wedge of lime.

Havana Banana Fizz

1½ ounces light rum
2 ounces pineapple juice
1 ounce lime juice (fresh or
    bottled)
⅓ ripe banana, peeled and sliced
Several dashes of bitters
1 scoop crushed ice
Cold bitter lemon soda

Mix all the ingredients, except the soda, in a blender. Blend until smooth. Pour the mixture into a chilled highball glass and top off with the bitter lemon soda.

Havana Special

1½ ounces light rum
2 ounces pineapple juice
2 splashes of maraschino liqueur
1 scoop crushed ice

Mix all the ingredients in a shaker. Strain the mixture into a highball glass half filled with crushed ice.

Hurricane

1 ounce light rum
1 ounce gold rum
½ ounce passion fruit syrup
½ ounce lime juice
1 scoop crushed ice

Mix all the ingredients thoroughly in a shaker. Strain the mixture into a chilled cocktail glass.

Italian Colada

1½ ounces light rum
¼ ounce amaretto
2 ounces pineapple juice
¼ ounce coconut cream
¾ ounces heavy cream
1 scoop crushed ice

Combine all the ingredients in a shaker and mix well. Pour the mixture into a highball glass.

Ixtapa

1 ounce dark rum
1 ounce gin
1 ounce dry red wine
1 ounce orange juice
1 scoop crushed ice
1 lime slice

Combine all the ingredients, except the lime slice, in a shaker. Mix briefly, just to combine. Pour the mixture into a chilled old-fashioned glass and garnish with the lime slice.

Jamaica Mule

1 ounce dark Jamaican rum
1 ounce light rum
½ ounce 151-proof rum
½ ounce Triple Sec or sugar
   syrup
½ ounce lime juice
1 scoop crushed ice
Ginger beer
1 fresh pineapple strip (optional)
1 section preserved ginger
   (optional)

Mix the rums, Triple Sec, lime juice, and ice thoroughly in a shaker. Pour mix into a chilled collins glass. Top off with cold ginger beer and stir gently. Garnish with the pineapple slice and ginger.

Jamaica Rum Fix

1 teaspoon granulated sugar
1 teaspoon water
1½ ounces dark Jamaican rum
1½ ounces light rum
2 teaspoons fresh lime juice
1 scoop crushed ice
Thin slice of ripe lime or twist of
   lime peel

In an old-fashioned glass, mix together the sugar and water. Add both kinds of rum and lime juice. Top off the glass with ice and stir lightly. Garnish with the lime or lime peel.

Kamehameha Rum Punch

1 ounce light rum
1 ounce dark rum
2 ounces pineapple juice
½ ounce lemon juice
½ ounce sugar syrup, or to taste
1 teaspoon blackberry brandy
1 teaspoon lemon juice
1 scoop crushed ice
1 fresh pineapple slice

Mix all the ingredients, except the pineapple slice, in a shaker. Pour mix into a chilled highball glass and top with a float of dark rum. Garnish with the pineapple slice.

Little Dix Mix

1½ ounces dark rum
½ ounce crème de banane
½ ounce lime juice
1 teaspoon curaçao
1 scoop crushed ice

Mix all the ingredients thoroughly in a blender. Pour the mixture into a chilled old-fashioned glass.

Luau Lullaby

Makes 2 servings

3 ounces light rum
2 ounces passion fruit syrup
2 ounces lime juice
1 egg white
2 scoops crushed ice
2 teaspoons 151-proof Demerara
  rum

Mix all the ingredients, except the 151-proof rum, in a shaker. Pour the mixture into whiskey sour glasses and top off with the high-proof rum.

Mai Kai No

1 ounce light rum
1 ounce dark rum
½ ounce 151-proof Demerara
  rum
1 ounce lime juice
½ ounce orgeat
½ ounce passion fruit juice
1 scoop crushed ice
Club soda
Pineapple or orange slice
Mint sprig (optional)

Mix all the ingredients, except the soda, fruit slice, and mint, in a shaker. Pour the mixture into a tall, chilled collins glass and top off with the club soda. Garnish with the fruit slice and the mint sprig.

Mauna Kea

1½ ounces light rum
½ ounce kirsch
1½ ounces passion fruit juice
1 ounce lemon juice
½ ounce sugar syrup, to taste
1 scoop crushed ice
1 coconut shell, halved
  (preparation below)
1 ounce dark rum
Red hibiscus and assorted tropical
  fruits (optional)

Mix all the ingredients, except the coconut, rum, and garnishes, in a blender. Pour the mixture into a coconut shell and top with a float of dark rum. Garnish with red hibiscus and assorted fruits.

Note: To prepare the coconut, puncture the "eyes" and drain the coconut milk. Save the milk for punches and other tropical rum drinks. Saw the coconut in half across its middle and steady it, open end up, in a cup, small dish, or ashtray to keep it stable when filled with liquid. If coconuts are not available, use any large decorative glass.

Mauna Lani Fizz

Makes 2 servings

4 ounces gold rum
1 ounce 151-proof rum
6 ounces pineapple, finely chopped
1 ounce lemon juice
1 ounce pineapple juice
1 ounce orgeat or sugar syrup to taste
1 egg white
Crushed ice
Club soda
Lime slices, seeded

Mix all the ingredients, except the club soda and lime slices, in a blender until smooth. Pour the mixture into chilled highball glasses and top off with club soda. Garnish with the lime slices.

Monaco

1½ ounces gold rum
½ ounce brandy
½ ounce pineapple juice
1 ounce lime juice
1 teaspoon Triple Sec
1 scoop crushed ice
Slice of lime, seeded

Mix all the ingredients, except the lime slice, in a shaker. Pour the mixture into a chilled collins glass and garnish with the lime slice.

Outrigger

2 ounces light rum
½ ounce Triple Sec
½ ounce pineapple or apricot liqueur
1 ounce lime juice
1 scoop crushed ice
1 lime slice, seeded

Mix all the ingredients, except the lime slice, in a shaker. Pour into a chilled old-fashioned glass and garnish with the lime slice.

Pinky Colada

2 ounces white rum
¾ ounce pineapple juice
¾ ounce grenadine
¾ ounce coconut cream
1½ ounces sweet cream or milk
1 scoop crushed ice

Combine all the ingredients in a shaker. Mix well and strain into a chilled wine goblet.

Polynesian Sour

1½ ounces light rum
½ ounce guava nectar
½ ounce orange juice
½ ounce lemon juice
1 scoop crushed ice

Combine all the ingredients in a blender. Mix until smooth and uniform in color. Pour the mixture into a chilled deep-saucer champagne glass.

Presidente

1½ ounces light rum
¼ ounce dry vermouth
¾ ounce sweet vermouth
Splash of grenadine
Maraschino cherry

In a stirring glass with ice, mix together all the ingredients. Strain the mixture into an iced cocktail glass and garnish with the cherry.

Robinson

1 ounce dark rum
1 ounce light rum
¾ ounce sugar syrup
Fruit of 1 papaya
Juice of ⅓ lime
1 scoop crushed ice
1 lime wedge, seeded

Combine all the ingredients, except the lime wedge, in a blender. Blend until smooth. Pour the mixture into a chilled highball glass over fresh crushed ice. Garnish with the lime wedge.

Rum Runner

1 ounce light rum
1 ounce dark rum
2¾ ounces pineapple juice
¼ ounce sugar syrup
A few splashes of bitters
Juice of ½ lime
Maraschino cherry
1 thin wedge of lime, seeded

Mix all the ingredients, except the cherry and lime wedge, in a shaker. Pour the mixture into a highball glass half filled with ice. Garnish with the maraschino cherry and lime wedge.

Sailfish Marina's Tipsy Turtle

¼ ounce dark rum
¼ ounce light rum
¼ ounce vodka
¼ ounce coconut liqueur
¼ ounce banana liqueur
Splash of grenadine
4 ounces pineapple juice
4 ounces orange juice
1 scoop crushed ice
1 slice fresh orange
1 slice fresh pineapple

Combine all the ingredients, except the orange and pineapple slices, in a blender and mix until smooth. Pour the mixture into a chilled highball glass and garnish with the fruit.

Strawberry Banana Colada

1½ ounces rum
2 ounces coconut cream
2 ounces fresh or frozen strawberries
½ banana, sliced
1 cup ice

Combine all the ingredients in a blender and blend until smooth. Pour the mixture into a chilled parfait glass.

Strawberry Colada

2 to 3 ounces gold rum
4 ounces piña colada mix
1 ounce fresh or frozen strawberries
1 scoop crushed ice
1 teaspoon strawberry schnapps or liqueur
1 fresh strawberry

Mix all the ingredients, except the schnapps and strawberry, in a blender until smooth. Pour the mixture into a chilled pilsner glass and top with strawberry schnapps or liqueur. Garnish with the strawberry.

Swimming Pool

1½ ounces light rum
¾ ounce vodka
2 ounces pineapple juice
¾ ounce coconut cream
¼ ounce heavy cream
1 scoop crushed ice
¼ ounce blue curaçao

Combine all the ingredients, except the curaçao, in a shaker and mix well. Pour the mixture into a highball glass and float the curaçao on top.

Tipsy Turtle

¼ ounce vodka
¼ ounce white rum
¼ ounce dark rum
¼ ounce coconut liqueur
¼ ounce banana liqueur
Splash of grenadine
4 ounces pineapple juice
4 ounces orange juice
1 scoop crushed ice

Combine all the ingredients in a blender. Blend well. Pour the mixture into a chilled highball glass.

Tropical Breeze

1 ounce rum
½ ounce crème de banane
1 ounce coconut cream
2 ounces orange juice
½ pineapple slice
1 scoop crushed ice

Combine all the ingredients in a blender and blend until smooth. Pour the mixture into a chilled parfait glass.

Zico

1 ounce light rum
1 ounce cachaca
2 ounces papaya juice
¾ ounce coconut cream
Juice of ¼ lime

Combine all the ingredients in a shaker with crushed ice. Shake well and strain into a chilled highball glass.

HOT DRINKS

Black Marie

¾ ounce dark rum
¾ ounce brandy
¼ ounce coffee liqueur
1 to 2 teaspoons superfine sugar
1 cup hot strong coffee or espresso

Combine the rum, brandy, and liqueur in a nonreactive saucepan and heat until warm, but do not boil. Add sugar to the heated mixture, stirring until it is dissolved. Pour into a heatproof punch glass and top off with hot coffee. Stir and serve.

Chocolate Sin

1½ ounces dark rum
½ ounce bourbon
½ ounce dark crème de cacao
4 ounces hot chocolate
2 ounces heavy cream, whipped

Pour all the ingredients, except the whipped cream, into an Irish coffee glass. Carefully spoon the cream on top of the drink.

Cidered Rum

2¼ ounces light rum
1 teaspoon cane or maple syrup
1 teaspoon granulated sugar
1 tablespoon fresh lime or lemon
    juice
1 slice of lemon or lime, pierced
    with 2 whole cloves
Hot apple cider

In a heavy mug or large cup, mix all the ingredients, except the lime slice and hot cider. Add the lime or lemon slice with cloves and top off the mug with cider.

Cuban Hot Coffee

1 ounce gold rum
¼ ounce brown crème de cacao
1 teaspoon superfine sugar
1 cup hot strong coffee

Combine the rum and liqueur in a nonreactive saucepan. Heat but do not boil. Add the sugar to the heated mixture and stir until dissolved. Pour into a heatproof punch glass and top off with hot coffee. Stir well before serving.

Goldie

1½ ounces dark rum
¼ ounce Galliano
¼ ounce heavy cream
1½ ounces milk
¾ ounce orange juice
1 to 2 teaspoons superfine sugar

Combine all the ingredients in a nonreactive saucepan and heat until warm, stirring gently. Pour into a heatproof punch glass and serve.

Hot Benefactor

1 teaspoon sugar syrup,
    or to taste
2 ounces Jamaican dark rum
2 ounces dry red wine
Lemon slice
Grated nutmeg

Put the syrup in a saucepan with a little hot water and stir. Add the rum and the wine. Heat the mixture until it begins to simmer. Pour into a warmed mug and garnish with the lemon slice. Sprinkle freshly grated nutmeg on top.

Hot Buttered Rum

1 teaspoon brown or white sugar
Boiling water
1½ ounces light or dark rum
Small piece of cinnamon stick
Pinch of ground allspice or
    nutmeg
Pat of butter

In preheated mug or large heavy
cup, dissolve the sugar in a small
amount of the boiling water. Stir in
the rum. Add the cinnamon stick
and the allspice or nutmeg. Top off
the mug with boiling water and a pat
of butter.

Hot Jamaican

½ ounce sugar syrup
Juice of one lime
2 ounces dark rum
Boiling water
½ cinnamon stick
1 lime wedge, seeded and studded
    with cloves

Warm the sugar, lime juice, and rum
in a nonreactive saucepan. Pour the
mixture into a heatproof punch glass
and top off with boiling water. Garnish with the cinnamon stick and the
lime wedge.

Hot MM

1½ ounces dark rum
¾ ounce coffee liqueur
2¾ ounces heavy cream
1 to 2 teaspoons sugar

Combine all the ingredients in a
nonreactive saucepan and heat until
warm, stirring gently. Pour into a
heatproof punch glass and serve.

Hot Rum Toddy

1 teaspoon honey
Boiling water
2 ounces white or light rum
1 lemon or lime slice, pierced with
    4 whole cloves
1 cinnamon stick

In a heavy mug, dissolve the honey
in a small amount of the hot water,
stirring constantly. Add the rum,
stirring gently, then add the lemon
or lime slice. Top off the mug with
boiling water and drop in the cinnamon stick.

Hot Spiced Cider

Makes 4 servings

1 quart apple cider
¼ cup granulated sugar
⅛ teaspoon salt
1 cinnamon stick, broken up
12 whole cloves
8 whole allspice berries
¾ cup light rum

Combine all the ingredients, except the rum, in a large saucepan and bring to a boil. Cool and let stand for at least 4 hours, stirring occasionally. Before serving, strain and reheat, stirring in the rum at the last moment. Serve in large mugs.

Jean Gabin

1½ ounces dark rum
¾ ounce Calvados
Sugar syrup or maple syrup, to taste
Hot milk
Freshly grated nutmeg

Warm the rum and Calvados in a nonreactive saucepan. Pour the mixture into a heatproof punch glass, stir in the syrup, and fill with hot milk. Sprinkle the grated nutmeg on top.

Southern Malt

1½ ounces dark rum
½ ounce Southern Comfort
4 ounces hot malted milk

Pour all the ingredients into a coffee mug and stir well.

Sweet and Hot

1½ ounces dark rum
¾ ounce coffee liqueur
¾ ounce heavy cream
2 ounces milk
1 whole clove
Lemon zest

Combine all the ingredients in a nonreactive saucepan; heat until warm. Pour into a heatproof punch glass.

Tom and Jerome

1 egg, separated
1 teaspoon confectioners' sugar
¼ teaspoon ground allspice
1½ ounces light rum
Hot milk
Freshly grated nutmeg

In a small bowl, whisk the egg yolk for about 30 seconds. Mix in the sugar, allspice, and rum. Continue to beat until mixture is smooth and has thickened. In another bowl, beat the egg white for a few seconds, then blend into the rum mixture. Turn the mixture into a preheated mug or large cup and top off with hot milk. Mix thoroughly. Dust with nutmeg and serve immediately.

PUNCHES

Blue Mountain Punch

Makes 12 servings

1 tablespoon powdered ginger
1 teaspoon grated nutmeg
7½ cups warmed beer
3 eggs
2 tablespoons molasses
½ cup light or dark rum

In a saucepan, mix the ginger and nutmeg with 6¾ cups of the beer. Heat until warm. Beat the eggs with the remaining beer and molasses. Slowly add the warm beer to the egg mixture, beating continuously. Add the rum and serve at once.

Creamy Rum Cider

Makes 8 servings

1 quart apple cider
1 cup dark rum
Cider ice cubes, as needed
Vanilla ice cream, to taste

In a large pitcher, combine the cider and rum and refrigerate. Just before serving, place a few cider ice cubes in a mug or glass. Add a scoop of vanilla ice cream and top off with the cold rum cider.

Eggnog I

Makes 24 servings

12 egg yolks
½ pound granulated sugar
1 quart whole milk
1 bottle (750 ml) light rum
1 quart heavy cream, whipped
    until stiff
Freshly grated nutmeg

Beat the egg yolks in a large bowl until they are light in color. Gradually add the sugar, beating until mixture thickens. Stir in the milk and rum. Cover the bowl and chill for 3 to 4 hours. Pour into a chilled punch bowl. Fold in the whipped cream and dust with the nutmeg.

Eggnog II

Makes 28 servings

12 whole eggs, separated
2 cups superfine sugar
1 pint Cognac
1 pint dark rum
3 pints milk
1 pint heavy cream
Freshly grated nutmeg

Beat the egg yolks and sugar together until the mixture becomes thick and the sugar is dissolved. Stir in the Cognac, rum, milk, and cream and chill in the refrigerator until needed. Just before serving, beat the egg whites until stiff and very gently fold them into the punch. Transfer to a chilled punch bowl and sprinkle with nutmeg.

Note: Do not put ice in the punch bowl; it will dilute the drink.

Fish House Punch I

Makes 40 (4-ounce) servings

10 cups water
Grated peel and juice of 5 limes
Grated peel and juice of 5 lemons
1½ cups brown sugar
6 cups dark rum
2 cups brandy
2 ounces Southern Comfort

Combine the water with the juices and grated peel of the lemons and limes in a large pot. Bring the mixture to a boil, stir in the brown sugar, and continue to boil until the liquid forms a light syrup. Add the rum, brandy, and Southern Comfort. Stir well and bring to a boil again. Serve immediately or store in sealed jars. You can also return the punch to the empty rum bottles and recap, leaving no air space. The punch can be stored for several days.

Note: Fish house punch may be served either hot or cold. When serving hot, use heatproof punch glasses. To serve cold, serve in a highball glass filled with crushed ice and float ¼ ounce 151-proof rum on top.

Fish House Punch II

Prepare as for Fish House Punch I, substituting 4 cups water and 6 cups black tea for the water.

Jamaican Eggnog

Makes 20 servings

12 egg yolks
1 cup granulated sugar
1 quart whole milk
1 bottle (750 ml) dark Jamaican rum
1 quart heavy cream
Freshly grated nutmeg

Beat the egg yolks until light in color. Add the sugar, and continue to beat until the mixture is thick and pale in color. Slowly stir in the milk and the dark rum. Chill in the refrigerator for 3 hours, stirring often. One hour before serving, whip the heavy cream until stiff. Turn the chilled mixture into a punch bowl, then fold in the whipped cream. Chill in the refrigerator for 1 more hour. Pour into collins glasses and sprinkle the nutmeg on top.

Jamaican Grand Punch

Makes 30 servings

Block of ice
1½ quarts dark Jamaican rum
1½ quarts unsweetened pineapple
  juice
1½ quarts mango nectar
1 cup lime juice
Soda water
½ peeled fresh pineapple, sliced
  into thin strips

Place the ice block in a big punch bowl and pour in the rum, pineapple juice, nectar, and lime juice. Add soda water to taste and garnish with the pineapple strips.

John's Mango Masterpiece

Makes 6 servings

1 cup light rum
1 cup mango purée (fresh or
  canned)
¼ cup fresh squeezed lime juice,
  strained
¼ cup water
Sugar syrup to taste
1 scoop crushed ice

Chill all the ingredients before starting. Mix the chilled ingredients and ice in a blender until smooth. Pour the mixture into chilled cocktail glasses.

Lindsay's Post-College Punch

1 bottle (750 ml) light rum
2 to 3 pints orange juice
2 to 3 pints cran-raspberry juice
Block of ice
1 liter ginger ale
Several sliced apples and oranges

Combine the rum and fruit juices in a punch bowl with the block of ice. Stir well. Add the ginger ale and fruit slices just before serving.

Martin's Rum-Orange Punch

1½ ounces dark rum
¾ ounce 151-proof dark rum
½ jigger Southern Comfort
2 teaspoons sugar
Juice of ½ lime
¾ ounce lime juice
1½ ounces orange juice
Wedges of lime and orange,
  seeded

Combine all the ingredients, except the lime and orange wedges, in a non-reactive saucepan; heat until warm. Pour into a heatproof punch glass and garnish with the wedges of lime and orange.

Philadelphia Fish House Punch

Makes 50 servings

2 cups brown sugar
2 quarts water
Peel and juice of 6 ripe lemons
1 bottle (750 ml) dark rum, or ½ bottle dark and ½ bottle light rum, combined
1 (750 ml) bottle brandy
½ bottle (375 ml) peach brandy

In a large heavy pot, heat the sugar and water until sugar has dissolved completely, stirring often with a wooden spoon. Add the lemon peel and juice, plus rum, brandy, and peach brandy. Mix well, remove from heat and allow to stand for several hours to absorb flavors. Strain over a large block of ice, about 1 hour prior to serving, in order to chill and also dilute slightly. Serve in chilled punch cups.

Thanksgiving Punch

Makes 10 servings

1 liter gold rum
½ teaspoon allspice
1 quart apple cider
3 cinnamon sticks
1 tablespoon butter

Heat all the ingredients together in a saucepan. Pour into warmed mugs.

Gin

London dry gins, such as Tanqueray, Beefeater, Gordon's, and Gilbey's, start with a grain formula that is three quarters corn and one quarter barley malt and other grains. The mixture is combined with water in a process called mashing. It is then cooked and finally fermented. This procedure is virtually identical to the early stages of the production of whiskey.

The resulting liquid is distilled to 180 proof (90% alcohol) in a column still, a device invented in 1830 by Dubliner Aeneas Coffey. The result is a strong and pure spirit that retains a hint of malty, whiskey-like flavor. It is then cut to 120 proof by the addition of distilled water. This slightly diluted spirit is then placed in a modified pot still called, appropriately, a "gin still," and redistilled in the presence of flavorings, primarily juniper berries. The gin still was developed in the late nineteenth century by James Burroughs, founder of the Beefeater distillery.

One can't help but be impressed with the cleanliness and order of the big gin distilleries. Unlike a winery, there are no wooden barrels and no damp cellars, just rows and rows of pipes and ranks of shiny stills. There is no season for gin—it is made throughout the year—nor is it aged for any appreciable amount of time. Clean water flows into the distillery from artesian wells and two weeks later it leaves, already bottled and ready for market. Another characteristic of a gin distillery is the seductive aroma of juniper and herbs that perfumes the air.

The juniper usually comes from northern Italy and Yugoslavia. In addition, distillers use many other herbs and botanicals including cassia bark, calamus, cardamom, bitter almonds, orris root, licorice, anise, cocoa nibs, lemon peel, caraway, orange peel, coriander from Essex, and angelica from Flanders. It is the small amounts of these ingredients that give each gin its individual brand distinction.

But gin is not made just in London. Unlike Scotch whisky, which is produced only in Scotland, gin can be made anywhere there is a still, some grain, and the requisite flavoring ingredients. A number of Stateside distillers have gotten into the act with great success, but American gins are slightly different than their English counterparts.

In America, laws require that gin be made from 100 percent neutral spirits. This means that the best domestic gins such as Gilbey's and Gordon's are crisp and clean tasting. They do not have the extra complexity of that slight hint of malt character that can be found in true London gins. American-made gin makes up for this difference by being quite a bit less expensive than the English product.

There are gins made in other parts of the world but, with one notable exception, they don't usually find their way into the U.S. market. The exception is the Scheidam gin of Holland, the original version of this unique drink.

The first gin was made in Holland about 1650 and it was a much more aromatic spirit than either the London or American versions that are so prevalent today. The Dutch continue to make gin in this same assertive style.

Dr. Sylvius was a respected Dutch physician and scientist in the mid-seventeenth century. He lectured and conducted chemical experiments at the University of Leiden. One of the substances that occupied his attention was oil of juniper, a popular diuretic. He sought to discover an easy way to administer this medicine to patients.

Eventually he hit upon the idea of blending juniper waters with neutral distilled spirits. He called his concoction "genever," from the French word for juniper, *genièvre*. Within a few months the good doctor's "medicine" was the rage of Holland. Not long afterward, the enterprising Bols firm in Amsterdam was marketing a commercial version.

Soon enough, English soldiers, returning from adventures in faraway places, passed through Holland and discovered what they called "Dutch courage." They triumphantly transported it back home where it soon became known as "gin," a corruption of genever. When Prince William of Orange, a Dutch grandson of the English Stuart kings, ascended to the British throne as King William III, gin became the stylish drink at The Court of St. James's.

Gin was an instant hit in England, especially around the port cities of Bristol, Plymouth, and Portsmouth. It soon became known as the "spirit of the masses," as opposed to the upscale and expensive ports and brandies that had been the darlings of the upper crust.

Over the next century or more, until the onset of the industrial revolution, gin was the engine that drove British society. Its use pervaded every level of English life, and by the mid-eighteenth century, a population of 6 million was imbibing more than 20 million gallons a year. London dry gin was being exported to all corners of the Empire.

Meanwhile back in Holland, the original style of gin continued to be made—and is made to this day. What causes this drink to be different is the fact that it is made from equal parts of barley, corn, and rye and distilled to a much lower proof than London gin. This leaves it with an intense whiskey flavor.

In Scheidam, a small Dutch town, there are more than 100 distilleries making this style of richly flavored gin, most of which is sold in Holland. The version most readily available in the American market is made by Bols and is packaged in a charming earthenware crock.

Plymouth gin, made in the English city of the same name, also has significant stylistic differences from London dry gin. This drink, which is made only by one firm, Coates & Company, is richer and more aromatic. It sacrifices the crispness and elegance of London gins for a somewhat heavier, rounder flavor that falls about halfway between Scheidam and London.

Of course gin's most popular usage, especially in the United States, is as the base for mixed drinks, and the classic gin mixed drink is the dry martini. This minimalist concoction, a healthy shot of gin kissed by dry vermouth and then gently stirred with ice, was a security blanket to an entire generation. A misleadingly simple cocktail, the martini put the roar in the Roaring Twenties and carried the nation full-throttle into a very wet Prohibition.

After the dry martini, there was a slew of mixed gin drinks that became popular. The ones that have stood the test of time include Tom Collins, gin and tonic, pink lady, Singapore sling, Ramoz fizz, americano, and negroni.

Although the past decade has not been a particularly good one for spirits, gin has managed to hold its own. This 300-year-old drink does not seem to have lost its appeal.

CLASSICS

Bronx Cocktail

1½ ounces gin
½ ounce dry vermouth
½ ounce sweet vermouth
1 ounce orange juice
1 scoop crushed ice

Combine all the ingredients in a shaker. Mix well and strain into a chilled cocktail glass.

Note: For a dry Bronx cocktail, omit sweet vermouth.

Dry Martini: The World's Greatest Cocktail

A couple of years ago, at the Napa auction, I rediscovered the dry martini. This was certainly unexpected, especially at a wine event, which made the experience all the more significant and memorable.

It had been one of those long, hot June days filled with deep purple Cabernet barrel samples and ladies in broad-brimmed sun hats. As the sun set I was feeling just a wee bit bilious as I trudged up the hill to one more winery. I had probably tasted more than sixty wines since ten that morning. The idea of yet another tasting left me less than delirious with anticipation.

I entered the winery determined to endure what was to come, quietly and with as much dignity as I could summon. I was greeted by a white-coated waiter with a silver tray. On the tray, glistening in the fading sunset, was a vision, a dream, my savior—a statuesque glass with a graceful stem and jaunty bowl holding a crystal clear liquid. A dry martini. I grabbed it like a drowning man grasping for a life preserver and, trying to not make a spectacle of myself, slowly drank it, appreciating every translucent drop. It refreshed my palate and cleansed my soul.

I remembered this drink from the days of Peter Arno cartoons and Uncle Miltie every Tuesday night. In the years after the war, when I was in grammar school, my father would make a dry martini every evening after my mother and I had retrieved him at our suburban train station. The mixing of this magical potion was a graceful and solemn ritual that filled the den with the gentle aroma of juniper and lemon zest.

For me, the martini has always had the aura of elegance. It reminds me of witty formal dinner parties and transatlantic crossings on the great Cunard liners, of beachside cocktail gatherings on breezy July evenings, and after-theater drinks at the "21" Club. It reminds me of Adolphe Menjou and Fred Astaire.

Actually, it all began in a very elegant environment. According to John Doxat, a British journalist who has made an exhaustive study of martini history, the first one was mixed in the bar at the old Knickerbocker Hotel in New York City on an evening in 1910. The inventor was the head bartender, one Martini di Arma di Taggia, and the first to taste his concoction was John D. Rockefeller, the then septuagenarian oil magnate.

The master mixologist poured some of his best imported London dry gin into a glass and added ice. He then poured an equal amount of dry vermouth into the glass and added a dash of orange bitters. He stirred the mixture and then strained it into a shallow cocktail glass. He squeezed a piece of lemon rind over the clear liquid and dropped in a green olive impaled on a wooden toothpick. Mr. Rockefeller was duly impressed and suggested naming the revolutionary new cocktail after its creator, and so the martini cocktail or, more correctly, the dry martini, was born.

Soon enough the Knickerbocker bar became renowned for this new drink and serious imbibers flocked there to taste Martini's cocktail. Not to be outdone, other bartenders at other watering holes began featuring the drink and adding their own personal modifications. And so began the endless evolutionary process that has made the dry martini both the most satisfying and the most exasperating of cocktails. It is one of the world's most popular mixed drinks, but at the same time no two people can ever agree completely as to how it should be made.

Martini drinkers of today, or even of the 1940s, would snicker at the idea of a dry martini being made in the proportions originally used by Martini di Arma di Taggia. Just before the beginning of World War II, the mixture went from equal parts of gin and vermouth to two parts gin and one part vermouth. After the war the formula changed again. My father's dry martini was four to one. By the 1960s the proportions had jumped to six to one, and in the 1970s eight to one was common.

Throughout this evolutionary process there was always a hard core that wanted to forget the vermouth altogether. These are the people who, while mixing, lean over their drink and whisper the word "vermouth," or just let the shadow of the unopened vermouth bottle fall across the glass. Winston Churchill used to simply bow in the direction of France while he made his martini.

But these shenanigans are just an excuse for drinking straight gin and that isn't a cocktail at all; it's just a vulgar "shot" or "belt" masquerading as a refined drink. True dry martini aficionados would never stoop to such foolishness.

There are also quite a few misguided souls who substitute vodka for gin. They are missing the point. The dry martini is built around the exquisite synergism of the juniper berry flavor of gin and the nutlike herbs of dry vermouth.

I asked some of my favorite bartenders and innkeepers how they make a dry martini. Doug Biederbeck at Bix in San Francisco swears by the five to one ratio and sneers at vodka martinis. "Real martini drinkers drink gin," he says. The five to one formula is also standard at the Ritz-Carlton in Chicago, but at the Beverly Wilshire in Los Angeles two to one is the rule.

Most top bartenders agree that, despite the predilections of one Mr. James Bond, the perfect dry martini should be stirred, not shaken. Purists will tell you that shaking "bruises the gin" and causes too much dilution from melting ice. Many experts will tell you that the sliver of lemon should be squeezed, skin side down, over the martini so that the bitter oils in the rind are added to the drink. Then the rind should be discarded. Some will tell you that the olive makes the drink salty, while others think it's essential.

All will tell you that top-quality ingredients are imperative. Save bargain gin for tonic; use only the best for your dry martini. Keep the drink well chilled and use the correct glass.

Even if you are not a regular cocktail drinker, a well-made dry martini can have an extremely salutary effect at occasional moments in your life. I keep finding more and more occasions.

2 ounces gin
½ teaspoon dry vermouth, or to taste
Olive or lemon twist

Stir the gin and vermouth in a mixing glass with plenty of ice. Strain the mixture into a chilled cocktail glass. Garnish with the olive or lemon twist.

Gimlet I

2 ounces gin
¼ ounce Rose's lime juice
1 scoop crushed ice
Lime slice

Mix the gin, lime juice, and ice in a shaker. Pour the mixture into a chilled old-fashioned glass and garnish with the lime slice.

Gimlet II

2 ounces gin
½ ounce fresh lime juice
1 scoop crushed ice
Lime peel

Mix the gin, lime juice, and ice in a mixing glass. Pour the mixture into a chilled old-fashioned glass. Twist the lime peel over the drink and drop it in before serving.

Gin and Bitters (Pink Gin)

2 to 3 ounces gin
½ teaspoon bitters

Mix the gin and bitters in a glass with ice cubes until chilled. Strain the mixture into a chilled old-fashioned glass without ice.

Gin and Tonic

2 ounces gin
Tonic water
Lime wedge

Pour the gin into a chilled collins glass with several ice cubes. Top off with tonic water. Squeeze the lime wedge over the drink and drop it in.

Gin Cobbler

2 ounces gin
1 teaspoon orgeat or sugar syrup
Club soda
Orange slice

Mix the gin and syrup in a double old-fashioned glass with ice. Top off the glass with cold club soda. Stir gently. Garnish with the orange slice.

Gin Daisy

2 to 3 ounces gin
1 ounce lemon juice
¼ ounce raspberry syrup or grenadine
½ ounce teaspoon sugar syrup, or to taste
1 scoop crushed ice
Club soda
Orange slice or mint sprigs

Mix all the ingredients, except the club soda and orange slice, in a blender. Pour the mixture into a chilled highball glass. Top off the glass with cold soda and garnish with the orange slice.

Gin Fizz

2 to 3 ounces gin
½ ounce sugar syrup
Juice of ½ lemon
Juice of ½ lime
Club soda
Maraschino cherry

Mix the gin, syrup, and juices in a shaker or blender. Pour the mixture into a chilled highball glass. Top off with cold club soda and garnish with the maraschino cherry.

Gin Sling

2 to 3 ounces gin
1 ounce lemon juice
½ ounce orgeat or sugar syrup, or to taste
1 scoop crushed ice
Club soda or water

Mix the gin, lemon juice, and syrup with crushed ice in a double old-fashioned glass. Top off with cold club soda or water. Stir well and serve.

Gin Sour

2 to 3 ounces gin
1 ounce lemon juice
1 teaspoon sugar syrup
1 scoop crushed ice
Orange slice
Maraschino cherry

Mix the gin, juice, and syrup in a shaker with crushed ice. Strain the mixture into a chilled whiskey sour glass. Garnish with the orange slice and maraschino cherry.

Melon Ball

1½ ounces gin
¾ ounce melon liqueur
½ ounce Triple Sec
½ ounce lemon juice
1 scoop crushed ice

Mix all the ingredients in a shaker. Strain the mixture into a chilled cocktail glass.

Negroni

2 ounces gin
½ ounce sweet vermouth
¾ ounce Campari
1 scoop crushed ice
Orange peel

Stir all the ingredients, except the orange peel, in a mixing glass. Strain the mixture into a chilled cocktail glass. Twist the orange peel over the drink, then use it as a garnish.

Orange Blossom

1½ ounces gin
1 ounce orange juice
1 scoop crushed ice
Orange slice

Mix the gin and orange juice in a shaker with crushed ice. Strain the mixture into a chilled cocktail glass. Decorate with the orange slice.

Pink Lady

Makes 2 servings

3 ounces gin
3 ounces applejack or Calvados
2 ounces lemon juice
2 teaspoons sugar syrup
2 teaspoons grenadine
1 egg white
Crushed ice

Mix all the ingredients in a shaker. Strain the mixture into chilled cocktail glasses.

Singapore Sling

2 ounces gin
1 ounce cherry brandy
Juice of ½ lemon
Dash of Benedictine
1 scoop crushed ice
Club soda
Lemon slice
Mint sprig (optional)

Mix the gin, brandy, lemon juice, Benedictine, and ice with a splash of soda or water in a shaker or blender. Strain the mixture into a chilled 12-ounce collins glass. Add ice cubes and top off the glass with cold club soda. Stir gently. Garnish with the lemon slice and mint sprig.

Tom Collins

2 to 3 ounces gin
1½ ounces lemon juice
½ ounce sugar syrup, or to taste
Club soda
Maraschino cherry

Mix the gin, lemon juice, and sugar
syrup in a tall collins glass with ice.
Top off the glass with club soda and
garnish with the cherry.

CREATIVE CONCOCTIONS

Admiral Growney

2 ounces gin
1 ounce dry vermouth
½ ounce lime juice
1 maraschino cherry (optional)

Combine the gin, vermouth, and
lime juice in a mixing glass with several ice cubes. Stir to mix ingredients. Strain the mixture into a chilled
old-fashioned glass and garnish with
the maraschino cherry.

Alaska

2 ounces dry gin
½ ounce green Chartreuse
½ ounce dry sherry (optional)
Lemon twist

Stir all the ingredients, except the
lemon twist, in a mixing glass with
ice. Strain the mixture into a cocktail
glass and garnish with the lemon
twist.

Alberto Tomba

1½ ounces gin
½ ounce plum brandy
½ ounce orange juice
½ ounce lemon juice
1 scoop crushed ice
Brandied cherry

Combine all the ingredients, except
the cherry, in a shaker. Mix well and
pour into a chilled cocktail glass.
Garnish with the cherry.

Alexander

1 ounce gin
1 ounce crème de cacao
1 ounce heavy cream
1 scoop crushed ice

Combine all the ingredients in a shaker. Mix well and strain into a chilled cocktail glass.

Alexander's Sister

1½ ounces gin
½ ounce white or green crème de menthe
¾ ounce heavy cream
1 scoop crushed ice

Mix all the ingredients in a shaker. Strain the mixture into a chilled cocktail glass.

Almond Cocktail

2 ounces gin
6 slivered almonds
½ ounce sugar syrup
1 ounce dry vermouth
1 teaspoon kirsch
½ ounce peach brandy

Warm the gin and add the almonds and sugar syrup. Chill and pour into an old-fashioned glass with several ice cubes. Add the remaining ingredients and stir well.

Almost Amanda

1½ ounces gin
½ ounce lime juice
½ ounce grapefruit juice
1 teaspoon sugar syrup
1 scoop crushed ice

Combine all the ingredients in a shaker. Mix well and strain into a chilled cocktail glass.

Amherst

1 ounce gin
½ ounce dry vermouth
1 teaspoon anisette
Generous dash of bitters
1 scoop crushed ice
Lemon peel

Mix all the ingredients, except the lemon peel, in a shaker. Strain the mixture into a chilled cocktail glass. Twist the lemon peel over the drink and drop it in.

Annapolis Fizz

1½ ounces gin
½ ounce lemon juice
1 teaspoon raspberry syrup
Several dashes of raspberry schnapps
1 scoop crushed ice
Club soda

Mix all the ingredients, except soda, in a shaker. Pour the mixture into a chilled highball glass. Top off the glass with ice cubes and club soda.

Anthony's Spur

1½ ounces gin
½ ounce dry vermouth
½ ounce sweet vermouth
1 ounce orange juice
1 egg yolk
1 scoop crushed ice

Combine all the ingredients in a shaker. Mix well and strain into a chilled cocktail glass.

Antibes

1½ ounces dry gin
½ ounce Benedictine
2 ounces grapefruit juice
1 scoop crushed ice
Orange slice

Mix all the ingredients, except the orange slice, in a shaker. Pour the mixture into a chilled old-fashioned glass and garnish with the orange slice.

Aruba

Makes 2 servings

3 ounces gin
1 ounce curaçao
2 ounces lemon juice
1 egg white
2 teaspoons orgeat or Falernum
Crushed ice

Combine all the ingredients in a shaker. Mix well and strain into chilled cocktail glasses.

Avalanche

1½ ounces gin
1 ounce white crème de cacao
1 ounce heavy cream
1 scoop crushed ice

Combine all the ingredients in a shaker. Mix well and strain into a chilled cocktail glass.

Aviation

1½ ounces gin
½ ounce lemon juice
½ teaspoon maraschino liqueur
½ teaspoon apricot brandy
1 scoop crushed ice

Combine all the ingredients in a shaker. Mix well and strain into a chilled cocktail glass.

Bay Bridge Cooler

2 ounces gin
3 ounces pineapple juice
½ ounce lime juice
1 teaspoon maraschino liqueur
Club soda, lemon-lime soda, or
   ginger ale
1 scoop crushed ice

Combine all the ingredients in a shaker. Mix well and pour into a chilled double old-fashioned glass.

Bermuda Highball

1 ounce gin
1 ounce brandy
1 ounce dry vermouth
Club soda or ginger ale

Pour the gin, brandy, and vermouth into a chilled highball glass with several ice cubes. Top off the glass with club soda or ginger ale.

Bermuda Triangle

1½ ounces gin
1 ounce apricot brandy
½ ounce lime juice
1 teaspoon sugar syrup
Dash of grenadine
1 scoop crushed ice
Orange peel
½ teaspoon curaçao

Mix all the ingredients, except the orange peel and curaçao, in a shaker. Pour the mixture into a chilled old-fashioned glass. Twist the orange peel over the drink and drop it in. Top with a float of curaçao.

Berry Fizz

2 ounces gin
½ ounce maraschino liqueur
1 ounce lemon juice
1 teaspoon raspberry syrup
Crushed ice
Club soda
2 raspberries

Mix all the ingredients, except the soda and fruit, in a shaker. Strain the mixture into a chilled highball glass. Top off the glass with club soda and stir gently. Garnish with the raspberries.

Big Kahuna

1½ ounces gin
½ ounce curaçao
2 ounces pineapple juice
1 teaspoon sweet vermouth
1 scoop crushed ice

Combine all the ingredients in a shaker. Mix well and strain into a chilled cocktail glass.

Bonnie Blush

1½ ounces gin
1 teaspoon curaçao
½ teaspoon lemon juice
1 teaspoon grenadine
1 scoop crushed ice

Combine all the ingredients in a shaker. Mix well and strain into a chilled whiskey sour glass.

Bonnie Prince

1½ ounces gin
½ ounce white wine
¼ ounce Drambuie
1 scoop crushed ice
Orange peel

Mix all the ingredients, except the orange peel, in a shaker. Strain the mixture into a chilled cocktail glass. Twist the orange peel over the drink and drop it in.

Boom Bang

1½ ounces gin
½ ounce amontillado sherry
1 scoop crushed ice
Lemon peel
1 ounce scotch

Mix the gin and sherry in a shaker with crushed ice. Pour the mixture into a chilled old-fashioned glass. Twist the lemon peel over the drink and drop it in. Float the scotch on top and serve.

Bridgehampton Fizz

1 ounce gin
1 ounce brandy
1 ounce dry vermouth
1 scoop crushed ice
Club soda
Lemon peel

Mix all the ingredients, except the soda and lemon peel, in a shaker. Pour the mixture into a chilled highball glass and top with club soda. Twist the lemon peel over the drink and drop it in.

Bulldog Cafe

½ ounce gin
½ ounce rye whiskey
½ ounce sweet vermouth
½ ounce brandy
Several dashes of Triple Sec or orange bitters
1 scoop crushed ice

Combine all the ingredients in a shaker. Mix well and strain into a chilled glass.

Bumblebee

1½ ounces gin
1 teaspoon honey
1 scoop crushed ice
Several dashes of lemon juice

Mix all the ingredients in a shaker or blender. Strain the mixture into a chilled cocktail glass. Add lemon juice to taste.

Burberry

1½ ounces gin
Several dashes of maraschino
    liqueur
Several dashes of orange bitters
Several dashes of sugar syrup
1 scoop crushed ice

Combine all the ingredients in a
shaker. Mix well and strain into a
chilled cocktail glass.

Cabaret

1½ ounces gin
1½ ounces Dubonnet rouge
Several dashes of bitters
Several dashes of Pernod
1 scoop crushed ice
Maraschino cherry

Mix all the ingredients, except the
cherry, in a shaker. Strain the mixture into a chilled cocktail glass and
garnish with the maraschino cherry.

Cablecar

1½ ounces gin
¾ ounce Triple Sec
1 ounce lemon juice
1 scoop crushed ice

Combine all the ingredients in a
shaker. Mix well and pour into a
chilled old-fashioned glass.

Caitlin's Cure

1½ ounces dry gin
Several dashes of grenadine
Several dashes of bitters
Several dashes of orange bitters
1 scoop crushed ice

Combine all the ingredients in a
shaker. Mix well and strain into a
chilled cocktail glass.

Cara Mia

1 ounce gin
¾ ounce dry vermouth
¾ ounce dry sherry
Dash of curaçao

Pour all the ingredients into a mixing glass with ice cubes. Stir and
strain into a chilled cocktail glass.

Central Park West

1½ ounces gin
½ ounce cherry brandy
½ ounce lime juice
¼ ounce maraschino liqueur
1 scoop crushed ice

Combine all the ingredients in a
shaker. Mix well and strain into a
chilled cocktail glass.

Claridge Cocktail

1½ ounces gin
1 ounce dry vermouth
½ ounce apricot brandy
½ ounce Triple Sec
1 scoop crushed ice

Mix all the ingredients in a shaker. Strain the mixture into a chilled cocktail glass.

Clover Club

Makes 2 servings

3 ounces gin
2 ounces lime juice
1 ounce grenadine
1 egg white
2 scoops crushed ice

Put all the ingredients in a shaker. Mix well and strain into chilled cocktail glasses.

Coco Chanel

1 ounce gin
1 ounce Kahlúa or other coffee
  liqueur
1 ounce heavy cream
1 scoop crushed ice

Combine all the ingredients in a shaker. Mix well and strain into a chilled cocktail glass.

Coit Tower Cooler

1½ ounces gin
1 ounce sloe gin
3 ounces grapefruit juice
½ ounce sugar syrup
Crushed ice
Club soda

Mix all the ingredients, except the soda, in a shaker. Pour the mix into a chilled collins glass. Top off the glass with cold club soda.

Colony Club

1½ ounces gin
1 teaspoon anisette
Several dashes of orange bitters
1 scoop crushed ice

Mix all the ingredients in a shaker. Strain the mixture into a chilled cocktail glass.

Company 19

1 ounce gin
½ ounce dry vermouth
½ ounce apricot brandy
1 teaspoon lemon juice
1 scoop crushed ice

Put all the ingredients in a shaker. Mix well and pour into a chilled old-fashioned glass.

Cooksie's Cooler

1½ ounces gin
3 ounces cranberry juice
½ ounce lemon juice
Several dashes of orange bitters
Club soda

Pour all the ingredients, except the soda, into a chilled highball glass with several ice cubes. Stir gently. Top off the glass with club soda.

Cool Toby

6 mint leaves
1½ ounces gin
½ ounce peppermint schnapps
½ ounce lemon juice
½ ounce sugar syrup
Lemon slice
Mint sprig

Muddle the mint leaves, gin, schnapps, lemon juice, and sugar syrup in a double old-fashioned glass with a little water. Add ice cubes and stir well. Garnish with the lemon slice and mint sprig.

Cornell Cocktail

Makes 2 servings

4 ounces gin
1 ounce maraschino liqueur
1 egg white
2 scoops crushed ice

Combine all the ingredients in a shaker. Mix well and strain into chilled cocktail glasses.

Daily Bruin

1 ounce gin
½ ounce apple brandy
½ ounce sweet vermouth
½ ounce lemon juice
Several dashes of grenadine
1 scoop crushed ice

Combine all the ingredients in a shaker. Mix well and strain into a chilled cocktail glass.

Dartmouth Green

1½ ounces gin
½ ounce green crème de menthe
¼ ounce kümmel
¼ ounce lemon juice
1 scoop crushed ice

Mix all the ingredients in a shaker. Strain the mixture into a chilled cocktail glass.

Dempsey

1 ounce gin
1 ounce applejack or Calvados
1 teaspoon sugar syrup
2 dashes of Pernod
2 dashes of grenadine
1 scoop crushed ice

Mix all the ingredients in a shaker.
Pour the mixture into a chilled old-
fashioned glass.

Devil's Advocate

1½ ounces gin
½ ounce applejack
¼ ounce lime juice
Several dashes of grenadine
1 scoop crushed ice

Mix all the ingredients in a shaker.
Pour the mixture into a chilled cocktail glass.

Diamond Head

Makes 2 servings

4 ounces gin
1½ ounces apricot brandy
2 ounces lemon juice
2 teaspoons sugar syrup
1 egg white
2 scoops crushed ice

Combine all the ingredients in a
shaker. Mix well and strain into
chilled cocktail glasses.

Doonesbury Dash

1½ ounces gin
1½ ounces medium sherry
½ ounce sweet vermouth
½ ounce dry vermouth
¼ ounce curaçao
¼ ounce cherry brandy
¼ ounce crème de cacao
1 ounce lemon or lime juice
1 scoop crushed ice

Mix all the ingredients in a shaker.
Pour the mixture into a large chilled
goblet.

Douglas Fairbanks

Makes 2 servings

4 ounces gin
1½ ounces apricot brandy
2 ounces lemon juice
2 teaspoons sugar syrup
1 egg white
Crushed ice

Mix all the ingredients in a shaker.
Strain the mixture into chilled cocktail glasses.

Drake Gin Sour

Makes 2 servings

4 ounces gin
2 teaspoons lemon juice
2 teaspoons orgeat or sugar syrup
1 egg white
Crushed ice

Mix all the ingredients in a shaker. Strain the mixture into a chilled whiskey sour glass.

Dutch Treat

Makes 2 servings

3 ounces gin
1 ounce aquavit
1 ounce lemon juice
2 teaspoons sugar syrup
2 teaspoons heavy cream
1 egg white
Crushed ice

Mix all the ingredients in a shaker. Pour the mixture into chilled old-fashioned glasses.

Everybody's Irish

2 to 3 dashes Angostura bitters
1 teaspoon green crème de menthe
2 to 3 ounces gin
Green cherry

In a shaker with crushed ice, mix together bitters, crème de menthe, and gin. Strain the mixture into a chilled cocktail glass and garnish with the green cherry.

Flipper

2 ounces gin
¾ ounce amaretto
½ ounce dry vermouth
½ ounce Campari
1 scoop crushed ice
Orange peel

Stir all the ingredients, except the orange peel, in a mixing glass. Pour the mixture into a chilled cocktail glass and garnish with the orange peel.

Georgetown

1 ounce gin
¾ ounce Dubonnet blanc
½ ounce apricot brandy
Dash of lemon juice
1 scoop crushed ice
Maraschino cherry

Combine all the ingredients, except the cherry, in a shaker. Strain the mixture into a chilled cocktail glass and garnish with the maraschino cherry.

Gin and Ginger

1½ ounces gin
Lemon peel
Ginger ale

Pour the gin into a chilled highball glass with several ice cubes. Twist the lemon peel over the drink and drop it in. Top off the glass with ginger ale and stir gently.

Gin Cassis

1½ ounces gin
½ ounce lemon juice
½ ounce crème de cassis
1 scoop crushed ice

Mix all the ingredients in a shaker. Pour the mixture into a chilled old-fashioned glass.

Gin Milk Punch

1½ ounces gin
5 ounces milk
1 teaspoon sugar syrup
1 scoop crushed ice
Pinch of grated nutmeg

Mix all the ingredients, except the nutmeg, in a shaker. Pour the mixture into a chilled highball glass. Sprinkle with the ground nutmeg.

Gin Rickey

1½ ounces gin
Club soda
Juice of ½ lime

Pour the gin into a chilled highball glass with several ice cubes. Top off with club soda and lime juice and stir gently.

Golden Fizz

2 to 3 ounces gin
1 ounce lemon or lime juice
1 teaspoon sugar syrup
1 egg yolk
1 scoop crushed ice
Club soda
Lemon or lime slice

Mix all the ingredients, except the soda and fruit slice, in a shaker. Pour the mixture into a chilled collins glass. Top off with cold club soda and stir gently. Garnish with the fruit slice.

Golden Rooster

1 ounce gin
½ ounce dry vermouth
½ ounce Triple Sec
½ ounce apricot brandy
1 scoop crushed ice
Maraschino cherry

Mix all the ingredients, except the cherry, in a shaker. Pour the mixture into a chilled old-fashioned glass. Decorate with the cherry.

Gradeal Special

1½ ounces gin
¾ ounce light rum
¾ ounce apricot brandy or
    liqueur
1 scoop crushed ice

Combine all the ingredients in a shaker. Mix well and strain into a chilled cocktail glass.

Grand Passion

2 ounces gin
1 ounce dry vermouth
1 ounce passion fruit liqueur
1 scoop crushed ice
Orange peel

Mix the gin, vermouth, and liqueur in a shaker with crushed ice. Strain the mixture into a chilled cocktail glass. Twist the orange peel over the drink and drop it in.

Green Jade

Makes 2 servings

2 ounces gin
1 ounce green crème de menthe
1 egg white
2 ounces cream
Green cherries
Mint sprigs

In a shaker with crushed ice, mix together the gin, crème de menthe,

egg white, and cream. Pour the mixture into cocktail glasses and garnish with the cherries and mint sprigs.

Groovy U.V.

1½ ounces gin
1 ounce lemon juice
½ ounce maple syrup
1 scoop crushed ice

Combine all the ingredients in a shaker. Mix well and pour into a chilled old-fashioned glass.

Guggenheim

1 ounce gin
1 ounce brandy
1 ounce Triple Sec
1 scoop crushed ice

Combine all the ingredients in a shaker. Mix well and strain into a chilled cocktail glass.

Harlem Cocktail

1½ ounces gin
1 ounce pineapple juice
1 teaspoon maraschino liqueur
1 tablespoon diced canned
    pineapple
1 scoop crushed ice

Mix all the ingredients in a shaker. Pour the mixture into a chilled old-fashioned glass.

Harvard Yard

1 ounce gin
3/4 ounce peppermint schnapps
1/2 ounce cranberry liqueur
Dash of Triple Sec
Orange slice

Mix all the ingredients, except the orange slice, in a shaker with ice. Strain the mixture into a chilled cocktail glass and garnish with the orange slice.

Hawaiian

Makes 2 servings

3 ounces gin
2 ounces pineapple juice
1 egg white
Several dashes of orange bitters
2 scoops crushed ice

Mix all the ingredients in a shaker. Strain the mixture into chilled cocktail glasses.

Headwall

1 ounce gin
1 ounce light rum
1 teaspoon lemon juice
Dash of grenadine
1 scoop crushed ice
Ginger ale

Mix all the ingredients, except the ginger ale, in a shaker. Pour the mixture into a chilled highball glass and top off with cold ginger ale.

Ivy Club

1 1/2 ounces gin
1/2 ounce amaretto
1/2 ounce lime juice
Dash of grenadine
1 scoop crushed ice

Mix all the ingredients in a shaker. Strain the mixture into a chilled cocktail glass.

Jamaica Glow

1 1/2 ounces gin
1/2 ounce dry red wine
1/4 ounce dark Jamaican rum
1/2 ounce orange juice
1 scoop crushed ice
Lime slice

Mix all the ingredients, except the lime slice, in a shaker. Strain the mixture into a chilled cocktail glass. Garnish with the lime slice.

Judge, Jr.

1 ounce gin
1 ounce light rum
½ ounce lemon juice
1 teaspoon grenadine
1 scoop crushed ice

Mix all the ingredients in a shaker. Strain the mixture into a chilled cocktail glass.

Jupiter Cocktail

1½ ounces gin
¾ ounce dry vermouth
1 teaspoon Parfait Amour or crème de violette
1 teaspoon orange juice
1 scoop crushed ice

Mix all the ingredients in a shaker or blender. Strain the mixture into a chilled cocktail glass.

Key Club Cocktail

1½ ounces gin
½ ounce dark rum
½ ounce Falernum
½ ounce lime juice
1 scoop crushed ice
Pineapple stick

Mix all the ingredients, except the pineapple, in a shaker. Strain the mixture into a chilled cocktail glass. Decorate with the pineapple stick.

Kyoto Cocktail

1½ ounces gin
½ ounce dry vermouth
½ ounce melon liqueur
Dash of lemon juice
1 scoop crushed ice

Mix all the ingredients in a shaker or blender. Strain the mixture into a chilled cocktail glass.

Leapfrog

1½ ounces gin
½ ounce lemon juice
1 scoop crushed ice
Ginger ale

Mix the gin and lemon juice in a tall highball glass with crushed ice. Top off the glass with cold ginger ale.

Little Devil

1 ounce gin
1 ounce gold rum
½ ounce Triple Sec
½ ounce lemon juice
1 scoop crushed ice

Mix all the ingredients in a shaker. Strain the mixture into a chilled cocktail glass.

London French "75"

1½ ounces gin
Juice of ½ lemon
1 teaspoon sugar syrup
1 scoop crushed ice
Brut champagne

Mix all the ingredients, except the champagne, in a shaker. Pour the mixture into a chilled collins glass. Top off the glass with cold champagne.

London Royal

1½ ounces gin
¾ ounce Triple Sec
½ ounce lemon juice
1 scoop crushed ice

Mix all the ingredients in a shaker. Pour the mixture into a chilled cocktail glass.

Maiden's Blush

2½ ounces gin
¾ ounce Pernod
½ teaspoon grenadine
1 scoop crushed ice

Mix all the ingredients in a shaker. Strain the mixture into a chilled cocktail glass.

Maiden's Prayer I

1½ ounces gin
¾ ounce Triple Sec
¼ ounce orange juice
¼ ounce lemon juice
1 scoop crushed ice

Mix all the ingredients in a shaker. Strain the mixture into a chilled cocktail glass.

Maiden's Prayer II

1½ ounces gin
½ ounce Lillet blanc
¼ ounce lemon juice
¼ ounce orange juice
1 scoop crushed ice

Mix all the ingredients in a shaker. Strain the mixture into a chilled cocktail glass.

Maple Tree

2 ounces gin
½ ounce light or gold rum
½ ounce lemon juice
½ ounce maple syrup
Crushed ice

Mix all the ingredients in a shaker or blender. Strain the mixture into a chilled cocktail glass.

Marmalade Cocktail

2 ounces gin
1 ounce lemon juice
1 tablespoon orange marmalade
1 scoop crushed ice

Mix all the ingredients in a shaker. Pour the mixture into a chilled cocktail glass.

Martha's Vineyard

2 ounces gin
1 ounce lemon juice
1 ounce lime juice
1 scoop vanilla ice cream
1 scoop crushed ice
Club soda

Mix all the ingredients, except the club soda. Shake or blend until the mixture is smooth. Pour the blend into a chilled double old-fashioned glass. Top off the glass with club soda and stir gently.

Martini Mint

2 ounces gin or vodka
1 ounce peppermint schnapps

Combine both ingredients in a mixing glass with ice cubes. Stir and strain into a chilled cocktail glass.

Midnight Rendezvous

1½ ounces gin
½ ounce kirsch
½ ounce Campari
1 scoop crushed ice
Lemon peel

Mix all the ingredients, except the lemon peel, in a shaker. Strain the mixture into a chilled cocktail glass. Twist the lemon peel over the drink and drop it in.

Mint Collins

2 ounces gin
½ ounce lemon juice
1 teaspoon white crème de menthe
1 teaspoon sugar syrup
1 scoop crushed ice
Club soda
Mint springs

Mix all the ingredients, except the club soda and mint sprigs, in a blender. Pour the mixture into a chilled collins glass. Top off the glass with cold club soda and stir gently. Garnish with the mint sprigs.

Moll Cocktail

1 ounce gin
1 ounce sloe gin
1 ounce dry vermouth
Dash of orange bitters
1 scoop crushed ice

Mix all the ingredients in a shaker. Strain the mixture into a chilled cocktail glass.

Moonstruck

1½ ounces gin
3 ounces clam juice
Dash of red pepper sauce

Combine all the ingredients in a mixing glass with several ice cubes. Strain the mixture into a chilled whiskey sour glass.

Morning Joy

1 ounce gin
1 ounce crème de banane
2 ounces orange juice
1 scoop crushed ice

Mix all the ingredients in a shaker. Strain the mixture into a chilled whiskey sour glass.

Mule's Hind Leg

¾ ounce gin
¾ ounce apple brandy
¾ ounce Benedictine
¾ ounce apricot brandy
¾ ounce maple syrup, or to taste
1 scoop crushed ice

Mix all the ingredients in a shaker. Pour the mixture into a chilled cocktail glass.

Nantucket Red

1½ ounces gin
¾ ounce apricot liqueur
½ ounce lemon juice
1 teaspoon grenadine
Dash of bitters
1 scoop crushed ice

Mix all the ingredients in a shaker. Strain the mixture into a chilled cocktail glass.

Newport Cooler

1½ ounces gin
½ ounce brandy
½ ounce peach liqueur
Several dashes of lime juice
Ginger ale or lemon-lime soda

Mix all the ingredients, except the ginger ale, in a chilled collins glass with ice cubes. Top off the glass with the ginger ale or lemon-lime soda.

Normandy Cocktail

1½ ounces gin
¾ ounce Calvados or applejack
½ ounce apricot brandy
Several dashes of lemon juice
1 scoop crushed ice

Mix all the ingredients in a shaker.
Pour the mixture into a chilled cocktail glass.

Opera

1½ ounces gin
¾ ounces Dubonnet rouge
½ ounces maraschino liqueur
1 scoop crushed ice
Orange peel

Mix all the ingredients, except the
orange peel, in a shaker. Strain the
mixture into a chilled cocktail glass.
Twist the orange peel over the drink
and drop it in.

Our Home

Makes 2 servings

2 ounces gin
2 ounces peach brandy
1 ounce dry vermouth
Dash of lemon juice
1 egg white
Crushed ice

Mix all the ingredients in a shaker.
Strain the mixture into chilled cocktail glasses.

Panda

1 ounce gin
1 ounce Calvados or applejack
1 ounce slivovitz
1 ounce orange juice
Dash of sugar or sugar syrup
1 scoop crushed ice

Mix all the ingredients in a shaker or
blender. Strain the mixture into a
chilled cocktail glass.

Passion Cup

2 ounces gin
2 ounces orange juice
1 ounce passion fruit juice
1 ounce piña colada mix or equal
    parts pineapple juice and
    coconut milk
1 scoop crushed ice
1 maraschino cherry

Mix all the ingredients, except the
cherry, in a shaker. Pour the mixture
into a chilled wine goblet and garnish with the cherry.

Peach Blow Fizz

2 to 3 ounces gin
1 ounce lemon juice
1 ounce heavy cream
1 teaspoon sugar syrup, or to taste
4 mashed strawberries
1 scoop crushed ice
Club soda

Mix all the ingredients, except the soda, in a shaker. Pour the mixture into a chilled highball glass. Top off the glass with club soda and stir gently.

Pedro

1 ounce gin
1 ounce apple brandy
1 ounce lemon juice
1 teaspoon sugar syrup
¼ teaspoon curaçao
1 scoop crushed ice

Mix all the ingredients in a shaker or blender with crushed ice. Strain the mixture into a chilled wine goblet.

Pegu Club Cocktail

1½ ounces gin
¾ ounces orange curaçao
1 teaspoon lime juice
Dash of bitters
Dash of orange bitters
1 scoop crushed ice

Mix all the ingredients in a shaker. Strain the mixture into a chilled cocktail glass.

Pendennis Club Cocktail

1½ ounces gin
¾ ounce apricot brandy
½ ounce lime juice
1 teaspoon sugar syrup
Several dashes of bitters
1 scoop crushed ice

Mix all the ingredients in a shaker. Strain the mixture into a chilled cocktail glass.

Pink Gin

2 to 3 ounces gin
Bitters to taste

In a mixing glass, stir together the gin, bitters, and ice cubes. Strain the mixture into a chilled cocktail glass.

Pink Panther

Makes 2 servings

3 ounces gin
1½ ounces dry vermouth
1 ounce crème de cassis
2 ounces orange juice
1 egg white
Crushed ice

Combine all the ingredients in a shaker. Mix well and strain into chilled cocktail glasses.

Pink Rose

1½ ounces gin
1 teaspoon lemon juice
1 teaspoon heavy cream
1 egg white
Several dashes of grenadine
1 scoop crushed ice

Mix all the ingredients in a shaker. Strain the mixture into a chilled cocktail glass.

Polish Sidecar

1 ounce gin
¾ ounce blackberry liqueur or
   blackberry brandy
¾ ounce lemon juice
1 scoop crushed ice
4 fresh blackberries (optional)

Mix the gin, brandy, and lemon juice in a shaker with crushed ice. Pour the mixture into a chilled glass. Garnish with the fresh blackberries.

Pré Catalan Cocktail

1½ ounces gin
1 ounce Parfait Amour
Several dashes of lemon juice
1 scoop crushed ice

Mix all the ingredients in a shaker. Strain the mixture into a chilled cocktail glass.

Princeton

1½ ounces gin
¾ ounce port
Several dashes of orange bitters
1 scoop crushed ice
Lemon peel

Mix all the ingredients, except the lemon peel, in a shaker. Strain the mixture into a chilled cocktail glass. Twist the lemon peel over the drink and drop it in.

Red Bluff

1 ounce gin
1 ounce cherry brandy
½ ounce dry vermouth
½ ounce lemon juice
Several dashes of orange bitters
1 scoop crushed ice

Mix all the ingredients in a shaker. Pour the mixture into a chilled old-fashioned glass.

Red Lion Cocktail

1 ounce gin
1 ounce orange liqueur
½ ounce orange juice
½ ounce lemon juice
1 scoop crushed ice

Mix all the ingredients in a shaker. Strain the mixture into a chilled cocktail glass.

Road Runner

1½ ounces gin
½ ounce dry vermouth
½ teaspoon grenadine
Several dashes of Pernod
1 scoop crushed ice

Mix all the ingredients in a shaker. Strain the mixture into a chilled cocktail glass.

Roma

¾ ounce gin
¾ ounce grappa
½ ounce Sambuca
½ ounce dry vermouth
1 scoop crushed ice
Green olive

Mix all the ingredients, except the olive, in a shaker or blender. Strain the mixture into a chilled cocktail glass and garnish with the olive.

Royal Gin Fizz

1½ ounces gin
½ ounce orange liqueur
1 ounce lemon juice
½ ounce sugar syrup
1 egg
1 scoop crushed ice
Club soda
Maraschino cherry

Mix all the ingredients, except the soda and cherry, in a shaker. Pour the mixture into a chilled collins glass. Top off the glass with cold club soda and garnish with the cherry.

Santa Barbara Sunset

2 ounces gin
¾ ounce apricot liqueur
2 ounces orange juice
Juice of ½ lime
Dash of grenadine or raspberry syrup
1 scoop crushed ice

Mix all the ingredients in a shaker. Strain the mixture into a chilled cocktail glass.

Savoy Hotel Special

1 ounce gin
½ ounce dry vermouth
2 dashes of grenadine
1 dash of Pernod
1 lemon peel twist

Combine all the ingredients, except the lemon twist, in a mixing glass with ice. Stir and strain into a chilled cocktail glass. Garnish with the twist of lemon peel.

Scarlet Letter

2 ounces gin
½ ounce lemon juice
1 teaspoon grenadine
1 scoop crushed ice
1 ounce port

Mix all the ingredients, except the port, in a blender. Pour the mixture into a chilled highball glass and top with a float of port.

Sea Ray

2 ounces gin
1 ounce light rum
3 ounces orange juice
1 ounce lemon juice
1 teaspoon orgeat or sugar syrup
Several dashes of maraschino
    liqueur
1 scoop crushed ice

Mix all the ingredients in a shaker. Pour the mixture into a chilled double old-fashioned glass.

Seville

1½ ounces gin
½ ounce fino sherry
½ ounce orange juice
½ ounce lemon juice
½ ounce sugar syrup
1 scoop crushed ice

Mix all the ingredients in a shaker or blender. Pour the mixture into a chilled old-fashioned glass.

Shepard's Suffering Bastard

Bitters
1½ ounces gin
1½ ounces brandy
1 teaspoon lime juice
Ginger beer
Mint sprig
Cucumber slice
Orange or lemon slice

Swirl the bitters around a chilled double old-fashioned glass so that the glass is thoroughly coated. Discard excess bitters. Add gin, brandy, and lime juice to the glass along with several ice cubes and mix well. Top off the glass with cold ginger beer and stir gently. Garnish with the mint, cucumber, and fruit slice.

Sloe Ball

1½ ounces sloe gin
½ ounce gin
½ ounce vodka
1 ounce orange juice
½ ounce lemon juice
1 teaspoon grenadine
1 scoop crushed ice

Combine all the ingredients in a shaker. Mix well and strain into a highball glass over ice cubes.

Socrates

1½ ounces gin
½ ounce dry vermouth
½ ounce sweet vermouth
1 ounce orange juice
1 egg white
1 scoop crushed ice

Mix all the ingredients in a shaker. Strain the mixture into a chilled cocktail glass.

Spanish Gold

1½ ounces gin
½ ounce dry red wine
¼ dark rum
½ ounce orange juice
1 scoop crushed ice
Lime slice

Mix all the ingredients, except the lime slice, in a shaker. Strain the mixture into a chilled cocktail glass and decorate with the lime slice.

Stanford Cocktail

1½ ounces gin
1 ounce strawberry liqueur
½ ounce lemon juice
Dash of Triple Sec
1 scoop crushed ice
Club soda
Lemon peel
1 whole strawberry

Mix all the ingredients, except the soda and fruit, in a shaker. Strain the mixture into a chilled collins glass. Top off the glass with club soda, then twist the lemon peel and drop it in. Garnish with the strawberry.

Steamboat

1½ ounces gin
¼ ounce crème de cassis
¼ ounce lemon juice
1 scoop crushed ice

Mix all the ingredients in a shaker. Pour the mixture into a chilled old-fashioned glass.

Stinson Beach Cooler

1½ ounces gin
3 ounces orange juice
Ginger ale

Pour the gin and orange juice into a chilled highball glass with ice cubes. Top off the glass with cold ginger ale and stir gently.

Sweet Jessica

1 ounce gin
1 ounce apricot brandy
1 teaspoon lemon juice
1/2 teaspoon sugar syrup
1/2 teaspoon grenadine
1 scoop crushed ice

Mix all the ingredients in a shaker. Strain the mixture into a chilled cocktail glass.

Tangier

1 ounce gin
1 ounce Triple Sec
1 ounce Mandarin Napoleon
1 scoop crushed ice
Orange peel

Mix all the ingredients, except the orange peel, in a shaker. Strain the mixture into a chilled cocktail glass. Garnish with the orange peel.

Tinsley Island

1 1/2 ounces gin
3/4 ounce gold rum
3 ounces orange juice
1/2 ounce lemon juice
Several dashes of 151-proof
    Demerara or light rum
1 scoop crushed ice

Mix all the ingredients in a shaker. Pour the mixture into a chilled old-fashioned glass.

Toby Twist

2 ounces gin
Mint leaves
1/2 ounce curaçao
1/2 ounce lime juice
Dash of orange bitters
1 scoop crushed ice
Club soda
Lemon slice
Several mint sprigs

Combine the gin, mint leaves, curaçao, lime juice, and bitters in a chilled old-fashioned glass and mix well. Add the crushed ice and a splash of club soda. Stir well. Garnish with the lemon slice and mint sprigs.

Triple A

1 ounce gin
1 ounce cherry liqueur
1 ounce lemon juice
1 scoop crushed ice

Mix all the ingredients in a shaker. Strain the mixture into a chilled cocktail glass.

Tutti-Frutti

3 ounces gin
1 ounce maraschino liqueur
1 ounce amaretto
2 ounces diced apples
2 ounces diced pears
2 ounces diced peaches
1 scoop crushed ice

Mix all the ingredients in a blender. Blend until smooth, then pour the blend into a chilled highball glass.

Ulanda

1½ ounces gin
¾ ounces Triple Sec
Several dashes of Pernod
1 scoop crushed ice

Mix all the ingredients in a shaker. Pour the mixture into a chilled cocktail glass.

Valencia Cocktail

1½ ounces gin
1 ounce dry sherry
Lemon peel

Pour the gin and sherry into a mixing glass with several ice cubes. Stir well and strain into a chilled cocktail glass. Twist the lemon peel over the drink and drop it in.

Verona Cocktail

1 ounce gin
½ ounce sweet vermouth
1 ounce amaretto
Dash or two of lemon juice
1 scoop crushed ice
Orange slice

Mix all the ingredients, except the orange slice, in a shaker. Pour the mixture into a chilled old-fashioned glass. Garnish with the orange slice.

Warday's Cocktail

1 ounce gin
1 ounce sweet vermouth
1 ounce Calvados or applejack
1 teaspoon yellow Chartreuse
1 scoop crushed ice

Mix all the ingredients in a shaker or blender. Strain the mixture into a chilled cocktail glass.

Wedding Belle

1 ounce gin
1 ounce Dubonnet rouge
½ ounce cherry brandy
1 ounce orange juice
1 scoop crushed ice

Mix all the ingredients in a shaker. Pour the mixture into a chilled cocktail glass.

White Baby

1 ounce gin
1 ounce Triple Sec
1 ounce heavy cream
1 scoop crushed ice

Mix all the ingredients in a shaker. Strain the mixture into a chilled cocktail glass.

White Lady

1½ ounces gin
¾ ounce Triple Sec
¾ ounce lemon juice
Crushed ice

Combine all the ingredients in a shaker. Mix well and strain into a chilled cocktail glass.

White Cargo I

2½ ounces gin
½ ounce maraschino liqueur
Dash of dry white wine
1 scoop vanilla ice cream

Mix all the ingredients in a blender until smooth. Pour the blend into a chilled wine goblet.

White Cargo II

2 ounces gin
Several dashes of cream sherry
¼ cup vanilla ice cream
Maraschino cherry

Mix the gin, sherry, and ice cream in a blender until smooth. Pour the blend into a chilled parfait glass. Garnish with the cherry.

White Lie

Makes 2 servings

3 ounces gin
1½ ounces maraschino liqueur
4 ounces orange juice
1 ounce lime juice
2 teaspoons sugar syrup
1 egg white
Crushed ice

Mix all the ingredients in a shaker. Strain the mixture into chilled cocktail glasses.

Xanadu

1 ounce gin
1 ounce cherry brandy
1 ounce yellow Chartreuse
1 scoop crushed ice

Mix all the ingredients in a shaker. Pour the mixture into a chilled cocktail glass.

Yale

1 ounce gin
1 ounce curaçao
1 ounce grapefruit juice
1 scoop crushed ice

Mix all the ingredients in a shaker or blender. Strain the mix into a chilled cocktail glass.

Youngblood

1½ ounces gin
½ ounce sweet vermouth
½ ounce dry vermouth
1 teaspoon strawberry liqueur
Several whole strawberries

Mix all the ingredients in a blender with crushed ice. When frosty, pour the blend into a chilled cocktail glass.

SIGNATURE DRINKS

Blond Bombshell

GORDON RESTAURANT, CHICAGO

1 ounce gin
1 ounce Lillet blanc
1 orange slice

Combine the spirits in a cocktail shaker. Chill well. Pour the mixture into a martini glass and garnish with the orange slice.

Bronx Cocktail (the Original)

WALDORF-ASTORIA, NEW YORK CITY

1½ ounces gin
½ ounce orange juice
Dash of dry vermouth
Dash of sweet vermouth
1 scoop crushed ice

Combine all the ingredients in a shaker. Mix well and strain into a chilled cocktail glass.

Cole Porter

WALDORF-ASTORIA, NEW YORK CITY

1½ ounces gin
3 to 4 small plum tomatoes, cooked and chilled
Dash of Angostura bitters
Dash of Worcestershire sauce
Dash of lemon juice
Crushed ice

Combine all the ingredients in a blender. Blend until smooth. Pour the blend into a chilled old-fashioned glass.

New England Martini

ASTA, SAN FRANCISCO

1¼ ounces gin
Splash of dry vermouth
3 olives
Vermont Cheddar cheese

In a mixing glass with ice, stir together the gin and vermouth. Strain the mixture into a chilled martini glass. Garnish with 3 olives and serve with a slice of Vermont Cheddar on the side.

Putting Green

THE COLONNADE HOTEL, BOSTON

¾ ounce gin
1 ounce melon liqueur
1½ ounces orange juice
1½ ounces lemon juice
Crushed ice
Green cherry
Orange slice

Mix all the ingredients, except the cherry and orange slice, in a shaker or blender. Pour the mixture into a frosted collins glass. Garnish with the cherry and the orange slice.

Ramos Gin Fizz

THE BALBOA CAFE, SAN FRANCISCO

1 ounce gin
2 teaspoons sugar
2 ounces half-and-half
Splash of orange juice
2 squirts of orange flower water
1 egg white
6 ice cubes
1 teaspoon vanilla extract
Club soda
Freshly ground nutmeg
Orange slice

Blend all the ingredients, except the club soda, nutmeg, and orange slice, on low speed. Pour a splash of club soda in the bottom of a tall collins glass and then add the blend. Sprinkle the freshly ground nutmeg on top and garnish with the slice of orange.

Small Dinger

LA FLORIDA BAR, HAVANA, FLORIDA

½ ounce gin
¼ ounce rum
¼ ounce grenadine
¼ ounce lemon juice
Crushed ice

Combine all the ingredients in a blender. Shake well and pour into a chilled cocktail glass.

South Camp Special

SOUTH CAMP ROAD HOTEL, KINGSTON, JAMAICA

¼ ounce dry gin
¼ ounce rum
¼ ounce scotch
Dash of lime juice
Dash of sweet vermouth
Dash of cherry brandy
1 scoop crushed ice
Maraschino cherry

Combine all the ingredients, except the cherry, in a shaker. Shake well and strain into a cocktail glass. Garnish with the maraschino cherry.

TROPICAL DRINKS

Bali Hai

1 ounce gin
1 ounce light rum
1 ounce okolehao (optional)
1 ounce lemon juice
3 ounces lime juice
1 teaspoon orgeat or sugar syrup
1 scoop crushed ice
Chilled champagne

Mix all the ingredients, except the champagne, in a shaker. Pour the mixture into a chilled collins glass and top off with champagne.

Blue Whale

1 ounce gin
¾ ounce curaçao
1 ounce coconut cream
1 cup ice

Combine all the ingredients in a blender and blend until smooth. Pour the blend into a chilled parfait glass.

Tequila

Most Americans have a stereotypical image of tequila: a powerful *macho* liquor with a cactus worm in its bottle. Others who have dared to sip tequila during visits to Mexico are not quite as bemused by tequila's mythic nature but, nevertheless, they look upon it as a seriously exotic drink—the kind of thing you consume when there, but only rarely at home. But there is much more to this complex beverage.

Tequila is a fresh-tasting liquor that is sold at 80 proof, the same alcohol level as gin and less than some vodkas and whiskeys. It has a delicious spicy, peppery flavor. Most tequila is clear, but there are a number of aged versions that have a slightly amber color.

Clear tequila, also known as white or silver tequila, is not aged. Rather, it is immediately bottled and sold for consumption. In contrast, gold tequila, gold because of its slight amber color, is aged in oak barrels for a minimum of one year. Gold tequila has a more robust and complex flavor than clear tequila.

Tequila is made in Jalisco province, a province that includes the small town of Tequila and the big city of Guadalajara. It is Mexico's most widely used liquor and, like Puerto Rico's rum and Scotland's whisky, it comes in different styles and qualities.

Guadalajara is a good place to start the process of finding out about tequila. Located 150 miles inland from the resort of Puerto Vallarta, Guadalajara is Mexico's second biggest city.

The highway into the town of Tequila winds through sugarcane and silver-blue fields of agave plants, the raw material of tequila. A large plant, agave is a member of the lily family. It takes eight years or more to reach maturity and grows to a height of seven feet with a core weighing as much as 150 pounds. The barbed outer leaves of maturing plants are severed with a razor-sharp machete.

The mature agave is cut off at its root and trimmed down to its heart with a sharp hoe-like implement called a *coa*. The heart, called the *piña* because of its resemblance to a large pineapple, is then transported to the factory to be cooked and distilled.

The tequila growing area is delimited by the government and, of many varieties, only the blue agave may be used for distillation. There are more than 100,000 acres of blue agave in the states of Jalisco, Michoacan, and Nayarit. (*Mezcal,* a crude distillate, can be made anywhere in Mexico and from any kind of agave. It is in *mezcal,* which is almost never exported, that one occasionally finds a maguay worm, put there as a macho sales gimmick. This harmless worm is *never* found in tequila.)

The agave must be cooked in order to yield the sugar that is needed for fermentation. To accomplish this, the piñas are steamed for forty-eight hours in large autoclaves, after which they cool for eight hours. The cooked agave tastes like a combination of pumpkin and artichoke.

After cooling, the piñas are transported by conveyor belt to a machine that shreds and crushes them to extract their juice (called *aguamiel,* or "honey water"). The juice is then pumped into large stainless steel fermentation vats. At this point, sugarcane can be added. Some distilleries produce tequila that is made from 100 percent blue agave, while others add cane sugar. Some produce both types. The government allows up to 49 percent sugar from sources other than blue agave. The difference between 100 percent agave tequilas and those that use cane sugar is similar to the comparison between single malt and blended Scotch whiskys; one is more assertively flavored and the other is softer and smoother.

The juice is fermented to 160 proof and then distilled. Unlike rum and gin, which are made in continuous column stills, tequila is made in copper pot stills, like the ones used in the making of Cognac and single malts. The clear liquor is double distilled to 150 proof, which means that the final product is extremely pure and clean.

Tequila is a spirit that deserves all the mainstream legitimacy of vodka, rum, or Scotch. It is uniquely flavored and particularly suited for mixed drinks.

CLASSICS

Coco Loco

1 coconut
1 scoop crushed ice
1 ounce tequila
1 ounce gin
1 ounce light rum
1 ounce pineapple juice
Simple syrup to taste
½ fresh lime

Open a fresh coconut by sawing off the top. Retain the coconut water in the husk. The coconut will be your cup. Add the crushed ice to the coconut and pour in all the liquid ingredients. Squeeze the lime over the drink and drop it in. Stir well, adding a little additional ice if necessary.

Frozen Margarita

Crushed ice
1½ ounces tequila
½ ounce Triple Sec
1 ounce lemon or lime juice
Lime slice
Coarse salt or mixture of sugar
    and salt in equal parts

Use 1½ to 2 scoops of crushed ice for each drink. Put the ice, tequila, Triple Sec, and juice in a blender. Blend until slushy, but not too watery. Moisten the rim of a large chilled cocktail glass or wineglass with the lime slice. Coat the rim with coarse salt or sugar and salt mixture. Pour the contents of the blender into the prepared glass and garnish with the lime slice.

Margarita

Lime slice
Coarse salt
1½ ounces tequila
1 ounce Triple Sec
1 ounce lime juice

Moisten the rim of a cocktail glass with the lime slice. Press the rim into the salt. In a shaker, combine the remaining ingredients with ice. Mix and strain into the glass. Garnish with the lime slice.

Matador

Coarse salt
1½ ounces tequila
½ ounce Triple Sec
Juice of ½ large or 1 small lime
1 scoop crushed ice

Moisten the rim of a chilled cocktail glass and press the rim into the coarse salt. Mix all other ingredients in a shaker. Strain the mixture into the prepared glass.

Tequila Neat

Sprinkle of coarse salt
1½ ounces tequila
1 lime wedge

Lick the back of the left hand between the thumb and index finger and sprinkle this area with salt. Hold a shot glass of tequila in the same hand. Hold the wedge of lime in the right hand. In one quick sequence, lick the salt on the back of the hand, drink the tequila, and bite into the lime wedge.

Tequila Sour

1½ ounces tequila
1 ounce lime or lemon juice
1 teaspoon confectioners' sugar
1 scoop crushed ice

Mix all the ingredients in a shaker. Strain the mixture into a chilled cocktail glass.

Tequila Sunrise I

1 scoop crushed ice
2 ounces tequila
¼ ounce grenadine
3 ounces orange juice

Fill a tall collins glass with crushed ice. Add the tequila and grenadine. Slowly fill the glass with orange juice and stir gently.

Tequila Sunrise II

1½ ounces tequila
Juice of ½ lime
½ ounce crème de cassis
1 scoop crushed ice
Club soda
Generous dash of orange liqueur
Lime slice

In a tall collins glass, mix the tequila, lime juice, cassis, and ice. Top off with soda and a dash of orange liqueur. Garnish with the lime slice and stir gently.

CREATIVE CONCOCTIONS

Acapulco Clam Digger

1½ ounces tequila
3 ounces tomato juice
3 ounces clam juice
½ teaspoon horseradish
Several dashes of Tabasco
Several dashes of Worcestershire
    sauce
Dash of lemon juice
1 scoop crushed ice
Lemon slice

Pour all the ingredients, except the lemon slice, into a double old-fashioned glass. Mix well and garnish with the lemon slice.

Beatie's Bloody Bull

1½ ounces tequila
3 ounces tomato juice
3 ounces beef consommé or
    bouillon
Dash of lemon juice
Several dashes of Worcestershire
    sauce
Pinch of celery salt (optional)
Pinch of white pepper
1 scoop crushed ice

Combine all the ingredients in a shaker. Mix well and pour into a double old-fashioned glass.

Blue Chimney Smoke

1½ ounces tequila
4 ounces orange juice, chilled
1 dash of blue curaçao

Place ice in a large, chilled wineglass. Add the tequila and orange juice and stir. Float the blue curaçao on top.

Blue Devil

1½ ounces mescal tequila
1 ounce Madeira
1 egg yolk
1 scoop crushed ice

Combine all the ingredients in a blender. Blend well and pour into an iced cocktail glass.

Bonanza

1½ ounces tequila
1 ounce applejack
½ ounce lemon juice
1 teaspoon simple syrup or maple
    syrup
Generous dash of Triple Sec or
    curaçao
1 scoop crushed ice
Lemon slice

Mix all the ingredients, except the lemon slice, in a shaker. Pour the mixture into a chilled old-fashioned glass and garnish with the lemon slice.

Brave Bull

1 ounce tequila
1 ounce coffee liqueur
Whipped cream

Mix the tequila and coffee liqueur in a stirring glass with ice cubes. Strain the mixture into a sherry glass and top with a dollop of the whipped cream.

Cactus Banger

1½ ounces tequila
Orange juice
½ ounce Galliano

Pour the tequila into a tall collins glass. Fill the glass with ice and orange juice. Top off with a float of the Galliano.

Carabinieri

1 ounce tequila
¾ ounce Galliano
1 egg yolk
2¾ ounces orange juice
¼ ounce lemon juice
1 scoop crushed ice

Combine all the ingredients in a shaker. Mix well and pour into a highball glass.

Changuirongo

1½ ounces tequila
Orange or lemon-lime soda or ginger ale
Lemon or lime wedge

In a tall highball or collins glass with ice cubes, pour in the tequila and soda. Stir gently and garnish with the lemon or lime wedge.

Chapala

1½ ounces tequila
¼ ounce Triple Sec
Splash of grenadine
1½ ounces orange juice
¾ ounce lemon or lime juice
1 scoop crushed ice

Mix all the ingredients, except the ice, in a shaker. Strain the mixture into a highball glass half filled with crushed ice.

Charro

1 ounce tequila
1⅓ ounces evaporated milk
⅔ ounce strong coffee
1 scoop crushed ice

Combine all the ingredients in a shaker and shake vigorously. Strain the mixture into a chilled old-fashioned glass.

Compadre

1 ounce tequila
⅓ ounce grenadine
4 drops maraschino liqueur
4 drops bitters
1 scoop crushed ice

Combine all the ingredients in a shaker. Shake vigorously and strain into a chilled cocktail glass.

Corcovado

1½ ounces tequila
1½ ounces Drambuie
1½ ounces blue curaçao
1 scoop crushed ice
Lemonade
Lemon or lime slice

Mix the spirits with ice cubes in a shaker. Strain the mixture into a highball glass filled with crushed ice. Top off with lemonade. Garnish with the lemon or lime slice.

Crazy Nun

1½ ounces tequila
1½ ounces anisette
1 scoop finely crushed ice

Fill an old-fashioned glass with finely crushed ice. Pour in the tequila and anisette and stir. Use less anisette for a drier drink.

Desert Glow

1 ounce tequila
4 ounces orange juice
1 ounce peach schnapps
Orange slice

Fill an old-fashioned glass with ice. Pour in tequila, orange juice, and peach schnapps. Stir well and garnish with the orange slice.

El Cid

1½ ounces tequila
1 ounce lemon or lime juice
½ ounce orgeat
1 scoop crushed ice
Tonic water
Grenadine
Lime slice

Pour the tequila, juice, and orgeat into a tall collins glass and mix well. Add crushed ice and top off the glass with tonic water and a dash or two of grenadine. Garnish with the lime slice.

El Diablo

1 scoop crushed ice
½ lime
1¾ ounces tequila
¾ ounce crème de cassis
Ginger ale

Fill a highball glass half full with crushed ice. Squeeze the lime over the ice, and add the lime half to the glass. Pour in the tequila and crème de cassis. Top off with the ginger ale and stir.

Frozen Cran Razz

Makes 5 (3-ounce) servings

6 ounces tequila
1 can (6 ounces) frozen cranberry juice concentrate
3 ounces raspberry liqueur

Combine all the ingredients in a blender. Add ice cubes and continue to blend until thick and slushy. Pour the blend into chilled wineglasses.

Frozen Matador

1¾ ounces tequila
¼ ounce Triple Sec
1 teaspoon sugar
Juice of ½ lime
1 scoop crushed ice
2 pineapple rings

In a shaker, mix all the ingredients, except the pineapple. Pour the mixture into a highball glass. Garnish with the pineapple rings.

Gentle Ben

1 ounce tequila
1 ounce vodka
1 ounce gin
3 ounces orange juice
1 teaspoon sloe gin (optional)
Orange slice

Mix all the ingredients, except the gin and orange slice, in a shaker or blender with crushed ice. Pour the mixture into a double old-fashioned glass. Float the sloe gin on top and garnish with the orange slice.

Gentle Bull

1 ounce cream
1½ ounces tequila
¾ ounces coffee liqueur
1 scoop crushed ice

Combine the cream, tequila, and coffee liqueur in a shaker with ice cubes. Shake vigorously and strain into a chilled brandy snifter filled with crushed ice.

Grapeshot

1½ ounces tequila
¾ ounce curaçao
1 ounce white grape juice
1 scoop crushed ice

Combine all the ingredients in a shaker. Mix well and strain into a chilled cocktail glass.

Horny Bull

1½ ounces white tequila
4 to 6 ounces orange juice, chilled

Pour the tequila into a cocktail glass filled with ice. Top off the glass with the orange juice and stir well.

Lemonaid

1 ounce tequila
5 ounces natural lemon-lime soda
1 tablespoon frozen lemonade
    concentrate
Lemon wedge

Fill a tall glass with ice. Add tequila, soda, and lemonade concentrate to the glass. Stir well and garnish with the lemon wedge.

Malcolm Lowry

Lime rind
Coarse salt
1 ounce tequila
¾ ounce light rum
¾ ounce Triple Sec
¾ ounce lemon or lime juice
1 scoop crushed ice

Using a lime rind, moisten the rim of an iced cocktail glass. Dip the rim in coarse salt. Combine the remaining ingredients in a shaker. Mix well and pour into the prepared glass.

Mexican Ruin

½ ounce tequila
1½ ounces coffee liqueur
1 scoop crushed ice

Stir all the ingredients in a mixing glass. Pour the mixture into a chilled cocktail glass.

Miguelito

1½ ounces tequila
Juice of 1 lime
1 teaspoon honey
Dash of bitters (optional)
1 scoop crushed ice

Mix all the ingredients in a shaker. Strain the mixture into a chilled cocktail glass.

Montezuma

1½ ounces tequila
1 ounce Madeira
1 egg yolk
1 scoop crushed ice

Combine all the ingredients in a blender. Blend well and pour into an iced cocktail glass.

Montezuma's Revenge

1½ ounces tequila
1 ounce fino sherry
1 egg yolk
1 scoop crushed ice

Combine all the ingredients in a shaker. Mix well and pour into a chilled cocktail glass.

Raspberry Margarita

1½ ounces tequila
1 ounce Triple Sec
1 ounce lime juice
½ cup frozen raspberries
Fresh raspberries

In a blender, combine all the ingredients, except the fresh fruit, with ½ cup ice. Blend until frothy. Pour the blend into a chilled highball glass and garnish with the fresh raspberries.

Note: When using only fresh raspberries, add sugar to taste.

Rocky Point

1½ ounces tequila
2 to 3 ounces grapefruit juice
1 teaspoon almond extract
Dash of lime juice
Dash of Triple Sec or curaçao
1 scoop crushed ice
Mint sprigs

Mix all the ingredients, except the mint, in a shaker or blender. Pour the mixture into a chilled wineglass and garnish with the mint.

Royal Matador

Makes 2 servings

Whole pineapple
3 ounces gold tequila
1½ ounces raspberry liqueur
Juice of 1 lime
1 teaspoon orgeat or amaretto

Remove the top of a pineapple and set it aside. Scoop out the pineapple, keeping the shell intact. Place the pineapple chunks in a blender and extract as much juice as possible. Strain the pineapple juice and return to blender. Add the tequila, raspberry liqueur, lime juice, orgeat or amaretto, and ice cubes. Mix well and pour into the pineapple shell, adding additional ice if needed. Replace the top and serve with straws.

Sangrita

Makes 14 (2-ounce) servings

2 cups tomato juice
1 cup orange juice
2 ounces lime juice
1 to 2 teaspoons Tabasco,
    or to taste
2 teaspoons finely minced onion
1 to 2 teaspoons Worcestershire
    sauce
Several pinches of white pepper
Celery salt or seasoned salt to taste
1½ ounces tequila per serving

In a large pitcher, blend all the ingredients, except the tequila. Strain the blend into a fresh pitcher and chill in the refrigerator. When ready to serve, pour the tequila into 1 shot glass and pour the sangrita into a second shot glass. Toss the tequila down your throat and chase it with the shot of sangrita. Sangrita can also be used for a spicy Bloody Mary.

Shellorama

1½ ounces tequila
½ teaspoon lemon juice
6 to 8 ounces grapefruit juice or
    grapefruit soda

Combine the tequila and lemon juice in a chilled highball glass with ice. Top off with grapefruit juice or soda and stir.

¡Sí!

1 ounce lemon juice
1 teaspoon sugar
1½ ounces tequila
3 to 4 ounces strong hot coffee

Combine the lemon juice and sugar in a chilled highball glass. Stir until the sugar is dissolved. Add tequila and stir again. Fill glass to ½ inch from the rim with ice. Top off with hot coffee and stir.

Silk Stockings

1 ounce tequila
1 ounce evaporated milk
1 ounce sweetened condensed
    milk
¼ ounce grenadine
1 scoop crushed ice
Powdered cinnamon

Blend all the ingredients, except the cinnamon, until smooth. Pour the blend into a champagne glass and sprinkle with the cinnamon.

Speedy Gonzalez

1½ ounces tequila
3 ounces grapefruit juice
1 teaspoon superfine sugar,
    or to taste
1 scoop crushed ice
Cold club soda

Mix all the ingredients, except the soda, in a shaker. Pour the mixture into a tall highball glass and top off with the club soda.

Sloe Poke Rodriguez

1 ounce tequila
1 ounce sloe gin
1 ounce lime juice
1 scoop crushed ice

Mix all the ingredients in a shaker. Strain the mixture into a chilled cocktail glass.

Sneaky Pete

Makes 2 servings

4 ounces tequila
1 ounce white crème de menthe
1 ounce pineapple juice
1 ounce lime or lemon juice
1 scoop crushed ice
Lime slices

Mix all the ingredients, except the lime slices, in a shaker. Strain the mixture into 2 chilled cocktail glasses. Garnish with the lime slices.

Steaming Bull

3 ounces beef consommé or
    bouillon
3 ounces tomato juice
Generous pinches of celery salt or
    celery seed
Generous dashes of Worcestershire
    sauce
½ teaspoon lemon juice (optional)
1½ ounces tequila

Heat all the ingredients, except the tequila, in a saucepan. Bring to the boiling point, stirring well. Pour the tequila into a heated mug. Fill the mug with the contents of the saucepan.

Submarino

1 large mug of beer
1 ounce tequila

Fill a mug with cold beer, leaving a few inches at the top. Drop a jigger of tequila into the mug. Some prefer to drink the tequila straight and follow it with a beer chaser.

Tequila Collins

1½ ounces light tequila
1 ounce lemon juice
Sugar syrup to taste
Cold club soda
1 maraschino cherry

Add the tequila, lemon juice, sugar syrup, and several ice cubes to a 14-ounce collins glass. Stir well. Top off with club soda and garnish with the cherry.

Tequila Fizz

1¾ ounces tequila
½ ounce sugar syrup
1 ounce lemon juice
1 scoop crushed ice
Cold club soda
Lemon slice or maraschino cherry

Combine all the ingredients, except the club soda and fruit, in a shaker.

Mix well. Pour the mixture into a highball glass and top off with the soda. Garnish with the lemon slice or maraschino cherry.

Tequila Grapefruit

1½ ounces tequila
½ ounce dry vermouth
4 ounces grapefruit juice
½ teaspoon sugar syrup, or to taste
1 scoop crushed ice
Orange slice

Mix all the ingredients, except the orange slice, in a shaker. Pour the mixture into a double-old fashioned glass. Garnish with the orange slice.

Tequila Julep

4 mint sprigs
1 teaspoon superfine sugar
1½ ounces tequila
4 to 6 ounces club soda, chilled

Fill a glass with ice. In a dish, crush 3 of the mint sprigs with sugar and add this mixture to the glass. Add tequila and stir. Top off with the soda. Stir gently until the glass is frosted. Garnish with the remaining mint sprig.

Tequila Manhattan (sweet)

1½ ounces tequila
¾ ounce sweet vermouth
2 dashes of bitters
1 maraschino cherry

Mix the tequila, vermouth, and bitters in a stirring glass with ice. Strain the mixture into a chilled cocktail glass. Garnish with the cherry.

Tequila Mockingbird

1½ ounces tequila
¼ ounce green crème de menthe
Juice of ½ lime
1 scoop crushed ice
Ice water or cold club soda

Mix all the ingredients, except the ice water or club soda, in a highball glass. Top off with ice water or soda and stir gently.

Tequila Maria

1½ ounces tequila
4 ounces tomato juice
Juice of ¼ lime
½ teaspoon freshly grated
    horseradish
Generous dashes of Worcestershire
    sauce
Generous dashes of Tabasco
Generous pinch of white pepper
Generous pinch of celery salt or
    celery seed
Generous pinch of tarragon,
    oregano, or dill
1 scoop crushed ice

In a mixing glass, stir all the ingredients together. Pour the mixture into a chilled double old-fashioned glass.

Tequini

1¾ ounces tequila
Dash of bitters
2 to 3 splashes of dry vermouth
Lemon twist or an olive

Mix all the ingredients, except the lemon, in a stirring glass with ice. Pour the mixture into a chilled cocktail glass. Serve with the lemon twist or olive.

TNT
(*Tequila 'n' Tonic*)

2 ounces tequila
½ ounce lime or lemon juice
About 6 ounces tonic water, chilled
1 strip lime or lemon peel

Fill a highball glass three quarters full with ice cubes. Add the tequila and lime or lemon juice. Top off the glass with tonic water and stir. Twist the lemon or lime peel over the drink and drop it in.

Toreador

1½ ounces tequila
½ ounce crème de cacao
2 tablespoons heavy cream
Whipped cream
Cocoa powder

Mix the tequila, crème de cacao, and heavy cream in a shaker with ice. Strain the mixture into a chilled cocktail glass or wineglass. Top with a dollop of whipped cream and sprinkle a little cocoa over the top.

Torridora Mexicano

1½ ounces tequila
¾ ounce coffee-flavored brandy
Juice of ½ lime
1 scoop crushed ice

Mix all the ingredients in a shaker. Strain the mixture into a chilled cocktail glass.

Yellow Boxer

1¾ ounces tequila
¼ ounce Galliano
¾ ounce orange juice
¾ ounce lime juice
¾ ounce lemon juice
1 scoop crushed ice

Mix all the ingredients in a shaker. Strain the mixture into a highball glass half filled with crushed ice.

SIGNATURE DRINKS

Austin Grill Swirlie

AUSTIN GRILL, WASHINGTON, D.C.

Makes 4 (10-ounce) servings

20 ounces Strawberry Margarita
(page 155)
20 ounces Frozen Lime Margarita
(right)
Lime wedge

Fill half a chilled margarita glass with Frozen Lime Margarita and top off the glass with Strawberry Margarita. Garnish with the lime wedge.

Berta's Special

BERTITA'S BAR, TAXCO, MEXICO

2 ounces tequila
Juice of 1 lime
1 teaspoon sugar syrup or honey
Several dashes of orange bitters
1 egg white
1 scoop crushed ice
Cold club soda
Lime slice

Mix all the ingredients, except the soda and lime slice, in a shaker. Pour this mixture into a 14-ounce collins glass. Top off with the club soda and stir gently. Garnish with the lime slice.

Cactus Kicker

THE DESERT MOON, SAN FRANCISCO

$\frac{1}{2}$ ounce tequila
$\frac{1}{2}$ ounce margarita schnapps
$\frac{1}{2}$ ounce pineapple juice
$\frac{1}{2}$ ounce blackberry or blueberry schnapps

Mix all the ingredients in a shaker with crushed ice. Strain the mixture into a shot glass.

Frozen Lime Margarita

AUSTIN GRILL, WASHINGTON, D.C.

Makes 2 servings

3 ounces gold tequila
1$\frac{1}{2}$ ounces Triple Sec
3 ounces freshly squeezed lime juice
1 ounce simple syrup
2$\frac{1}{2}$ cups ice
Lime wedge

Mix all the ingredients, except the lime wedge, in a blender and blend until smooth. Pour the blend into a chilled wineglass or margarita glass. Garnish with the lime wedge.

Frozen Melon Head

SOUTHERN CULTURE,
CHARLOTTESVILLE, VIRGINIA

1½ ounces gold tequila
¾ ounces Triple Sec
1½ ounces melon liqueur
Juice of 1 lime
1 scoop crushed ice

Combine all the ingredients in a blender. Blend until frothy. Pour the blend into a margarita glass.

Mango Gorilla

HARRY DENTON'S, SAN FRANCISCO

½ ounce tequila
½ ounce Grand Marnier
½ ounce pineapple juice
Splash of lime juice

Pour all the ingredients into a shot glass.

Prairie Dog

THE BALBOA CAFE, SAN FRANCISCO

1½ ounces tequila
3 squirts of Tabasco

Pour both ingredients into a shot glass.

Stargarita

STARS, SAN FRANCISCO

½ ounce gold tequila
½ ounce Triple Sec
½ ounce fresh lime juice
Splash of Campari
2 teaspoons superfine sugar
Coarse salt
Lime wheel

Combine all the ingredients, except the lime and salt, in a shaker with ice. Shake well and strain into a salt-rimmed balloon glass. Garnish with the lime wheel.

Strawberry Margarita

AUSTIN GRILL, WASHINGTON, D.C.

Makes 2 servings

Lime rind
Coarse salt or mixture of sugar
    and salt in equal parts
3 ounces gold tequila
1½ ounces Triple Sec
2 ounces freshly squeezed lime
    juice
2½ cups ice
½ ounce simple syrup
4 ounces puréed strawberries
    (fresh or frozen)
2 fresh strawberries

Moisten the rim of 2 wineglasses with the lime rind and roll the rims in coarse salt or a salt-sugar mixture.

Combine all other ingredients, except the strawberry garnish, in a blender and blend until smooth. Pour the blend into the prepared wineglasses. Garnish with the fresh strawberries.

Sunset

SU CASA RESTAURANT, CHICAGO

Sugar
1 ounce tequila
1½ ounces pineapple juice
1½ ounces orange juice

Moisten the rim of a chilled wineglass and press the rim into sugar. Combine the remaining ingredients in a blender and blend until frothy. Pour the blend into the prepared glass.

Tequila Sunset

SU CASA RESTAURANT, CHICAGO

Sugar
1 ounce white or gold tequila
1½ ounces orange juice
1½ ounces pineapple juice
1 scoop crushed ice

Moisten the rim of a large wine glass and frost it with sugar. Combine the remaining ingredients in a blender and blend at medium speed for about 30 seconds.

Top Shelf Margarita

CRESCENT COURT, DALLAS

1½ ounces gold tequila
2 ounces sweet 'n' sour mix
Splash of Rose's lime juice
Splash of Grand Marnier
Splash of Triple Sec
Splash of Drambuie

Pour all the ingredients into a shaker with crushed ice. Shake and strain the mixture into a chilled collins glass over fresh ice.

TROPICAL DRINKS

Gringo Swizzle

2 ounces tequila
½ ounce crème de cassis, or to
   taste
1 ounce lime juice
1 ounce pineapple juice
1 ounce orange juice
2 scoops crushed ice
Cold ginger ale

Mix all the ingredients, except the ginger ale, in a shaker or blender. Pour this mixture into a 14-ounce collins glass. Top off the glass with the ginger ale and add a few ice cubes.

Latin Lover

1½ ounces tequila
¾ ounce spiced rum
2 ounces pineapple juice
¾ ounce lime juice
¼ ounce lemon juice
2 scoops crushed ice
Pineapple slice
1 maraschino cherry

Mix the tequila, rum, and fruit juices in a shaker with 1 scoop of crushed ice and shake vigorously. Strain the mixture into a highball glass half filled with crushed ice. Garnish with the pineapple slice and the cherry.

Mexicana

1¾ ounces tequila
Splash of grenadine
1½ ounces pineapple juice
¾ ounce lemon or lime juice
1 scoop crushed ice

Mix all the ingredients in a shaker. Strain the mixture into a highball glass over fresh crushed ice.

Mexicolada

1½ ounces tequila
¾ ounce coffee liqueur
2 ounces pineapple juice
¼ ounce coconut cream
¾ ounce sweet cream
1 scoop crushed ice

Mix all the ingredients in a shaker or blender. Pour the mixture into a highball glass.

Pepe

1 ounce tequila
¾ ounce cachaca
Splash of Triple Sec
1½ ounces grapefruit juice
¼ ounce lemon or lime juice
2 scoops crushed ice

Mix all the ingredients in a shaker
with 1 scoop of crushed ice. Strain
the mixture into a highball glass half
filled with fresh crushed ice.

Piña

1½ ounces tequila
3 ounces pineapple juice
1 ounce lime juice
1 teaspoon superfine sugar

Combine all the ingredients with 3
or 4 ice cubes in a shaker. Shake
vigorously and strain into a tall
chilled collins glass. Add fresh ice
cubes.

Piñata I

1½ ounces tequila
4 ounces pineapple juice
Pineapple spear

Fill a short or stemmed glass with
ice. Add the tequila and top with
juice. Stir well and garnish with the
pineapple spear.

Piñata II

1½ ounces tequila
1 tablespoon banana liqueur
1 ounce lime juice
1 scoop crushed ice

Combine all the ingredients in a
blender and blend at medium speed
until smooth. Pour the blend into a
chilled whiskey sour glass.

Note: You can add strawberries or
peaches for different flavors.

Tequila Tropical

1 scoop crushed ice
1½ ounces tequila
½ ounce grenadine
3 ounces orange juice, chilled
1 teaspoon lemon juice
½ orange slice
1 maraschino cherry

Fill a highball glass three quarters
full with crushed ice. Add the
tequila, grenadine, and fruit juices
and stir. Garnish with the orange
slice and cherry.

HOT DRINKS

Cranberry Lodge Toddy

1 ounce tequila
1 ounce Triple Sec
½ ounce apple schnapps
1 cup hot cranberry juice

Pour all the spirits into a mug of hot cranberry juice. Stir well before serving.

Mexican Coffee

1½ ounces tequila
¾ ounce coffee liqueur
1 cup hot strong coffee or
   espresso
Whipped cream

Mix the tequila and coffee liqueur in a large mug. Add hot coffee or espresso. Top off with a dollop of the whipped cream.

Mountain Melter

1 ounce tequila
½ ounce Triple Sec
Dash of cinnamon schnapps
1 cup hot cocoa

Pour the tequila, Triple Sec, and cinnamon schnapps into a mug of hot cocoa. Stir well.

Tequila Tea

1½ ounces tequila
Hot tea
Sugar
Lemon slice

Pour the tequila into a large mug. Fill the rest of the mug with hot tea and add sugar to taste. Garnish with the lemon slice.

Toe Warmer

½ ounce tequila
½ ounce cream-based whiskey
   liqueur
½ ounce coffee brandy
½ ounce hazelnut liqueur
Hot coffee

Pour all the ingredients, except the coffee, into a cocktail glass. Top with the hot coffee and serve.

PUNCHES

Pitcher Peach Piñata

Makes about 6 (6-ounce) servings

4 ounces tequila
4 ounces peach schnapps
3 cups pineapple juice
Fresh pineapple spears

Mix all the ingredients, except the pineapple spears, in a 2- to 3-quart pitcher. Add ice and garnish with the pineapple.

Premium Punch

Makes 12 (4-ounce) servings

16 ounces tequila
16 ounces cranberry juice
1 can (6 ounces) frozen lemonade
    concentrate
10 ounces club soda

Chill all the ingredients. In a punch bowl, combine tequila, cranberry juice, and lemonade concentrate. Mix in the club soda. Add ice before serving.

Aquavit and Schnapps

A group of people are clustered around a table for a typical lunch that will include several courses and a clear, fiery drink. The host pours the ice cold liquid into frosty, chilled, conical-shaped glasses. He raises his glass, at which point the diners turn to one another and make eye contact. "Skoal," calls out the host, and everyone takes another sip. Again there is eye contact, and then the glasses are set on the table, not to be lifted again until the host raises his. The liquid is aquavit, and the ritual is virtually the same throughout Scandinavia.

Aquavit is a distilled spirit that is much like vodka. What makes it different from that neutral flavor are extracts of herbs and spices added to the spirit. There are versions that taste of cinnamon, Madeira, coriander, lemon, dill, and—most popular of all—caraway.

The development of aquavit is an example of how distilled spirits took very different courses in different countries. From similar beginnings, hundreds of spirits have evolved, their variances based mainly on the diversity of the local agriculture.

Distillation has been around since ancient times. "Sea water can be rendered potable by distillation," wrote the Greek philosopher Aristotle. His discovery was allegedly based on the simple observation that steam from hot food condenses on the inner surface of the cover placed over the dish. Early civilizations learned how to create medicines, perfumes, and flavorings using simple distillation. Herbs, spices, and plants were cooked, macerated, or infused to make concentrates that were easy to use and store. The ancient Chinese created a unique spirit from rice and beer, and in the East Indies as long ago as 800 B.C. something called arrack was made with fermented sugarcane and rice.

A MODERN HISTORY

Despite the long-standing awareness of the distillation effect, it was not until the early Middle Ages that the distillation of alcohol became a widespread practice and the modern history of this remarkable process began.

It was the Arabs who started it all. They even invented the word "alcohol." It seems that for centuries the Arabs had been (and, in fact, still are) making eye makeup using black powder that was liquefied, vaporized, and solidified again. They called it kohl. When wine was first distilled, the name of this cosmetic was used to describe the result—"al koh'l"—since the procedure was so similar.

In the Latin-speaking regions of Europe during the Middle Ages, the newly discovered spirit was called *aqua vitae* ("water of life"). The reason for this rather grandiose name was the fact that, at first, distilled spirits were used mostly by alchemists, and many of these scientists thought that they had finally found the elusive "elixir of life." In the thirteenth century, for example, the Majorcan chemist and philosopher Raymond Lully wrote that aqua vitae was "an emanation of the divinity, an element newly revealed to men, but hid from antiquity, because the human race was then too young to need this beverage destined to revive the energies of modern decrepitude."

As this knowledge of distillation spread, the Latin name was translated into the local language. In France, it became known as *eau de vie,* while on the Irish peat bogs it was gaelicized into *visige beatha,* which eventually was corrupted into "whiskey." In Russia, "water of life" evolved into "vodka" from the Russian word for water, *voda*.

Only in Denmark, Sweden, and other Scandinavian countries did the original Latin name remain relatively unscathed. True, the phrase was shortened slightly, but the essence of the word remains—"aquavit."

DISTILLATION CATCHES ON

Fifteenth-century Europe saw distillation take hold and spread like wildfire. It was completely unregulated, and anyone who understood how the process worked could build a primitive still and produce his own aquavit. For raw materials, these cottage distillers used whatever was inexpensive and in good, constant supply. In Ireland and Scotland, whiskey got its distinctive character from barley and a dose of smoky peat. In France, Spain, and Italy, wine was plentiful, and it formed the basis for locally made brandies. Barley, corn, and rye were the backbone of gin in Holland. Later, Caribbean sugarcane was made into rum and the Mexican century plant was used in tequila.

In Sweden, at first, aquavit (or sometimes "akavit" or "akevit") was made by distilling wine. The problem was that all the fruit had to be imported from more temperate countries because no grapes were grown in Sweden. This made the aquavit so expensive that it could be consumed only sparingly. Its use was limited almost entirely to medicinal purposes.

Later on, when the Swedes discovered how to produce the spirit from grain, aquavit became less costly and easier to obtain. But grain was not the ideal raw ingredient either. Because of the country's harsh weather, the crop was often cut short by the early arrival of winter. To avoid a grain shortage, the government occasionally had to prohibit the distilling of aquavit.

The Swedes had grown accustomed to their "snaps," so frequent interruptions in its supply were quite unacceptable. Distillers experimented with myriad substitutes for grain, including roots and berries, but nothing seemed to yield satisfactory results. Finally, in the eighteenth century, it was discovered that the common potato was ideal for the purpose. It was plentiful, inexpensive, relatively unaffected by variances in weather, and consistent in quality. Most aquavit has been made from potatoes ever since.

A LIVELY DISPUTE

The Swedes and the Danes like to dispute which country was the first to produce aquavit. Both countries have a good case; in fact, it is quite possible that distillation began independently in both places at about the same time. The first Swedish license to sell aquavit was granted in Stockholm in 1498. Danish distilling can be traced to some time around 1400, and in 1555 King Christian III of Denmark established a royal distillery.

Today in Denmark, where aquavit is known as "schnapps," distilling is centered in Aalborg, a town of 160,000 in northern Jutland. There, Danish Distilleries Ltd. produces half the world's supply of aquavit. Twelve brands, each flavored with a different herb, are made in the same distillery, including the biggest seller, caraway-flavored Aalborg Taffel Akvavit, and another readily available in this country, dill-flavored Jubilaeums.

Most Swedish distilleries are located in the southern province of Skane. The best-known Swedish brand is O.P. Anderson, which is flavored with caraway seed, fennel seed, and aniseed. There is also a small industry in Norway.

The manufacture of aquavit is simple and straightforward. Potatoes are cleaned and then boiled. The resulting starch mass is combined with a grain malt, which helps the starch convert to sugar. Yeast is added and the sugar is fermented into alcohol. Then the spirit is rectified and distilled, after which a flavoring is added.

In Scandinavia, aquavit is often accompanied by a beer chaser. It is not unusual for a Dane or a Swede to drink three or four shots of this icy 90-proof liquor during the course of a meal. Try aquavit with such typical smorgasbord fare as gravlax, caviar, and herring.

Using this spirit in mixed drinks requires some experience. Aquavit in a martini or combined with tonic might not be too well received, but a Bloody Mary made with either a dill, lemon, or caraway version is quite delicious. There is also no law that says that aquavit cannot be served over ice. In fact, people who drink vodka on the rocks may find this an exciting new alternative. Everything considered, aquavit, no matter how you choose to drink it, is surely one of the most delightful of all distilled spirits.

A popular new twist on the traditional flavored aquavits are flavored schnapps. Clear and sweetened, these recent additions to the bar could also be classified as liqueurs. These very popular spirits are excellent for mixed drinks and they provide a whole new avenue for creative mixologists.

AQUAVIT · CREATIVE CONCOCTIONS

Aquaman

1 ounce aquavit
1 ounce gin
Dash of dry vermouth
Olive

In a mixing glass with ice, stir together the aquavit, gin, and vermouth. Strain the mixture into a chilled cocktail glass and drop in the olive.

Aquavit Clam

3 ounces aquavit
1½ ounces clam juice
1 teaspoon lemon juice
½ teaspoon Worcestershire sauce
Salt, black pepper, and cayenne

In a mixing glass with ice, stir together all the ingredients. Chill thoroughly. Strain into an old-fashioned glass containing fresh ice cubes.

Aquavit Martini

2 to 3 ounces aquavit
Dash of dry vermouth
Olive

In a mixing glass with ice, mix together the aquavit and vermouth. Strain the mixture into a chilled cocktail glass and drop in the olive.

Bullfight

2 ounces aquavit
6 ounces beef bouillon
1 teaspoon lemon juice
½ teaspoon Worcestershire sauce
1 celery rib

Mix all the ingredients, except the celery, in a mixing glass with ice. Strain the mixture over fresh ice cubes in a collins glass. Garnish with the celery.

Flaming Glogg

Makes 15 servings

1½ pints aquavit
1 bottle (750 ml) red wine
1 cup orange juice
Cardamom seeds
Fresh, peeled gingerroot
6 whole cloves
1 cinnamon stick
Dried fruits: apricots, peaches,
    plums, apples
Grated citrus rind
½ grapefruit
Sugar

Saving 1 cup of the aquavit, mix all
the other ingredients, except the
grapefruit and sugar, in a saucepan.
Bring the mixture to a simmer, but
do not boil. Pour the heated mixture
into a chafing dish. Scoop out the
inside of the grapefruit half. Moisten
the rim and the inside of the shell
with aquavit and press the shell into
sugar. Float the shell on the glogg.
Fill it with the remaining aquavit.
Light the spirit and let it burn for a
few minutes before overturning the
shell into the glogg.

Gerry Fjord

½ ounce aquavit
1 ounce brandy
1 ounce orange juice
½ ounce lime juice
1 teaspoon grenadine
1 scoop crushed ice

Combine all the ingredients in a
shaker. Mix well and strain into a
chilled cocktail glass.

Northern Exposure

1½ ounces aquavit
1 ounce grapefruit juice
½ ounce lemon juice
1 teaspoon sugar syrup, or to taste
Dash of grenadine
1 scoop crushed ice
Orange slice

Mix all the ingredients, except the
orange slice, in a shaker or blender.
Pour the mixture into a chilled cocktail glass. Garnish with the orange
slice.

Viking

1½ ounces Swedish Punsch
  liqueur
1 ounce aquavit
1 ounce lime juice
1 scoop crushed ice

Mix all the ingredients in a shaker. Strain the mixture into a chilled cocktail glass.

SCHNAPPS · CREATIVE CONCOCTIONS

Apple Pie

1½ ounces apple schnapps
1½ ounces cinnamon schnapps
1 orange slice

Pour apple and cinnamon schnapps into a chilled cocktail glass with ice cubes. Garnish the glass with the orange slice.

Blue Cool

1½ ounces peppermint schnapps
¾ ounce blue curaçao
Cold lemon-lime soda
Lemon slice

In a chilled highball glass, stir together the schnapps, curaçao, and several ice cubes. Top off the glass with soda and stir. Garnish with the lemon slice on the rim of the glass.

Frozen Peachy Orange Colada

1½ ounces peach schnapps
2 ounces coconut cream
2 ounces orange juice
½ ounce grenadine
1½ cups crushed ice

Combine all the ingredients in a blender and blend until smooth. Pour the mixture into a chilled parfait glass.

Galway Bay

3/4 ounce peppermint schnapps
3/4 ounce coffee liqueur
3/4 ounce Irish cream
3/4 ounce cream

Mix all the ingredients in a blender and blend until smooth. Pour the mixture into a chilled wineglass with several ice cubes.

Miami Ice

3/4 ounce peach schnapps
3/4 ounce rum
1/2 ounce coconut cream
4 ounces pineapple juice
1/4 ounce grenadine
2 ounces club soda

Combine all the ingredients, except the club soda, in a shaker with crushed ice. Shake and strain into a tall collins glass filled with fresh ice. Top off the glass with club soda and stir gently.

Patagonia

1 ounce peppermint schnapps
3/4 ounce coffee liqueur
1/2 ounce bourbon
1/2 ounce vodka

Combine all the ingredients in a mixing glass half filled with ice cubes. Stir well and strain into a chilled cocktail glass.

Peaches 'n' Cream

1 1/2 ounces peach schnapps
2 ounces half-and-half or milk

In a shaker with crushed ice, mix together both the ingredients. Strain the mixture over fresh ice cubes in an old-fashioned glass.

Sweet Navel

1 1/2 ounces peach schnapps
Orange juice, chilled

Pour schnapps into a chilled highball glass with several ice cubes. Top off with orange juice.

Tropical Peach

1 ounce banana liqueur
1 ounce peach schnapps
1 ounce coconut cream
1 scoop crushed ice
2 ounces orange juice

Combine all the ingredients in a blender. Blend until smooth. Pour the mixture into a chilled wineglass.

SCHNAPPS · SIGNATURE DRINKS

Apple Juice Cooler

MICKEY'S PLACE, BALDWIN, NEW YORK

1 ounce vodka
2 ounces apple schnapps
2 ounces cranberry juice
Cold club soda
Apple wedge

Combine the vodka, apple schnapps, and cranberry juice over ice in a tall glass. Top off with club soda and garnish with the apple wedge.

Brain Hemorrhage

THE BALBOA CAFE, SAN FRANCISCO

1 ounce peach schnapps
½ ounce Irish cream
Splash of grenadine

Pour the peach schnapps into a shot glass. Add Irish cream to the glass so that it clouds up. Finish with a healthy splash of grenadine. Do not stir. (The grenadine will simulate the drink's name.)

Deathmint

JASPER'S, BOSTON

1½ ounces green Chartreuse
½ ounce peppermint schnapps

Chill both ingredients. Combine the Chartreuse and schnapps in a shaker with crushed ice. Mix well and strain into a small wineglass.

Frozen Peachtree Road Race

RITZ-CARLTON, ATLANTA

1¼ ounces peach schnapps
1¼ ounces vodka
2 ounces peach purée
2 ounces orange juice
2 cups crushed ice
Cranberry juice

Mix all the ingredients, except the cranberry juice, in a blender. Blend at high speed for a few seconds. Pour the mixture into a chilled collins glass. Top off with a cranberry juice float.

Ginger Peach

MICKEY'S PLACE, BALDWIN, NEW YORK

1 1/2 ounces peach schnapps
1 ounce gin
Ginger ale
Peach wedge

In a highball glass filled with ice, mix together the schnapps and gin. Top off the glass with the ginger ale and garnish with the peach wedge.

Wild Thing

THE DESERT MOON, SAN FRANCISCO

1/2 ounce wildberry schnapps
1/2 ounce bourbon
1/2 ounce cranberry juice
1/2 ounce sweet 'n' sour mix

Mix all the ingredients in a shaker with crushed ice. Strain the mixture into a shot glass.

Smurf Berry

RED ARROW TAP, BENTON HEIGHTS, MICHIGAN

1 1/2 ounces blueberry schnapps
1/2 ounce Triple Sec
2 to 3 dashes of blue food coloring
Cream
1 maraschino cherry

Pour the schnapps, Triple Sec, and food coloring into a cocktail glass with ice. Top off the glass with cream. Stir well and garnish with the cherry.

BROWN GOODS

Bourbon and American Blended Whiskey

The four whiskeys that make up the "brown goods" segment of the American spirits market—bourbon, scotch, Canadian, and blended whiskey—account for 40 percent of the total market.

As recently as 1960 this segment represented nearly three quarters of all American liquor business, but the boom in "white goods," particularly vodka and rum, and the popularity of cordials and liqueurs have diminished its market share over the past three decades.

The history of America is very closely tied to the history of its distilled spirits, especially whiskey. The still was brought to the New World from Europe by the Spanish and its first product was probably a crude spirit distilled in the sixteenth century from the agave plant in Mexico; this drink was a rudimentary precursor of tequila.

By the mid-seventeenth century, commercial rum production had begun in Massachusetts. This development had a profound effect on the future of the young American nation. First of all, rum figured directly in the infamous slave triangle between Africa, the Caribbean, and New England. It was also responsible for the establishment of a network of taverns that later served as the gathering places for colonial revolutionaries. And it was the onerous English taxes in 1733 on the molasses used for making rum that began the colonists' march toward independence.

In the early 1700s, as a result of religious persecution, recurring famine, and falling wages, a large group of Scotch-Irish emigrated to America from Ulster County, Ireland. Many of these settlers migrated to the wilderness of western Pennsylvania, where they planted grain and set up their stills to make whiskey. They found that corn, rye, and barley were the easiest crops to grow and these grains became the base for their American whiskey.

After fighting valiantly against the hated British in the Revolutionary War, the western Pennsylvania settlers returned to their farms and their stills to enjoy their newly won liberty. Unfortunately, the long war had left the treasury of the new country quite bare. Treasurer Alexander Hamilton proposed some fund-raising methods, one of which was an Excise Tax on Spiritous Liquors.

The Scotch-Irish of Pennsylvania, who used whiskey as their medium of exchange, were outraged by this incursion into their daily lives. They took drastic action to express their displeasure. Between 1791, when the law was passed, and 1794 there were countless incidents in which tax collectors were threatened, intimidated, and in several instances, tarred and feathered.

Finally, in 1794, the western Pennsylvanians mounted an insurrection. This being the first crisis for the new American government, the Whiskey Rebellion army of 15,000 was met by a small militia force commanded by President Washington himself. This impressive show of force put the rebels to rout and, as hoped, resulted in no bloodshed.

Many of the rebellious farmers decided to pack their families and stills into wagons and move to an area that was less accessible to the hated taxman. They left the friendly valleys of the Ohio, Monongahela, and Allegheny Rivers and trekked more than four hundred miles westward to settle in the virgin lands of Bourbon County. This vast and unspoiled region eventually became the north central part of Kentucky as well as sections of Virginia and West Virginia.

Thanks to abundant clean water and a more lenient atmosphere, distilling flourished in Bourbon County. The Federal Excise Tax was abolished in 1802 and then reinstated in 1814 for three years. From 1817 to 1862, until the next tax was instituted, was a golden age for American whiskey. Distilleries operated in Kentucky, Tennessee, Indiana, Illinois, and a number of other states. Americans developed a love for assertively flavored country whiskey made from corn, rye, and barley.

Hearty bourbon (whiskey made from at least 51 percent corn) and rye (whiskey made from at least 51 percent rye) became an integral part of American life through the industrial revolution, the Civil War, and past the turn of the century. But all the time that most Americans were enjoying whiskey and other alcoholic beverages, the forces of prohibitionism were gathering strength.

For fifty years the temperance movement pursued a relentless campaign against alcohol and saloons. This intense effort took the form of a persuasive public relations blitz and extremely effective political action. Before they knew what hit them, the majority—who favored the continued use of alcohol—were finding that a minority of rural legislators had been gradually turning state after state "dry." On January 16, 1919, a resolution written by prohibitionist congressman Volstead and subsequently vetoed by President Wilson, then reconfirmed by congress, became the Eighteenth Amendment to the United States Constitution. One year later it became the law of the land.

What followed was one of the greatest disasters in the history of social legislation. Instead of turning the United States into a righteous, churchgoing nation, Prohibition created a land of speakeasies, crime, corruption, and bootleg hooch. Meanwhile, every legitimate winery and distillery was padlocked.

In 1928 a Canadian distillery executive, looking over the chaos in the U.S., became convinced that Prohibition's repeal was inevitable. To back up this thinking, he increased production and began stockpiling whiskey in Canada. The name of this man was Samuel Bronfman and the name of his company was Distillers Corporation-Seagrams, Ltd.

Between 1928 and Repeal on December 5, 1933, Seagram created the largest stock of Canadian-made American whiskey in the world. While other distillers had to start from scratch after Repeal, Seagram was ready with mature, high-quality whiskey for the U.S. market.

Mr. Bronfman had another interesting idea: "When I found, following Repeal, that many U.S. distillers had decided to make straight bourbon or rye and to sell their products as straight whiskey, it was time for a major decision," he wrote in 1971, at the time of his eightieth birthday. "Quality Canadian and Scotch whiskeys generally were all blended. I appreciated that by blending we could produce a better-tasting product, the quality of which would be uniform year after year, and decided that we would produce blended whiskey in America."

AMERICAN BLENDED WHISKEY

American blended whiskey is a smooth and mellow mixture of straight whiskeys and grain neutral spirits or light whiskeys. It has become a fundamental part of the U.S. distilled spirits market, yet it is a relatively new product, having been introduced here only after the repeal of Prohibition in 1933.

The idea of blended American whiskey is a natural. Taking fiesty American bourbons and removing some of their aggressiveness by combining them with soft, neutral-flavored spirits is a very logical concept. Such a coalition was almost a necessity just after Repeal since most distillers had to start from scratch and had no mellow older whiskeys to bottle. But I am getting ahead of the story. The government has set down guidelines for the manufacture of blended whiskey. There must be a minimum of 20 percent straight whiskeys in the blend and the rest can be grain neutral spirits, grain spirits, or light whiskeys. Grain neutral spirits are distilled out at a very high proof and have no noticeable flavor or aroma. Grain spirits are neutral spirits that have been aged in used oak barrels to give them a subtle, soft flavor. Light whiskeys are similar to grain spirits, they are just distilled out at a lower proof.

Most blended whiskeys are 80 proof. The finest ones are soft and balanced, mellow and smooth. The suggested way to consume blended whiskey is on the rocks or with a splash of water. People also use them extensively in cocktails and mixed drinks, most notably the "seven and seven," a mixture of Seven Crown and 7-Up, a combination that is, for many, the first alcoholic drink they ever taste.

A number of people who drink blends call them "rye." This is a complete misnomer; rye is a whiskey made from at least 51 percent rye. A true rye, such as Old Overholt, is an aggressive, strong drink that would probably horrify the people who normally drink blends. Likewise, Canadian whiskey is often incorrectly referred to as rye whiskey. The grains used in Canadian whiskey include corn, rye, wheat, and barley malt and none are more than 50 percent.

Southern Comfort is a blend of bourbon whiskey, peach liqueur, and fresh peaches. This American product can be listed as either a liqueur or a blended whiskey. This blend is 100 proof, but is mellowed by the liqueur and fruit. It was originally created in 1875, and was first known as Cuff and Buttons. Louis Herron, a bartender in St. Louis, changed the name to Southern Comfort.

American blended whiskey is a gentle and charming product that allows consumers to savor the rich tastes of good bourbon whiskey without having to experience the harsh, burning sensation that often accompanies these whiskeys. At their best, American blends are among the most refined and subtle of all distilled products.

BOURBON · CLASSICS

Allegheny

1 ounce bourbon
1 ounce dry vermouth
¼ ounce blackberry-flavored
  brandy
¼ ounce lemon juice
Dash of bitters
Lemon twist

Stir together all the ingredients, except the lemon twist, in a mixing glass with ice. Pour the mixture into a cocktail glass and garnish with the lemon twist.

Bourbon Collins I

1½ ounces bourbon
½ ounce lime juice
1 teaspoon sugar syrup, or to taste
1 scoop crushed ice
Club soda
Lime peel

Mix the bourbon, lime juice, and sugar syrup in a shaker with crushed ice. Pour the mixture into a chilled 12-ounce collins glass and top off the glass with club soda. Twist the lime peel over the glass and drop in.

Bourbon Collins II

2 ounces 100-proof bourbon
½ ounce lemon juice
1 teaspoon sugar syrup, or to taste
Several dashes of bitters
Crushed ice
Club soda
Lemon slice (optional)

Mix all the ingredients, except the soda and lime, in a shaker. Pour the mixture into a chilled highball glass and top off the glass with club soda. Decorate with the lemon slice.

Bourbon Daisy

1½ ounces bourbon
½ ounce lemon juice
1 teaspoon grenadine
1 scoop crushed ice
Club soda
1 teaspoon Southern Comfort
Orange slice
Pineapple stick

Mix the bourbon, lemon juice, and grenadine in a shaker with crushed ice. Pour the mixture into a chilled highball glass and top off with club soda and a float of Southern Comfort. Garnish with the fruit and serve.

Bourbon Eggnog

2 ounces bourbon
8 ounces milk
1 teaspoon superfine sugar
1 egg
1 scoop crushed ice
Grated nutmeg

Combine all the ingredients, except the nutmeg, in a shaker. Shake well and strain into a tall glass. Sprinkle the freshly grated nutmeg on top.

Bourbon Sour

2 ounces bourbon
Juice of ½ lemon
½ teaspoon sugar or sugar syrup
1 scoop crushed ice
Orange slice

Mix all the ingredients, except the orange slice, in a shaker. Strain the mixture into a chilled whiskey sour glass and garnish with the slice of orange.

Classic Mint Julep

6 small mint leaves
2 ounces bourbon
1 ounce lemon juice
1 ounce sugar syrup
1 scoop finely crushed ice
Mint sprig

Muddle the mint leaves with bourbon, lemon juice, and syrup in a bar glass. Put this mixture in a blender with finely crushed ice. Mix at high speed for about 15 seconds, or until ice becomes mushy. Pour the blend into a chilled double old-fashioned glass and garnish with the mint sprig.

Commodore Cocktail

1½ ounces bourbon
¾ ounce white crème de cacao
½ ounce lemon juice
1 scoop crushed ice

Mix all the ingredients in a shaker. Strain the mixture into a chilled cocktail glass.

Dixie Old-Fashioned

1 teaspoon superfine sugar
2 dashes of bitters
1½ ounces bourbon
1 orange slice
Twist of lemon peel
Maraschino cherry

Mix the sugar and bitters in an old-fashioned glass with ¾ ounce water. Add bourbon and ice and stir. Garnish with the orange slice, a twist of lemon peel, and the cherry.

Manhattan, Bourbon

1½ to 2 ounces bourbon
½ ounce sweet vermouth
Dash of bitters
Ice cubes
Maraschino cherry

Combine all the ingredients, except the cherry, in a large mixing glass.

Stir well and strain into a chilled cocktail glass. Garnish with the cherry.

Quick and Easy Mint Julep

Several mint sprigs
1 teaspoon superfine sugar
1 teaspoon water
1 scoop finely crushed ice
3 ounces bourbon

Muddle the mint sprigs in a double old-fashioned glass with sugar and water until sugar is dissolved. Fill the glass with finely crushed ice and add bourbon. Stir briskly with an iced tea spoon. Garnish with the mint sprig.

Sazerac

2 scoops crushed ice
1 sugar cube
2 dashes of bitters
2 ounces rye whiskey
Dash of Pernod
Lemon peel

Fill 2 old-fashioned glasses with the crushed ice to chill the glasses. Remove the ice from 1 glass. Place the sugar cube and a little water in the glass. Add bitters and crush the sugar cube with a muddler until the sugar is well dissolved. Add the whiskey, along with several ice cubes, and stir well. Empty the second glass of ice. In the second glass, pour a generous dash of Pernod to coat the inside of the glass thoroughly. Pour out the excess Pernod. Add the mixture from the first glass. Twist the lemon peel over the drink but do not drop it in.

Easy Sazerac

¼ teaspoon Pernod or other absinthe substitute
½ teaspoon sugar
1 tablespoon water
Dash of bitters
2 ounces bourbon, rye, or blended whiskey
Lemon peel

Coat the inside of an old-fashioned glass with Pernod. Add the sugar, water, and bitters and muddle until the sugar is dissolved. Add bourbon, rye, or blended whiskey with ice cubes and stir well. Twist the lemon peel over the drink and drop it in.

BOURBON · CREATIVE CONCOCTIONS

Admiral Highball

1½ ounces bourbon
1½ ounces Tokay wine
Dash of pineapple juice
Dash of lemon juice
Club soda

Stir together all the ingredients, except the soda, in a mixing glass with ice. Pour the mixture into a highball glass with one ice cube. Top off the glass with chilled club soda.

Anchor Splash

1 ounce bourbon
2 teaspoons Triple Sec
2 teaspoons peach brandy
2 teaspoons maraschino liqueur
2 tablespoons heavy cream
Several drops of maraschino cherry juice
1 scoop crushed ice

Combine all the ingredients in a shaker. Mix well and pour into a chilled old-fashioned glass.

Artist's Special

1 ounce bourbon
1 ounce sherry
½ ounce lemon juice
¼ ounce grenadine

Stir together all the ingredients in a mixing glass with ice. Pour the mixture into a cocktail glass.

Banana Bird

1 ounce bourbon
2 teaspoons crème de banane
2 teaspoons Triple Sec
1 ounce heavy cream

Mix together all the ingredients in a shaker with crushed ice. Strain the mixture into a cocktail glass.

Bianco

1½ ounces bourbon
½ ounce dry vermouth
Dash of Angostura bitters
Lemon twist

Stir together all the ingredients, except the lemon twist, in a mixing glass with ice. Pour the mixture into a fresh cocktail glass and garnish with the lemon twist.

Bishop

1 ounce bourbon
½ ounce sweet vermouth
1 ounce orange juice
Dash of yellow Chartreuse

Mix together all the ingredients in a shaker with crushed ice. Pour the mixture into a chilled cocktail glass.

Blizzard

1 scoop crushed ice
1½ ounces bourbon
1½ ounces cranberry juice
½ ounce lime juice
½ ounce grenadine
1 teaspoon sugar

Place the crushed ice in a blender and add ingredients in the order listed. Blend on a slow speed for 15 to 30 seconds or until frozen stiff. Pour the blend into a chilled highball glass.

Blue Grass Cocktail

1½ ounces bourbon
1 ounce pineapple juice
1 ounce lemon juice
1 teaspoon maraschino liqueur
1 scoop crushed ice

Mix together all the ingredients in a shaker. Strain the mixture into a chilled cocktail glass.

Boomerang

¾ ounce bourbon (or rye
   whiskey)
¾ ounce Swedish punsch liqueur
¾ ounce dry vermouth
Dash of Angostura bitters
Dash of lemon juice

In a mixing glass with ice, stir together all the ingredients. Pour the
mixture into a chilled cocktail glass.

Bordever

2 ounces bourbon
½ ounce ginger ale
Lemon twist

Stir together the bourbon and ginger ale in a mixing glass with ice.
Pour the mixture into a chilled cocktail glass and garnish with the lemon
twist.

Bourbon Cobbler

1½ ounces bourbon
1 ounce Southern Comfort
1 teaspoon peach-flavored brandy
2 teaspoons lemon juice
1 teaspoon sugar syrup
1 scoop crushed ice
Club soda
Peach slice

Mix all the ingredients, except the
soda and peach slice, in a shaker or
blender. Pour the mixture into a

chilled highball glass. Add ice cubes,
top off with soda, and decorate with
the peach slice.

Bourbon Cooler

3 ounces bourbon
½ ounce grenadine
1 teaspoon sugar syrup, or to taste
Several dashes of peppermint
   schnapps
Several dashes of orange bitters
1 scoop crushed ice
Club soda
Pineapple stick
Orange slice
Maraschino cherry

Mix all the ingredients, except the
soda and fruit, in a shaker. Pour the
mixture into a chilled, tall collins
glass and top off the glass with club
soda. Garnish with the fruit.

Bourbon Flip

1½ ounces bourbon
1 egg
1 teaspoon confectioners' sugar
2 teaspoons sweet cream
   (optional)
1 scoop crushed ice
Freshly grated nutmeg

Mix all the ingredients, except the
nutmeg, in a shaker. Strain the mixture into a 5-ounce flip glass. Sprinkle the freshly grated nutmeg on
top.

Bourbon Milk Punch

1½ ounces bourbon
3 ounces milk or half-and-half
1 teaspoon honey or sugar syrup
Dash of vanilla extract
1 scoop crushed ice
Nutmeg, grated

Mix all the ingredients, except the nutmeg, in a shaker. Pour the mixture into a chilled old-fashioned glass. Sprinkle with the nutmeg before serving.

Bourbon Orange

1½ ounces bourbon
½ ounce Triple Sec
1 ounce orange juice
1 scoop crushed ice
Lemon peel

Mix together all the ingredients, except the lemon peel, in a shaker. Pour this mixture into a chilled old-fashioned glass. Twist the lemon peel over the drink and drop it in.

Bourbon Satin

1 ounce bourbon
1 ounce white crème de cacao
1 ounce heavy cream
1 scoop crushed ice

Mix all the ingredients in a shaker. Strain the mixture into a chilled cocktail glass.

Bourbon Sidecar

1½ ounces bourbon
¾ ounce Triple Sec
½ ounce lemon juice
1 scoop crushed ice

Mix all the ingredients in a shaker or blender. Strain the mixture into a chilled cocktail glass.

Bourbon Sloe Gin Fizz

1 teaspoon sugar syrup, or to taste
½ teaspoon lemon juice
1½ ounces bourbon
¾ ounce sloe gin
Club soda
Lemon slice
Maraschino cherry

Pour all the ingredients, except the soda and fruit, into a 14-ounce collins glass. Add some ice and mix well. Add additional ice and top off the glass with club soda. Garnish with the lemon slice and the cherry.

Bourbonnaise

1½ ounces bourbon
½ ounce dry vermouth
½ ounce crème de cassis
Dash of lemon juice

In a mixing glass with ice, stir together all the ingredients. Pour the mixture into a chilled cocktail glass.

Bourborita

1½ ounces bourbon
1½ ounces sweet 'n' sour mix
½ ounce Triple Sec
½ ounce pineapple juice
1 scoop crushed ice

Mix together all the ingredients in a shaker. Strain this mixture into a sour glass or pour over ice cubes into an old-fashioned glass.

Bull and Bear

1½ ounces bourbon
¾ ounce curaçao
1 tablespoon grenadine
Juice of ½ lime
1 scoop crushed ice
1 maraschino cherry
1 orange slice

Combine all the ingredients, except the cherry and orange slice, in a shaker. Shake and strain this mixture into a chilled cocktail glass. Garnish with the cherry and the orange slice.

Dan'l Boone

1½ ounces bourbon
½ ounce orange liqueur
3 ounces chilled grapefruit juice

Pour the bourbon over ice cubes into an 8-ounce glass. Add the orange liqueur and the grapefruit juice. Stir well before serving.

Dry Mahoney

2½ ounces bourbon
½ ounce dry vermouth
Lemon peel

In a mixing glass with ice, stir together the bourbon and vermouth. Strain the mixture into a chilled cocktail glass. Twist the lemon peel over the drink and drop it in. Serve with an ice cube or two in an additional glass.

Flintstone

1½ ounces bourbon
½ ounce applejack
1 teaspoon lemon juice
Several dashes of grenadine
Several dashes of peppermint
    schnapps
1 scoop crushed ice

Mix together all the ingredients in a shaker. Strain the mixture into a chilled cocktail glass.

Forester

1½ ounces bourbon
¾ ounce maraschino liqueur
1 teaspoon lemon juice
1 scoop crushed ice
Maraschino cherry

Mix together all the ingredients, except the cherry, in a shaker. Pour the mixture into a chilled old-fashioned glass. Garnish with the cherry.

French Kiss

1½ ounces bourbon
¾ ounces apricot liqueur
½ teaspoon lemon juice
1 teaspoon grenadine
1 scoop crushed ice

Put all the ingredients in a shaker. Mix well and strain into a chilled cocktail glass.

Golden Boy

1½ ounces bourbon
½ ounce rum
2 ounces orange juice
1 teaspoon lemon juice
Sugar syrup to taste
1 scoop crushed ice
Dash of grenadine

Mix all the ingredients, except the grenadine, in a shaker. Strain the

mixture into a chilled cocktail glass. Top with a dash of grenadine.

Green Derby

2 ounces bourbon
1 ounce green crème de menthe
Juice of ½ lime
1 teaspoon sugar syrup, or to taste
6 small mint leaves
Club soda
Mint sprig

Put the bourbon, crème de menthe, lime juice, syrup, and mint leaves in a bar glass. Muddle leaves well. Add the mixture to a blender with some crushed ice and mix well. Pour this mix into a chilled collins glass and top off the glass with soda. Garnish with the mint sprig.

Hampton Punch

1 ounce bourbon
1 ounce Cognac
¾ ounce Benedictine
Juice of ½ lemon
Juice of ½ orange
1 teaspoon sugar syrup, or to taste
1 scoop crushed ice
Club soda
Orange slice

Mix all the ingredients, except the soda and orange slice, in a shaker.

Pour the mixture into a chilled high-ball or collins glass. Top off the glass with soda and stir gently. Garnish with the orange slice.

Hawaiian Eye

1½ ounces bourbon
1 ounce vodka
1 ounce coffee liqueur
½ ounce Pernod
1 ounce cream
1 egg white
2 ounces maraschino cherry juice
1 scoop crushed ice
Pineapple chunk
Maraschino cherry

Whirl all the ingredients, except the pineapple and cherry, in a blender until smooth. Pour the blend into an old-fashioned glass. Garnish with the pineapple chunk and the cherry.

Holiday Sparkle Punch

Makes 2 (6-ounce) servings

6 tablespoons frozen
  cranberry-raspberry juice
4 ounces bourbon
½ tablespoon concentrated frozen
  lemonade
2 ounces club soda

Mix all the ingredients in a shaker, without ice. Pour the mixture into ice-filled cocktail glasses. This cocktail can be frozen or made into a slush by filling the shaker half full with crushed ice and adding 2 more tablespoons of juice, as well as an extra ounce of bourbon.

Home Run

1 ounce bourbon
1 ounce light rum
1 ounce brandy
2 teaspoons lemon juice
Sugar syrup to taste

Mix together all the ingredients in a shaker. Strain the mixture into a chilled cocktail glass.

Imperial

1¼ ounces bourbon
Splash of club soda
1¼ ounces orange liqueur
Splash of simple syrup
1 scoop crushed ice

Mix together all the ingredients in a shaker. Strain the mixture into an old-fashioned glass over ice cubes. Top off the glass with club soda.

Jessica's Julep Mist

1 scoop crushed ice
1½ ounces bourbon
½ ounces crème de menthe
Mint leaf

Pack a cocktail glass with crushed ice. In a mixing glass, combine the bourbon and the crème de menthe. Add this mixture to the cocktail glass and garnish with the mint leaf. Serve with short straws.

Kentucky Cappuccino

1 ounce bourbon
1 ounce coffee liqueur
4 ounces heavy cream (milk or skim milk can be used)
1 teaspoon instant coffee
2 ounces club soda
Dark chocolate shavings
Whipped cream (optional)

Mix all the ingredients, except the chocolate shavings and the optional whipped cream, in a blender without ice. Pour the blend into a tall glass with ice. Garnish with the dark chocolate shavings.

If a warm after-dinner drink is desired, heat the cream or milk and dissolve the coffee in it. Then proceed to the blender. Pour the blend into a small stem glass with a dollop of whipped cream if desired and the chocolate shavings.

Kentucky Cooler

1½ ounces bourbon
¾ ounce brandy
1 ounce lemon juice
2 teaspoons sugar syrup, or to taste
1 scoop crushed ice
Club soda
Barbados or other medium-weight rum

Mix together all the ingredients, except the soda and rum, in a shaker. Pour the mixture into a chilled 14-ounce collins glass. Add fresh ice and top off the glass with club soda and a float of rum.

Kentucky Sunrise

1½ ounces bourbon
3 ounces chilled orange juice
1 teaspoon grenadine

Pour the bourbon into an 8-ounce glass filled with ice cubes. Add orange juice and stir. Add grenadine, but do not stir before serving.

Louisville Lady

1 ounce bourbon
¾ ounce crème de cacao
¾ ounce cream

In a shaker, mix together all the ingredients with ice. Strain the mixture into a cocktail glass.

Man o' War

2 ounces bourbon
1 ounce orange curaçao
½ ounce sweet vermouth
Juice of ½ lime
1 scoop crushed ice

Mix all the ingredients in a shaker with crushed ice. Pour the mixture into a chilled cocktail glass.

Miami Beach

1½ ounces bourbon
1 ounce orange juice
1 ounce pineapple juice
1 teaspoon lemon juice
Several dashes of bitters
Sugar syrup to taste
1 scoop crushed ice

Mix together all the ingredients in a shaker. Pour the mixture into a chilled old-fashioned glass.

Millionaire Cocktail

Makes 2 servings

3 ounces bourbon
1 ounce Pernod
Several dashes of curaçao
Several dashes of grenadine
1 egg white

Mix all the ingredients in a shaker with crushed ice. Strain the mixture into chilled cocktail glasses.

New Orleans Cocktail

1½ ounces bourbon
½ ounce Pernod
Dash of orange bitters
Several dashes of bitters
Dash of anisette
Sugar syrup to taste
1 scoop crushed ice
1 lemon peel twist

Mix all the ingredients, except the lemon peel, in a shaker. Pour the mixture into a chilled old-fashioned glass and garnish with the lemon peel twist.

Painless Paul

1½ ounces bourbon
½ ounce apricot liqueur
1 ounce grapefruit juice
1 teaspoon lemon juice
Several dashes of bitters
1 scoop crushed ice

Mix together all the ingredients in a shaker. Pour the mixture into an old-fashioned glass.

Peppermint Patty

1½ ounces bourbon
½ ounce peppermint schnapps
1 tablespoon lemon juice
1 teaspoon sugar syrup, or to taste
1 scoop crushed ice
Mint sprig (optional)
Maraschino cherry

Stir together all the ingredients, except the mint sprig and cherry, in a mixing glass. Pour the mixture into an old-fashioned glass. Garnish with the mint sprig and the cherry.

Polo Dream

1½ to 2 ounces bourbon
1 ounce orange juice
¾ ounce orgeat, or to taste

Mix all the ingredients in a shaker with crushed ice. Strain this mixture into a chilled cocktail glass.

Presbyterian

2 to 3 ounces bourbon
Ginger ale
Club soda

Pour the bourbon into a chilled highball glass. Add ice cubes. Top off the glass with equal parts of ginger ale and soda.

Rebel Party Sour

6 ounces bourbon
6 ounces beer
1 can (6 ounces) concentrated
    lemon juice
1 scoop crushed ice
Maraschino cherry
Orange slice

Combine all the ingredients, except the fruit, in a blender. Pour the blend into a sour glass. Garnish with the cherry and the orange slice.

Rebel Ringer

1 ounce gold crème de menthe
1 ounce bourbon
1 scoop crushed ice
1 lemon twist

Mix together all the ingredients, except the lemon, in a shaker. Strain the mixture into a chilled cocktail glass. Garnish with the lemon twist and serve.

Reverend Craig

1½ ounces bourbon
1½ ounces concentrated frozen
   lemonade
6 ounces beer

Mix together all the ingredients in a shaker. Shake well. Pour the mixture into a large beer glass filled with ice.

Rhett Butler Slush

1½ ounces bourbon
1 teaspoon Triple Sec
Juice of ½ lime
Juice of ¼ lemon
½ teaspoon sugar
1 scoop crushed ice

Whirl together all the ingredients in a blender. Pour the blend into a chilled champagne glass.

Royal Roost

¾ ounce bourbon or rye
¾ ounce Dubonnet rouge
Several dashes of curaçao
Several dashes of Pernod
Pineapple slice
Orange slice
Lemon peel
Generous dashes of bitters

Mix all the ingredients, except the fruit and bitters, in a mixing glass with crushed ice. Strain the mixture into a chilled old-fashioned glass with several ice cubes. Garnish with the fruit and top with bitters.

Shanty Hogan

2 ounces bourbon
1 ounce simple sugar
1 ounce lemon juice
1 scoop crushed ice
Maraschino cherry
6 mint leaves

Combine the bourbon, sugar, lemon juice, and ice in a blender. Blend until smooth. Pour the blend into a zombie glass with a straw. Garnish with the cherry and mint leaves.

Sherry Twist

1½ ounces bourbon or blended
   whiskey
¾ ounce cocktail sherry
Lemon peel

Pour the bourbon or blended whiskey and sherry into a shaker with crushed ice and stir. Strain the mixture into a chilled cocktail glass. Twist the lemon peel over the drink and drop it in.

Skyscraper

2 ounces bourbon
1 teaspoon fine sugar
1 tablespoon lime juice
Dash of bitters
1 scoop crushed ice
1 cup chilled cranberry juice
1 cucumber rind peeling

In a shaker, mix together all the ingredients, except cranberry juice and cucumber. Strain this mixture into a highball glass with ice cubes. Top off the glass with chilled cranberry juice and garnish with the cucumber peeling.

Sloe 'n' Bouncy

1½ ounces bourbon
½ ounce sloe gin
½ ounce lemon juice
1 teaspoon sugar syrup
Lemon slice
Peach slice (optional)

Mix all the ingredients, except the fruit slices, in a shaker with crushed ice. Strain the mixture into a chilled cocktail glass. Garnish with the lemon and, if desired, the peach slice.

Snowman

3 ounces bourbon
1 ounce cranberry juice
1 tablespoon lemon juice
2 tablespoons sugar syrup
1 scoop crushed ice

Mix all the ingredients in a blender until the drink is frosty. Pour the blend into a chilled highball glass.

Sonoma Fizz

1½ ounces bourbon
1 teaspoon lemon juice
1 teaspoon lime juice
1 teaspoon sugar syrup, or to taste
1 egg white
1 scoop crushed ice
Club soda
Maraschino cherry

In a shaker, mix together all the ingredients, except the soda and cherry. Pour the mixture into a chilled highball glass and top off with cold club soda. Garnish with the cherry.

Southern Ginger

1½ ounces 100-proof bourbon
1 teaspoon ginger-flavored brandy
1 teaspoon lemon juice
1 scoop crushed ice
Ginger ale
Lemon twist

Mix all the ingredients, except the ginger ale and lemon twist, in a shaker. Pour the mixture into a doubled old-fashioned glass. Top off the glass with ginger ale. Twist the lemon peel over the drink and drop it in.

Southern Maiden

1¼ ounces bourbon
¾ ounce Triple Sec
2 ounces orange juice
12 ounces pineapple juice
Splash of grenadine

Combine the bourbon, Triple Sec, orange juice, and pineapple juice in a tall glass with ice. Top off the glass with a splash of grenadine. Stir once and serve.

Spinner

1½ ounces bourbon
1 ounce orange juice
1 tablespoon lime juice
1 teaspoon superfine sugar
1 scoop crushed ice
1 orange slice

Combine all the ingredients, except the orange slice, in a shaker. Shake briskly and strain the mixture into a cocktail glass or over fresh ice in an old-fashioned glass. Garnish with half a slice of orange.

Sunday Brunch

1½ ounces bourbon
2 ounces tomato juice
2 ounces canned beef bouillon
Dash of Worcestershire sauce
1 tablespoon lemon juice

Pour the bourbon into a tumbler filled with ice cubes. Add the remaining ingredients and stir well before serving.

Sweet and Sour Bourbon

1½ ounces bourbon
4 ounces orange juice
Pinch or two of sugar
Pinch of salt
1 scoop crushed ice
Maraschino cherry

Mix all the ingredients, except the cherry, in a shaker. Pour the mixture into a whiskey sour glass. Garnish with the cherry.

Waldorf Cocktail

1½ ounces bourbon
¾ ounce Pernod
½ ounce sweet vermouth
Dash of bitters

In a mixing glass, stir together all the ingredients with ice. Strain the mixture into a chilled cocktail glass.

Ward Eight

1½ to 2 ounces bourbon
1 ounce lemon juice
1 ounce orange juice
Sugar syrup to taste
Dash of grenadine

Mix all the ingredients in a shaker with crushed ice. Strain the mixture into a chilled cocktail glass.

Whirlaway

2 ounces bourbon
1 ounce curaçao
Several dashes of bitters
1 scoop crushed ice
Club soda

Mix all the ingredients, except the soda, in a shaker. Pour the mixture into a chilled old-fashioned glass and top off with club soda.

BOURBON · SIGNATURE DRINKS

Boiler Maker

THE BALBOA CAFE, SAN FRANCISCO

1 shot of bourbon
½ pint of beer

Pour the bourbon into a small shot glass. Drop the entire shot glass into a ½ pint glass of beer.

Cool Mint Julep

SOUTHERN CULTURE,
CHARLOTTESVILLE, VIRGINIA

1½ ounces bourbon
¾ ounce peppermint schnapps
2 ounces water
2 cups ice
4 fresh mint leaves

Combine all the ingredients, except the mint, in a blender. Blend until frothy. Pour the blend into a chilled old-fashioned glass and garnish with the fresh mint.

Geesto's Manhattan

ASTA, SAN FRANCISCO

1¼ ounces bourbon
½ ounce sweet vermouth
Splash of cherry juice
Dash of bitters
2 maraschino cherries

Combine all the ingredients, except the cherries, in a mixing glass with ice. Stir and strain into a chilled martini glass. Garnish with the maraschino cherries.

Occidental "Statist" Coffee

OCCIDENTAL GRILL, WASHINGTON, D.C.

1 pint heavy cream
1½ teaspoons granulated sugar
1 teaspoon ground allspice
½ teaspoon ground cloves
Hot coffee
1½ ounces Kentucky bourbon
½ ounce coffee liqueur
Lemon twist

Whip the heavy cream at high speed, adding granulated sugar. Whip in allspice and cloves. Whip until the cream holds its peaks. Fill a 10-ounce glass or snifter with hot coffee. Add bourbon and coffee liqueur. Top off with clove-scented whipped cream. Garnish with the lemon twist.

Old-Fashioned

ASTA, SAN FRANCISCO

2 maraschino cherries
2 orange slices
5 dashes of bitters
1 teaspoon sugar
1½ ounces bourbon
Splash of soda

In a rocks glass, place 1 cherry, ½ slice of orange, bitters, and sugar. Muddle until the mixture is well ground. Add the bourbon and a splash of soda while still mixing. Fill the glass with ice. Garnish with the remaining cherry and orange slices.

Tropical Itch

MAUNA LANI BAY HOTEL, BIG ISLAND, HAWAII

Crushed ice
½ lime
½ ounce bourbon
2 dashes of bitters
Dash of orange curaçao
½ ounce dark rum
Tropical fruit juice
1¼ ounces 151-proof rum
Maraschino cherry
Mint sprig

Fill a hurricane glass with crushed ice. Squeeze the lime into the glass and leave the rind in the glass. Separately, blend together the bourbon, bitters, curaçao, and rum. Add this blend to the glass. Fill with tropical fruit juice just below the neck of the glass. Mix with a bar spoon and add more crushed ice. Float the rum on top. Garnish with the maraschino cherry and the mint sprig.

Tumbleweed

"21" CLUB, NEW YORK CITY

2 ounces bourbon
Splash of Pernod
1 scoop crushed ice
Club soda
Lemon twist

Combine the bourbon and Pernod in a shaker with crushed ice. Strain the mixture into an old-fashioned glass. Top off the glass with club soda and drop in the lemon twist.

BOURBON · HOT DRINKS

Hot Brick Toddy

¼ teaspoon powdered cinnamon
1 teaspoon sugar syrup
1 butter pat
Boiling water
2 ounces bourbon (rye, Canadian, or blended whiskey can be used)

Rinse an old-fashioned glass in hot water. Add the cinnamon, syrup, butter, and enough boiling water to thoroughly mix the ingredients. Add the whiskey. Top off the glass with boiling water.

CANADIAN WHISKEY · CREATIVE CONCOCTIONS

Bix Manhattan

BIX, SAN FRANCISCO

1½ ounces Canadian whiskey
½ ounce Carpano (Italian sweet
  vermouth)
Dash of bitters
Crushed ice
Maraschino cherry

Mix all the ingredients, except the cherry, in a shaker. Shake vigorously. Strain the mixture into a 5-ounce chilled, stemmed martini glass. Garnish with the maraschino cherry.

Dark Canadian Colada

FOUR SEASONS HOTEL, TORONTO

1½ ounces Canadian whiskey
1 ounce coconut cream
2 ounces cream
½ ounce dark crème de cacao
1 cup ice

Combine all the ingredients in a blender and blend until smooth. Pour the blend into a chilled parfait glass.

Old Pepper

1½ ounces Canadian whiskey
1 ounce lemon juice
Dash of Worcestershire sauce
Dash of chili sauce
2 dashes of Angostura bitters
Dash of Tabasco
1 scoop crushed ice

Combine all the ingredients in a shaker. Mix well and strain into a sour glass.

Note: You can substitute ¾ ounce rye and ¾ ounce bourbon for the Canadian whiskey.

Opening Cocktail

½ ounce Canadian whiskey
¼ ounce sweet vermouth
¼ ounce grenadine

Mix all the ingredients in a shaker with crushed ice. Strain the mixture into a chilled cocktail glass.

RYE WHISKEY · CREATIVE CONCOCTIONS

Fancy Free

Lemon juice
Confectioners' sugar
1½ ounces rye whiskey
2 dashes of maraschino liqueur
Dash of orange bitters
Dash of Angostura bitters

Moisten the rim of a cocktail glass with lemon juice. Press the moistened rim into confectioners' sugar. In a shaker with crushed ice, mix together the whiskey, maraschino, and bitters. Strain the mixture into the prepared glass.

SOUTHERN COMFORT · CREATIVE CONCOCTIONS

Down Comforter

1½ ounces Southern Comfort
½ ounce gin
½ ounce lemon juice
1 ounce orange juice
1 scoop crushed ice

Combine all the ingredients in a shaker. Shake well and strain into a chilled cocktail glass.

Plump Peach

2 ounces Southern Comfort
1½ ounces peach brandy
Dash of bitters
1½ ounces heavy cream
Slice of fresh peach

In a shaker, mix all the ingredients, except the peach slice, with ice. Strain the mixture, over ice cubes, into an old-fashioned glass. Garnish with the peach slice.

Rhett Butler

1½ ounces Southern Comfort
1 ounce orange curaçao
¾ ounce lime juice
¾ ounce lemon juice
½ ounce orange juice
1 scoop crushed ice
Soda
Orange slice and mint sprig

Shake the Southern Comfort, curaçao, and juices with ice cubes. Strain the mixture into a highball glass filled with crushed ice. Top off the glass with soda and garnish with the orange slice and mint sprig.

Scarlett O'Hara

1½ ounces Southern Comfort
1½ ounces cranberry juice
½ ounce lime juice

In a mixing glass with ice, stir together all the ingredients. Strain the mixture into a chilled cocktail glass.

Southern Frost

1½ ounces Southern Comfort
1½ ounces amaretto
1 ounce Galliano
3 ounces orange juice
3 ounces pineapple juice
1 scoop crushed ice

Mix all the ingredients in a blender. Pour the blend into a hurricane glass.

Scotch Whisky

Scotland is a lumpy mass of land that juts out of the northernmost part of England. On a map it is a jagged hunk sliced and spliced by lakes (lochs), inlets, bays, firths, rivers, and streams. Some parts of it seem to have been so carved up by the omnipresent water that they have broken entirely from the land and floated out to sea as islands.

The northern part of the country is hilly and rocky, while the southern part is flat and moist. The upper region, the Highlands, is separated from the lower, the Lowlands, by an imaginary line that cuts across the country from Dundee to Greenock. Highlanders consider themselves to be the true, modern inheritors of the rugged character born of Scotland's tumultuous past.

In 1746, after the defeat of Bonnie Prince Charlie at Culloden Moor, the British crown, attempting to bring independent-minded Scotland under its thumb, banned kilts and other traditional clothes; and in 1814, distillation from any stills with less than 500 gallons' capacity was outlawed in Scotland. Both these prohibitions caused anger and defiance among the Scots. The kilt and Highland dress are an integral part of the Scottish character, and so is "a wee dram" of whisky. Any meddlesome restrictions placed on these would have to constitute a grievous insult to each and every true Scot.

But, as in many other instances throughout history, this adversity only helped create a Scottish character that was stronger and more emphatically independent than ever before. The home stills of the Highlands not only remained, but also grew into flourishing businesses.

"Malt" whisky is the product of these distilleries. The term refers to the spirit produced from malted barley. When a distillery bottles the whisky it produces, without any other whiskies being added, the product is called a "single malt whisky." These single malts have pronounced individual characteristics and complexity of flavor just like fine wines, due to the individual ways in which they are produced.

There are several Scottish regions that produce distinct styles of malt whisky, but of the eighty-one single malt distilleries operating today most are located in the Highlands, north of the "Highland Line." Highland malts are generally considered to be Scotland's best.

To make whisky, the Scots gather top-quality barley and then steep it in water, causing it to germinate and sprout. This changes the barley's starch into sugar, which eventually is converted to alcohol during fermentation. Then the sprouting barley is dried in a kiln that is heated by peat fire, after which it is crushed in preparation for fermentation.

This procedure requires substantial space and some rather heavy equipment. As you might imagine, this part of the process can present a considerable hardship for tiny Highland distilleries. To answer this problem, malting has been concentrated—as of the early 1960s—at a relatively small number of plants that were expressly built for the intake, storage, and processing of barley malt; one plant supplies malted barley to several distilleries.

No amount of reading or study prepared me for the wonderful smell of the malting plant—a moist, toasty perfume that permeates the air. There is something comforting and tremendously appealing about the basic, earthy aroma of gently roasting grain infused with the spicy smoke of a peat fire. Now, every time I taste scotch, I am reminded of that delicious sensory experience.

All Scots will tell you that it is the Highland water that makes their whisky special. The water, flowing in profusion out of the hills, is softened as it passes over granite and through vegetation. It also takes on a round, almost sweet flavor.

Each distillery has its own natural water supply—a spring or a stream gurgling out of the hills. The water source at each facility is tended and protected but never tampered with (despite the fact that the water does take on a slight brownish tinge as a result of its contact with peat). In fact, it was the water source that dictated where each distillery was located.

The main reason for the differences among the brands is the type of oak barrel each distillery uses for aging. One distiller puts the clear whisky into "refill" sherry casks. These are relatively neutral and add little flavor to the spirit over time, allowing the whisky's true malty character to shine forth. At another, the whisky is aged in casks that have held two vintages of Oloroso or cream sherry. The result, after a number of years of aging, is a dark spirit that has absorbed a great degree of complexity and richness from the inside walls of the aging barrel.

There is no right or wrong way to age whisky; it is all just a question of style. Some aim for a subtle, dry, and elegant style, while others prefer to make a sweeter, richer whisky. Some distillers compromise between the two extremes by aging a percentage in used sherry casks and part in refills.

By the same token, some find that their whisky hits its peak after eight years, while others prefer to allow theirs to slumber for ten, twelve, or eighteen years. These barrel and aging decisions, plus the rate (temperature) of distillation, the shape of the still, and the water are what determine the character of a single malt whisky.

One production director told me that between 70 and 80 percent of the distillery's production is sold for blending. "The vast majority of the Scotch whisky sold in the world is blended," he said. Blending is a skillful procedure that might combine eight or ten different single malts with a portion of grain whiskey. The resulting product can be more balanced and more complex than a typical single malt, but it lacks the assertive individualism and profound flavor.

In grain whisky, the basic ingredients are barley, wheat, and/or corn instead of just barley. The whisky is distilled in seventy-foot tall continuous stills to a much higher proof than single malts. The resulting whisky is soft, smooth, and fairly neutral in flavor.

Grain whisky is the base for all blended Scotch whiskies. A fifth-generation master blender let me taste a Highland malt—spicy, dense, complex, and elegant; a Lowland malt—light and crisp; an Islay malt—smoky, salty, peaty, and intense; and a grain whisky. Then he blended them. The end result was balanced, silky, and attractive. It held hints of all of its various ingredients, but they had blended smoothly into a whole.

* * *

According to 1988–1989 domestic sales figures, while overall alcohol consumption was slipping by 1.7 percent, top single malts were increasing their business by 31 percent. All the best bars were laying in a good supply of malt whiskies. "We used to carry only three or four single malts," says Kevin Or, bar manager at Smith and Wollensky's in New York. "Today we have more than a dozen. Malts have come of age in the last few years."

Scotland has its regions similar to those found in the wine country of France or California. Each of these places produces scotch with recognizable regional style and flashy characteristics. The study of these distinctive whiskies is fascinating and can offer a lifetime of enjoyment. Each one speaks clearly of its origins and its history.

The drinks that follow are just fine when made with good blended scotch (such as Johnny Walker, Ballantine's, Cutty Sark, Dewar's, or White Horse). If you have a favorite single malt, however, using it in these drinks adds an exciting dimension to the mixture.

CLASSICS

Hopscotch

1½ ounces scotch
½ ounce sweet vermouth
Several dashes of orange bitters
1 scoop crushed ice
Olive

Mix the scotch, vermouth, bitters, and ice in a shaker. Pour the mixture into a chilled cocktail glass and drop in the olive.

Remsen Cooler

2 to 3 ounces scotch
1 teaspoon sugar syrup
Club soda
Lemon peel

Put the scotch, sugar syrup, and several ice cubes in a chilled collins glass. Top off the glass with the club soda and stir. Twist the lemon peel over the drink and drop it in.

Rob Roy

1½ to 2 ounces scotch
½ ounce sweet vermouth
Dash of orange bitters
1 maraschino cherry

In a mixing glass with ice, stir together the scotch, vermouth, and bitters. Strain the mixture into a chilled cocktail glass and garnish with the cherry.

Rob Roy Dry

1½ to 2 ounces scotch
½ ounce dry vermouth
Dash of bitters (optional)
Lemon peel

In a mixing glass with ice cubes, stir together the scotch, vermouth, and bitters. Strain the mixture into a chilled cocktail glass. Twist the lemon peel over the drink and drop it in.

Scotch Sour

1½ ounces scotch
½ ounce lemon juice
1 teaspoon sugar syrup
1 scoop crushed ice
Orange slice
1 maraschino cherry

Mix together all the ingredients, except the fruit, in a shaker. Shake and then strain the mixture into a chilled whiskey sour glass. Garnish with the orange slice and the cherry.

CREATIVE CONCOCTIONS

Aberdeen Sour

2 ounces scotch
1 ounce orange juice
1 ounce lemon juice
½ ounce Triple Sec
1 scoop crushed ice

Combine all the ingredients in a shaker or blender. Mix well and pour into a chilled old-fashioned glass.

Affinity Cocktail

1 scoop crushed ice
1 ounce scotch
1 ounce dry sherry
1 ounce port
Several dashes of bitters
Lemon peel
1 maraschino cherry

In a mixing glass with ice, stir together the scotch, sherry, port, and bitters. Strain the mixture into a chilled cocktail glass. Twist the lemon peel over the drink and drop it in. Garnish with the cherry.

Blackwatch

1½ ounces scotch
½ ounce curaçao
½ ounce brandy
Lemon slice
Mint sprig

Pour the scotch, curaçao, and brandy over ice cubes in a chilled highball glass. Stir and then garnish with the slice of lemon and the mint sprig.

Caracas Cocktail

2 ounces scotch
½ ounce lemon juice
1 teaspoon sugar syrup
Several dashes of curaçao
Dash of amaretto
1 scoop crushed ice

Combine all the ingredients in a shaker. Mix well and strain into a chilled cocktail glass.

Christian's Cocktail

1 ounce scotch
1 ounce medium sherry
1 teaspoon lemon juice
1 teaspoon orange juice
½ teaspoon sugar syrup
1 scoop crushed ice

Put all the ingredients in a shaker or blender. Mix well and strain into a chilled cocktail glass.

Farmer's Milk

5 ounces heavy cream
2 ounces scotch
1 scoop crushed ice
1 whole egg
1 teaspoon sugar syrup
Freshly grated nutmeg

Combine the cream and scotch in a shaker with the crushed ice. Beat the egg and sugar syrup together in a bowl, then add to the shaker. Shake vigorously. Pour the mixture into a chilled old-fashioned glass and sprinkle with the nutmeg.

Harry Lauder

1¼ ounces scotch
1¼ ounces sweet vermouth
½ teaspoon sugar

In a mixing glass with ice, stir together all the ingredients. Strain the mixture into a chilled cocktail glass.

Hawaiian Bull

1½ ounces scotch
Crushed ice
Fresh pineapple
½ ounce orgeat

Pour the scotch into a double old-fashioned glass. Fill the glass with crushed ice and fresh pineapple wedges. Top off with a float of the orgeat.

Heathcliff

1 ounce scotch
1 ounce Calvados
½ ounce dry gin
1 teaspoon heather honey or sugar
  syrup
1 scoop crushed ice

Mix all the ingredients in a shaker. Strain the mixture into a chilled cocktail glass.

Highland

1½ ounces scotch
3 ounces milk
1 teaspoon sugar
1 scoop crushed ice
Freshly grated nutmeg

Mix the scotch, milk, sugar, and ice in a shaker. Pour the mixture into a chilled old-fashioned glass and sprinkle the nutmeg on top.

Horseshoe

1 lemon, peeled in a long spiral
2 to 3 ounces scotch
½ ounce sweet vermouth
½ ounce dry vermouth
1 scoop crushed ice

Place the lemon peel in a chilled collins glass, leaving one end of it hanging over the rim. Pour in the scotch and the vermouths. Add the crushed ice and stir well. Let the drink stand for a few minutes before serving.

Knucklebuster

1½ ounces scotch
¾ ounce Drambuie

Fill an old-fashioned glass with ice cubes. Pour both ingredients into the glass and stir well.

Marylou

3 ounces scotch
½ ounce lime juice
Ginger ale
Lemon slice

Pour the scotch and lime juice into a chilled collins glass filled with ice cubes. Top the glass with ginger ale and stir. Garnish with the lemon slice.

Miami Beach Cocktail

1 ounce scotch
1 ounce dry vermouth
1 ounce grapefruit juice
1 scoop crushed ice

Mix all the ingredients in a shaker. Strain the mixture into a chilled cocktail glass.

Prince Edward

1½ ounces scotch
½ ounce vermouth-based apéritif
    such as Lillet or St. Raphael
¼ ounce Drambuie
1 scoop crushed ice
Preserved orange slice

Mix all the ingredients, except the orange slice, in a shaker. Pour the mixture into a chilled old-fashioned glass and garnish with the orange slice.

Saucy Sue

2 to 3 ounces scotch
¼ ounce lime or lemon juice
1 scoop crushed ice
Cold ginger ale
Lime or lemon wedge

Mix the scotch and lime juice in a mixing glass with crushed ice. Strain the mixture into a chilled highball glass. Top off with ginger ale and garnish with the lime or lemon wedge.

Scotch Orange Fix

2 ounces scotch
½ ounce lemon juice
1 teaspoon sugar syrup
1 scoop crushed ice
Orange peel cut in a long spiral
1 teaspoon curaçao

Mix together the scotch, juice, syrup, and ice in a shaker. Mix vigorously. Pour the mixture into a double old-fashioned glass. Add additional ice and drop in the orange peel. Top with a float of the curaçao.

Scotch Sangaree

1 teaspoon heather honey,
    or to taste
1½ ounces scotch
Lemon twist
Club soda
Freshly grated nutmeg

Mix the heather honey and a little water or club soda in a double old-fashioned glass until the honey is dissolved. Add the scotch, a lemon twist, and ice cubes. Top off the glass with club soda and sprinkle the nutmeg on top.

Scotch Smash

Heather honey or sugar syrup
6 mint leaves
1 scoop crushed ice
2 to 3 ounces scotch
Dash of orange bitters
Mint sprig

Muddle the honey or sugar syrup with mint in a double old-fashioned glass. Fill the glass with crushed ice. Add the scotch and mix well. Top off with the orange bitters and the mint sprig.

Shogun Fizz

2 ounces scotch
2 ounces dry red wine
½ ounce lemon juice
1 teaspoon sugar syrup
1 scoop crushed ice
Cold club soda
Pineapple spear

Mix all the ingredients, except the soda and pineapple, in a shaker. Pour the mixture into a chilled highball glass, then top off with club soda. Decorate with the pineapple spear.

Starboard

1 ounce scotch
1 ounce grapefruit juice
1 ounce dry vermouth
1 scoop crushed ice

Mix all the ingredients in a shaker. Pour the mixture into a chilled old-fashioned glass.

University

2 ounces scotch
6 ounces chocolate milk
1 teaspoon curaçao
1 scoop crushed ice
Grated chocolate

Mix the scotch, milk, and curaçao in a shaker with crushed ice. Pour the mixture into a chilled double old-fashioned glass and sprinkle the chocolate on top.

HOT DRINKS

Oxford Grad

Makes 2 servings

4 ounces scotch
4 ounces boiling water
2 teaspoons sugar
2 small lemon peels

Pour the scotch and boiling water into separate warm mugs. Ignite the scotch. While the scotch is blazing, pour it back and forth between the two mugs. Extinguish the scotch and serve the drink in two mugs. Add 1 teaspoon sugar to each mug and stir well. Garnish with the lemon peels.

Note: You might want to practice once or twice with cold water.

Irish Whiskey

Irish whiskey was the first and, for a time, the only distilled spirit made in the British Isles. Today the best known whiskey from the region is, of course, scotch, but Irish whiskey has been around a good deal longer and certainly has many fans.

Some zealous constituents assure us that this heady spirit dates to the sixth century when missionary monks brought the art of distillation to the Emerald Isle. Others insist that there was enough *uisge beatha* (Celtic for "water of life") on hand in the twelfth century for Henry II's invading troops to take a supply home with them. Actually, the first recorded reference to Irish whiskey goes back to the early 1400s, which means that the spirit still predates scotch by nearly a century. In fact, many believe that distillation was brought to Scotland from Ireland.

In the beginning of the seventeenth century, none other than Sir Walter Raleigh became a devotee of Ireland's mellow spirits, whiskey in particular. On his last visit to the West Indies, Raleigh stopped to visit his friend the Earl of Cork, and he happily reported in his diary that he was given "a supreme present"—a 32-gallon keg of home-distilled whiskey. Queen Elizabeth I was also fond of Irish spirits.

Soon, as a result of its burgeoning popularity in England, the spirit underwent a name change and the Celtic spelling was anglicized into "whiskey." Oddly enough, there is a spelling difference between the whiskeys of the world. Irish spirits, along with those from the American continent, are named "whiskey," while the Scots drop the "e" and call theirs "whisky."

It was during the reign of Elizabeth's successor, James I, that Sir Thomas Phillips, the king's deputy in the Irish province of Ulster, was given the authority to grant distilling licenses. Those were simpler days: Ignorant of such modern ethical considerations as conflict of interest, Sir Thomas immediately granted himself the first license. In 1608, Phillips built his distillery on the banks of the Bush River in County Antrim, Northern Ireland. The world's first licensed distillery, he christened it "Bushmills."

Whiskey distilling flourished in Ireland in the seventeenth century, but most stills were small cottage industries. There were many attempts—some of them violent—made to control and tax these distilling activities. But, as in Scotland and America, most of these efforts were unsuccessful.

The true beginnings of the modern Irish whiskey business came about in the late eighteenth century when a group of large commercial distilleries were built. Brands that have survived include John Jameson, which opened its distillery in 1780, and John Power, which appeared in 1791. Both of these firms were established in Dublin. Later, in 1825, the Murphy brothers built a distillery in Midleton, near Cork. Here they installed the world's largest pot still—3,000 gallons in volume. It wasn't until 1975, on the still's 150th birthday, that it was taken out of service.

There are important differences between the ways Scotch and Irish whiskeys are made. Both methods use pot stills, but the Irish stills are much bigger. In addition, the Irish spirit is distilled three times, Scotch just twice. As a result, Irish whiskey is purer and quite a bit more forceful coming off the still. By adding distilled water, both whiskeys are brought down to a lower proof before bottling.

Another major difference between the two goes back to the treatment of the grain malt in the initial stages of the whiskey-making process. In both cases, the grain is moistened, after which it begins to germinate. Scottish malt is dried in kilns over open peat fires, a process that gives the resulting whiskey its distinctive smoky flavor. Irish malt is toasted over peat in enclosed kilns, which adds no noticeable character to the eventual distillate.

Scotch malt is made entirely from malted barley, while Irish whiskey is made from a blend of malted and unmalted barley, oats, rye, and wheat. Irish whiskey is aged—often for ten to twelve years—in oak casks that previously held either bourbon, rum, or sherry. These well-seasoned barrels give the whiskey additional complexity.

Irish whiskey gained worldwide acceptance in the nineteenth and early twentieth centuries. In America, it was the spirit of choice until the advent of Prohibition in 1919. But that bleak thirteen-year period, plus the effects of a depression that had spread throughout the world, seriously damaged the industry.

During World War II, the Irish government restricted whiskey export sales. As a result, American GIs returned home from Europe singing the praises of scotch.

The Irish whiskey industry remained in the doldrums until the mid-1960s, when all the distilleries in Ireland merged to form one big company, Irish Distillers Group, Limited (I.D.G.). Many of the old distilleries had become outmoded; some of them were finding it difficult to obtain a consistent supply of good water. The Dublin operations, once situated on the outskirts of the city, were slowly being engulfed by urban expansion.

After much research, it was decided to build a big new complex at Midleton. Completed in 1975, this plant now produces all Irish whiskey except Old Bushmills. The company's directors assure us that this operation is "capable of producing all the famous whiskeys in exactly the way they have always been made and ensures that their unique flavors and characteristics are preserved."

Old Bushmills, although part of I.D.G. since 1975, continues to make its whiskey in the ancient County Antrim distillery on the edge of St. Columb's Rill in Northern Ireland.

Like other whiskeys, Irish is consumed mostly on the rocks or with water or soda. The spirit has a gentle, warm, nutlike flavor with plenty of shadings. This complexity gives it considerable staying power and a taste that doesn't pale when sipped over the course of a long evening.

Irish whiskey can also be used with mixers or in any of the cocktails that are ordinarily made with scotch, bourbon, Canadian, or blended whiskeys. Of course the most famous of all Irish whiskey drinks is Irish coffee. This delicious blending of coffee, sugar, and whiskey topped with whipped cream was allegedly created by Joe Sheridan, who was the chef at Shannon Airport. Legend has it that it made its first American appearance in 1952 at the Buena Vista Cafe on San Francisco's Fisherman's Wharf, and there is a plaque outside the restaurant to commemorate the event.

But Irish can stand on its own without mixers of any sort. This historic spirit has a distinct character and a style that is unique. Different from scotch or bourbon, Irish whiskey deserves a place on every bar.

CLASSICS

Hot Irish Coffee

1 ½ ounces Irish whiskey
Strong, hot coffee
Brown sugar
Whipped cream

Pour the Irish whiskey into a warm glass coffee mug. Fill the mug with hot coffee and add brown sugar to taste. Stir to combine. Top off with a dollop of freshly whipped cream.

Iced Irish Coffee

4 ounces strong, hot coffee
1 ½ ounces Irish whiskey, warmed
1 to 2 teaspoons brown sugar
Lightly whipped heavy cream

Pour freshly brewed coffee into a glass container. Add the Irish whiskey and sugar. Stir well until the sugar is dissolved. Chill. When ready to serve, pour the cold mixture into a stemmed glass. Gently pour the lightly whipped cream over the back of a spoon, held just above the coffee's surface, so that the whipped cream floats on top. Do not stir before serving.

CREATIVE CONCOCTIONS

Ballylickey Belt

½ teaspoon heather honey,
    or to taste
1 ½ ounces Irish whiskey
Cold club soda
Lemon peel

In a cocktail glass, mix the honey with a little water or club soda until it dissolves. Add the whiskey and several ice cubes, then fill the glass with club soda. Twist the lemon peel over the drink and drop it in.

Blackthorn

1 ½ ounces Irish whiskey
1 ½ ounces dry vermouth
Several dashes of Pernod
Several dashes of bitters
1 scoop crushed ice

Combine all the ingredients in a shaker or a blender. Mix well and pour into a chilled old-fashioned glass.

Brainstorm

2 ounces Irish whiskey
½ ounce dry vermouth
¼ ounce Benedictine
Orange peel

In a mixing glass, stir together the whiskey, vermouth, and Benedictine. Pour the mixture into a cocktail glass and garnish with the orange peel.

Connemara Clammer

2 ounces Irish whiskey
2 ounces clam juice
3 ounces V-8 juice
1 teaspoon lime juice
Several dashes of Worcestershire sauce
½ teaspoon grated horseradish
Several pinches of freshly ground black or white pepper
1 scoop crushed ice

Combine all the ingredients in a shaker. Mix and strain into a chilled double old-fashioned glass.

Dublin Sour

1½ ounces Irish whiskey
½ ounce Triple Sec
1 ounce lime juice
1 scoop crushed ice
¼ ounce raspberry liqueur

Mix the whiskey, Triple Sec, and lime juice in a shaker with crushed ice. Strain the mixture into a chilled cocktail glass. Top off with a float of raspberry liqueur.

Four-Leaf Clover

1½ ounces Irish whiskey
1½ ounces green crème de menthe
2 ounces heavy cream
1 scoop crushed ice
1 maraschino cherry

Mix all the ingredients, except the cherry, in a shaker. Pour the mixture into a chilled old-fashioned glass and garnish with the cherry.

Green-Eyed Monster

1¼ ounces Irish whiskey
1 ounce sweet vermouth
¼ ounce green crème de menthe
1 dash of bitters

In a mixing glass with ice, stir together all the ingredients. Pour the mixture into a chilled cocktail glass.

Irish Fix

2 ounces Irish whiskey
½ ounce Irish Mist
½ ounce lemon juice
½ ounce pineapple syrup or
    pineapple juice
1 scoop crushed ice
Orange slice
Lemon slice

Mix all the ingredients, except the fruit slices, in a blender. Pour the mixture into an old-fashioned glass. Garnish with the orange and lemon slices.

Note: If you use pineapple juice in place of syrup, add a little sugar syrup to taste.

Irish Kilt

2 ounces Irish whiskey
1 ounce scotch
1 ounce lemon juice
1½ ounces sugar syrup, or to
    taste
Several dashes of orange bitters
1 scoop crushed ice

Mix all the ingredients in a shaker. Strain the mixture into a chilled cocktail glass.

Leprechaun

1½ ounces Irish whiskey
½ ounce sloe gin
½ ounce light rum
1 ounce lemon juice
1 teaspoon sugar syrup
2 peach slices, diced
1 scoop crushed ice
5 to 6 fresh raspberries
1 maraschino cherry

Mix all the ingredients, except the fruit, in a blender. Pour the mixture into a chilled old-fashioned glass. Garnish with the raspberries and a cherry.

Lucky Shamrock

1½ ounces Irish whiskey
¾ ounce dry vermouth
1 teaspoon green Chartreuse
1 teaspoon green crème de
    menthe

Combine all the ingredients in a mixing glass filled with ice. Stir well and strain into a chilled cocktail glass.

Marco's Polo

1½ ounces Irish whiskey
¾ ounce Triple Sec
1 ounce lemon juice
1 scoop crushed ice

Combine all the ingredients in a shaker or blender. Shake or blend and strain into a chilled cocktail glass.

Murphy Fizz

1½ ounces Irish whiskey
1 ounce medium sherry
½ ounce crème de noyaux
½ ounce lemon juice
Cold club soda

Pour all the ingredients, except the soda, into a chilled highball glass with ice cubes. Top off the glass with club soda and stir gently.

Paddy Cocktail

1½ ounces Irish whiskey
¾ ounce sweet vermouth
Several dashes of bitters
1 scoop crushed ice

Mix all the ingredients in a shaker. Pour the mixture into a chilled cocktail glass.

Transamerica

1½ ounces Irish whiskey
1 ounce coconut syrup
3 ounces pineapple juice
1 teaspoon lemon juice
1 scoop crushed ice
Cold club soda

Pour the whiskey, coconut syrup, fruit juices, and crushed ice into a blender. Blend well. Pour the mixture into a chilled highball glass along with several ice cubes. Top off the glass with club soda and stir gently.

SIGNATURE DRINKS

Warm Creamy Bush

THE FILLMORE BAR & GRILL,
SAN FRANCISCO

½ ounce warm coffee
¾ ounce Bailey's Irish Cream
¾ ounce Bushmill's Irish whiskey

Pour all three ingredients into a shot
glass.

HOT DRINKS

Spirited Coffee Lopez

½ ounce Irish whiskey
8 ounces hot coffee
½ ounce coconut cream

Stir all the ingredients in a warm
mug.

Brandy

Brandy is made virtually everywhere wine is produced or fruit is grown.
It is, quite simply put, distilled fermented fruit juice. In most cases, that
fermented fruit juice is wine made from grapes.

The many brandies of the world have specific characteristics, brought
about by variations in distilling techniques and aging procedures, but
basically they are made the same way.

Quality wine-based brandies are produced in France, Italy, Spain,
Germany, Portugal, and the United States, among other countries.
Most every brandy produced in these places will be quite acceptable
when used in the mixed drinks that follow. However, if you are planning
to drink brandy in the more traditional manner—without ice, water, or
other additives, straight up in a snifter—you should probably stick to the
better (and more expensive) brandies.

When it comes to selecting a top quality brandy, the choice narrows.
There are some excellent boutique brands being made in California,
great Spanish brandies, and exquisite brandies called Armagnac made in
southwestern France. But all of these must be held up to the standard
set by Cognac.

What is it that sets Cognac apart from these others? What's so special about Cognac anyway?

Actually there are several things that make this brandy unique. Each of these elements is important on its own, but in combination they can make magic.

Let's start with location. The Cognac producing region is directly north and east of the best vineyards of Bordeaux. But even more important is the fact that its growing area extends to the banks of the Gironde River, which enters from the Atlantic Ocean and opens out into a wide and well-protected waterway. This unusually serene and inviting marine thoroughfare became, early on, a popular trading stop for ships from Holland, Scandinavia, and Britain. The secure Atlantic port of La Rochelle also attracted many vessels.

It is because of the Dutch trade that there was any brandy made in the region at all. (The word itself comes from the Dutch "brandewijn," which means "burnt wine.") In the sixteenth century, Charentais wine merchants, looking for a way to reduce taxes and shipping costs to Holland, decided to distill their tart and rather ordinary white wine, thereby reducing its weight. Since the distillation essentially dehydrated the wine, they theorized that all they would have to do was add water at the other end of the voyage to reconstitute it. Of course this didn't work; what resulted instead was the first Cognac brandy.

Interest in this distilled wine was immediate, especially from the British Isles. Mr. Hine arrived from Dorset, Mr. Martell came from the Channel Islands, and Mr. Hennessy appeared, having traveled from his home in Ireland. The Cognac business had begun. This strong British presence in Cognac has been an extremely important influence on the development of the unique style of the region's brandy. The English obsession with elegance and finesse dictated right from the beginning what Cognac was to become.

Next, let's talk about soil. Although the grapes used to make the rather pedestrian wine that eventually becomes Cognac are considered incidental to the final product, the soil in which they are grown is crucial. (For the record, the grapes are mostly Ugni Blanc, with some Folle Blanche and Colombard mixed in.)

The stony, chalky, lime-rich earth around the town of Cognac and along the southern banks of the Charente River produces the brandy with the greatest finesse and the finest bouquet. This small sub-region, with 32,100 acres of white wine vineyards, is called *grande champagne* and its brandies are Cognac's most highly prized. *Petite champagne* (39,500 acres) is the next best area and it forms a collar around Grande Champagne. *Borderies* (9,900 acres) to the north of the river and to the west of Cognac is next.

These three prime areas are surrounded by three lesser subdivisions, *fins bois, bons bois,* and *bois ordinaires* (154,400 acres total), which produce coarser, earthier, less complex spirits from soils that are heavier and contain less limestone. (By contrast, in Bas-Armagnac—the best section of the only other region that is ever mentioned in the same breath as Cognac—the soil is mostly sandy.)

Another unique aspect of Cognac's soil is the special yeast that grows there, which provides a complete and natural fermentation as well as adding a singular note to the brandy's bouquet.

Technique is another important element in the Cognac story. Nearly all distilled spirits and most brandies (including Armagnac) are made in a continuous or column still, a fast, efficient, and relatively inexpensive process. Cognac, on the other hand, is made in distinctive, onion-shaped copper pot stills.

The distillation procedure, known as *double chauffe,* requires that the wine be distilled twice. This method allows for greater control and also, because the alembic pot stills are small, permits individual growers to distill their own brandy.

There are some 50,000 winegrowers in the Cognac region that was delimited by the French government in 1909. Most of these take their grapes to one of 250 small distilleries or cooperatives in the region. There are 6,000 growers, however, who actually distill their own brandy.

It is a lonely task for those who choose to be their own distillers. The wood fire that keeps the still operating must never be allowed to go out, and it must be tended, day and night, during the many cold weeks of the wintertime distillation period. The resulting Cognac, made in a way that has been handed down from father to son for generations, is produced drop by drop.

Wood is a significant element in the production of Cognac. After distillation the clear, white eau-de-vie is put into small barrels made from oak that comes from the forests of Limousin or Troncais, not far to the northeast of the Cognac district. This oak is highly porous and quite low in the harsh wood tannins that can add an unwelcome bitterness to a young brandy.

There are some 300 cooperages in the Cognac district. Most important, distillers operate and strictly oversee their own barrel-making operation. Cognac barrels are made entirely by hand from staves that have been air-dried for at least four years. The staves are carefully bent with the use of heat and fitted together. No nails may be used in making barrels because, if any metal were to come in contact with the brandy, its effect on flavor could be disastrous.

Now we come to one of the most important of all ingredients in fine Cognac—age. The early brandies of the region were sold fresh from the still—harsh, fiery white liquors that were rather difficult to stomach.

It was the Wars of the Spanish Succession that changed the course of Cognac history. This conflict effectively stopped the brandy trade with England during its twelve-year run. When it ended, in 1713, with the Treaty of Utrecht, merchants discovered that the eau-de-vie they had barreled back in 1701 had turned a lovely golden color and had lost much of its harshness.

Since then, aging has become a standard part of Cognac production. The raw young brandy is put into new oak barrels and stored in a well-ventilated warehouse, known as a *chai*. Then a subtle but remarkable natural procedure begins. The brandy extracts tannins, color, and taste from the wood while, at the same time, the alcohol gradually evaporates through the porous oak. The annual amount of evaporation, called by some "the angel's share," is equivalent to one quarter of the annual world consumption of Cognac. Also, as a result of this, the air around the city of Cognac, where many of these *chais* are located, has a persistent but delightful perfume.

The youngest Cognac that may be sold must have aged for a minimum of two and a half years. The least expensive Cognac, 3-star, is a blend that actually averages closer to five years of age. Some houses call their 3-star brandies "V.S." (Very Superior). Most Cognacs of this type cost about $20.

The next step on the age scale is V.S.O.P. (Very Superior Old Pale), which by law must be at least four and one-half years old, but is usually closer to seven to ten years of age. These Cognacs cost in the neighborhood of $30.

Next comes X.O. (Extra Old) or Napoleon. The law says these must contain no brandies that are less than five and one-half years old, but most of them average between fifteen and twenty-five years of age. You can expect to ante up about $50 for these.

Finally there are the Grande Réserves. These are not defined by law, but most of them average fifty years of age. Some of the best known of this group are Hennessy Paradis, Martell Extra, Remy Martin Louis VIII, and Delamain Réserve de la Famille. They range in price from $125 to $450, depending on the elaborateness of the container.

Incidentally, Cognac ages only when it is in oak. Unlike wine, once brandy is bottled it doesn't change; it neither deteriorates nor improves.

The last and ultimately the most important aspect of Cognac production is people. The Cognacais take their local brandy seriously and they are willing to expend the extra effort required to make it special. There is the vast network of growers, the hard-working distillers, and, most remarkable of all, the tasters.

Each of the 320 Cognac houses has a head taster on staff. He is the keeper of the flame. His taste buds are responsible for the success (or failure) of the house product. His job is to taste and judge the thousands of samples brought to him each year by local growers and distillers. From these he selects and buys sound brandies that, eventually, will find their way into one of the house Cognacs.

Each year, although there may be dramatic differences in the vintage, the head taster and his staff must construct a blend that is completely consistent with the house style. Cognacs are not vintaged because they represent a blend of brandies from many different years. Thus, although two bottles of Cognac may have been blended several years apart, there will be nothing on the label to distinguish them from each other and, ideally, they will be identical in flavor.

Each house, not unlike key champagne producers, has its own distinctive style. A consumer who enjoys a glass of a particular Cognac in Paris should be able to buy the same brandy in Chicago and have the identical sensory experience. This distinctive characteristic of good Cognac is the result of the head taster's talents.

When the master taster decides to make a super-premium Cognac he goes to the *paradis,* the cellar where the oldest brandies are stored. From the barrels there he selects a blend—the oldest Cognacs for complexity and oaky richness, some others for smoothness and finesse, perhaps younger ones for fruit and liveliness. The result is superb, a true artistic expression.

Cognac has been called "the distilled quintessence of wine." In fact, there is no more perfect finale to a succession of good wines than a toasty, rich, softly fruity, intensely perfumed few ounces of this unique liquid. Swirling shimmering amber up the walls of a graceful glass, one can appreciate all the things that make this elegant brandy so special: the location of its vineyards, the Charente soil, the time-honored techniques, the wood, the aging, and the people who have devoted their lives to making Cognac the world's finest brandy.

It used to be that the only brandy made in the United States was the mass-produced kind, brewed in tall column stills. These brandies, which still represent the lion's share of the domestic brandy market, are usually simple and a little sweet, pleasant in mixed drinks and for cooking.

But in the last decade some new and different brandies have begun to appear. A few hardy souls have attempted to reproduce the hand-made, oak-aged, pot still brandies that have made Cognac so renowned, and some have also set about to make serious pomace brandies.

Although limited to very few producers and tiny production, the boutique brandy business is beginning to be noticed and appreciated by consumers. The reason for this growing interest is that brandies have appeared that can hold their own in the company of some of the best distilled products of Europe.

One of the world's best brandies is made from the distillation of fermented apple juice. It is made in Normandy, where there are many more apple trees than grape vines, and called Calvados. Apple brandies are made in other places as well. Versions made in the United States are often called "applejack."

Another recent trend has been the manufacture of flavored brandies. These are generally young, wine-based brandies with fruit flavorings added. Although not particularly interesting on their own, these products work well in mixed drinks.

Finally, I would be remiss if I did not mention pomace brandies. Pomace is a term that includes the pits, stems, skins, and pulps of the grape. Pomace brandies are the less-polished stepsisters of the brandies mentioned above. They are made by distilling the remnants of the winemaking process, the pomace, and they can be strong and fiery. The best known pomace brandies are grappa and marc.

Grappa is an unaged brandy made from the residue of winemaking. When grapes are pressed in the beginning stages of the winemaking process, the juice is put into a fermenting tank where it continues the dramatic progression of transformation from grape juice to wine. Left behind, after the pressing, is a dense mass of grape skins, pulp, and seeds plus stems and leaves. This residue, or pomace, is called *vinaccie* in Italian.

Since the grapes are not pressed so hard that all the juice is extracted, the remains still contain liquid. This pomace can be fermented and then distilled. The result, in Italy, is called grappa. In France, it is called *marc* (pronounced "marr").

Grappa is directly descended from the medicines and digestive tonics of the Middle Ages. It was a rough, completely unrefined country brandy, almost like moonshine, that was until 1933 sold directly from the barrel. In that year, it was decreed that this traditional spirit must be bottled.

Today's grappa can be very different. Yes, there still is plenty of fiery grappa around that tastes like a fermented compost heap, but the real action is with carefully made, premium grappas. This whole new type of grappa is what has captured the interest of connoisseurs. Modern grappa is carefully made from the moment the grapes are first crushed. The pomace is only lightly pressed, kept fresh, and quickly distilled—preferably within six hours—to minimize oxidation and to preserve fresh perfumes and flavors.

In the old days, very little attention was paid to the variety of grapes used to make grappa. Whatever residue was left after winemaking was combined and eventually processed. Pomace from various crushings were customarily distilled together. The result was a distillate that was high in alcohol but missing specific flavor and complexity.

Today, a sizable number of the best grappas are made from an individual grape variety, and frequently they derive from a particular vineyard. A few of them are even vintaged. Many of the finest versions carry some very well-known wine names. Lungarotti, Ceretto, Gaja, Marchesi de Gresy, Monte Vertine, and many other notable Italian wineries now release their own branded grappas.

There are grappas made from Nebbiolo (the red grape from Barolo and Barbaresco), Sangiovese (the red grape from Chianti), Chardonnay, Barbera, Moscato, and Prosecco (the sweet white grape that is made into sparkling wine in the Veneto). Some grappas are made from pomace that comes from specific cuvées for certain wines such as Chianti Classico (a blend of Sangiovese, Canaiolo, Malvasia, and Trebbiano) or Rubesco Torgiano (Sangiovese, Canaiolo, Trebbiano, and Ciliegiolo), while others are vineyard designated such as Ceretto's grappa from Brunate, a Barolo vineyard.

Until 1970, winemakers had stills on their own property and made their own grappas. That year, however, a law was passed forbidding distillation on a winery estate. Most wineries either arranged to have their pomace turned into grappa by a reliable local distiller, or they built their own distillery off the property but nearby.

The growth of independent distillers and the increased popularity of grappa in the United States has belatedly introduced consumers to an extremely important name—Nonino. This remarkable family has been distilling grappa in Friuli since 1897.

Nonino has been a leader in the metamorphosis of the grappa industry. In the 1960s, when grappa first became widely known among consumers and sales began to increase, most distillers switched from the slow, discontinuous stills—similar in style to the pot stills used in the production of Cognac—to speedy continuous column stills. They managed to produce the quantity of spirits the market demanded, but quality slipped significantly. The Noninos, on the other hand, added more costly *bagna-Maria* (double boiler) stills and decided to focus on quality.

In 1974 Nonino introduced the first varietal grappa, made from Picolit, Friuli's rarest grape. It was packaged in a graceful, hand-blown clear glass cruet designed by one of Italy's best architects. This bottle, topped with a plated stopper, has become the Nonino trademark.

The Noninos have been fastidious in encouraging the cultivation of varieties that are in danger of becoming extinct. They now produce a whole line of grappas from these obscure varieties: Fragolino, Ribolla, Tacelenghe, Verduzzo di Ramandolo, Pignola, and Schiopettino. The company has also invented a completely new drink called *ue* (the Italian word for "grape"), which is made by distilling whole, uncrushed grapes.

There are a number of special grappas on the market that contain various kinds of fruit or herbs. After several months of steeping, the brandy will begin to pick up the flavors of whatever it contains. Many northern Italians like to make their own flavored grappas. They buy a good clean grappa and pour it into a wide-mouthed jar, add fresh fruit, seal it, and allow it to stand for a year or two. Several American restaurants have amassed fine collections of this type of grappa.

In the past, grappas were never aged; they were sold almost right out of the still. The new trend is to age the top-of-the-line grappa for a year or two in oak or some other type of wood. This mellows and softens the brandy's harshness.

In addition to the lovely Nonino grappas, there are a number of other fine, high-quality versions that I have tried. Here are my favorites:

- *Lungarotti Rubesco* is distilled from the pomace of this famous Umbrian wine. It is rich and clean with complex, refined licorice flavors.

- *Zardetto* makes a stunningly soft and elegant grappa from Prosecco grapes grown in the Cartizze section of the Veneto.

- *Andrea da Ponte* makes another lovely Prosecco grappa that is aged three years in wood.

- *Ceretto* grappa is made entirely from Nebbiolo grapes grown in Piedmont for the production of Barolo and Barbaresco. This spirit is spicy and dry with an appealing herbal quality.

- *Ceretto Grappa delle Brunate* is also produced from Nebbiolo. The difference is that this earthy, rich, and herbal spirit is made from the fruit of one single vineyard. The Ceretto firm makes grappa in its own distillery.

- *Marchesi di Gresy Grappa Martinenga* (1985) is made from Nebbiolo grown in the Martinenga Vineyard in Barbaresco. This exquisite grappa, currently my favorite, is soft and rich with a lovely peppery quality.

- *Gaja Costa Rusi* is a crisp and austere Nebbiolo grappa made from a single Barbaresco vineyard.

Other excellent grappas include *L'Aquavite de Castello; Castello di Querceto* (Tuscany); *Grappa di Capezzana* (Tuscany); *Monte Vertine* (Tuscany); *Conte di Cavour* (Piedmont); *Zeni* (Friuli); *Jermann* (Friuli); and *Castello di Gabbiano* (Tuscany).

Because of its current market success, grappa can be quite expensive. Regular, mass-produced grappas are in the $18 to $25 range. But the special small-production grappas mentioned above can cost between $30 and $80 a bottle.

Those traveling in the north of Italy will quickly become aware of grappa in restaurants and wine shops. A delightful side trip in the Veneto is Bassano del Grappa, a charming small city that has been the traditional center of the grappa trade. The town has a picturesque wooden bridge that crosses the Brenta River and there always seems to be the perfume of grappa in the air.

As imported grappa became more and more popular, some American producers decided to make grappas of their own. The results have been quite good. Bonny Doon, Creekside, and St. George Spirits have made very attractive versions.

CLASSICS

Betsy Ross

1½ ounces brandy
1½ ounces port
1 egg yolk
1 teaspoon sugar syrup,
    or to taste
Several dashes of curaçao
Several dashes of bitters
1 scoop crushed ice
Freshly ground nutmeg

Mix all the ingredients, except the nutmeg, in a shaker. Strain the mixture into a chilled cocktail glass. Top with a sprinkle of nutmeg.

Bob Danby

1 ounce brandy
2 to 3 ounces Dubonnet rouge

Put both ingredients in a mixing glass filled with ice cubes. Stir well and strain into a chilled cocktail glass.

Brandy Alexander

1½ ounces brandy
1 ounce crème de cacao
1 ounce heavy cream
1 scoop crushed ice

Mix all the ingredients in a shaker. Strain the mixture into a chilled cocktail glass.

Brandy Daisy I

2 ounces brandy
1¼ ounces lemon juice
½ teaspoon sugar
¼ ounce grenadine
Crushed ice

Mix all the ingredients in a shaker. Shake well and pour into a large cocktail glass.

Brandy Daisy II

2 to 3 ounces brandy
Juice of ½ lemon
½ ounce raspberry syrup or
    grenadine
1 teaspoon sugar syrup
1 scoop crushed ice
Cold club soda
Dash of Pernod
Peach slice or orange slice
Pineapple stick
1 maraschino cherry

Mix the brandy, lemon juice, syrups, and ice in a shaker. Pour the mixture into a chilled wineglass and add additional ice. Stir briskly until the glass is frosted. Top off with club soda and a dash of Pernod. Garnish with the fruit.

Brandy Eggnog

2 to 3 ounces brandy
½ ounce sugar syrup, or to taste
1 cup milk
1 egg
1 scoop crushed ice
Freshly grated nutmeg

Mix all the ingredients, except the nutmeg, in a shaker. Strain the mixture into a chilled highball glass. Sprinkle the nutmeg on top.

Brandy Manhattan

2 ounces brandy
½ ounce sweet or dry vermouth
Dash of bitters
1 maraschino cherry

In a mixing glass, stir the brandy, vermouth, and bitters. Strain the mixture into a chilled cocktail glass and garnish with the cherry.

Brandy Old-Fashioned

1 sugar cube
Several dashes of bitters
3 ounces brandy
Lemon peel

Place the sugar cube in a chilled old-fashioned glass. Add bitters and a dash of cold water and stir until the sugar cube is dissolved. Add ice cubes and brandy. Twist the lemon peel over the drink and drop it in.

Brandy Sour

2 ounces brandy
1 ounce lemon juice
½ ounce orange juice (optional)
1 teaspoon sugar syrup, or to taste
1 scoop crushed ice
1 maraschino cherry

Combine all the ingredients, except the cherry, in a shaker. Mix well and strain into a chilled whiskey sour glass. Garnish with the cherry.

CREATIVE CONCOCTIONS

Alabama

1 ounce brandy
1 ounce curaçao
½ ounce lime juice
½ teaspoon sugar syrup, or to
    taste
1 scoop crushed ice
Orange peel

Combine all the ingredients, except the orange peel, in a shaker. Mix well and strain into a chilled cocktail glass. Twist the orange peel over the drink and drop it in.

American Rose

1½ ounces brandy
1 teaspoon grenadine
½ fresh peach, peeled and mashed
Several dashes of Pernod
1 scoop crushed ice
Champagne or sparkling wine

Mix all the ingredients, except the champagne, in a shaker. Pour the mixture into a chilled wineglass. Top off with the champagne and stir gently.

Apple Blossom

1½ ounces brandy
1 ounce apple juice
1 teaspoon lemon juice
1 scoop crushed ice
Lemon slice

Mix all the ingredients, except the lemon slice, in a shaker. Strain the mixture into a chilled cocktail glass and garnish with the lemon slice.

Apple Brandy Cooler

2 ounces brandy
1 ounce light rum
4 ounces apple juice
½ ounce lime juice
1 teaspoon sugar syrup, or to taste
1 scoop crushed ice
1 teaspoon dark rum
Lime slice

Mix all the ingredients, except the dark rum and lime slice, in a shaker. Pour the mixture into a chilled collins glass. Top off with a float of dark rum and garnish with the lime slice.

Banana Peel

1½ ounces brandy
¾ ounce crème de banane
½ ounce lemon juice
1 scoop crushed ice
Cold club soda
Lemon wedge
Banana slice

Mix all the ingredients, except the soda and fruit, in a shaker. Pour the mixture into a chilled collins glass. Top off with the club soda and stir gently. Decorate with the lemon wedge and the banana slice.

Beach Street Cooler

1½ ounces brandy
½ ounce curaçao
½ ounce lemon juice
1 scoop crushed ice
Cold cola

Mix all the ingredients, except the cola, in a shaker. Pour the mixture into a chilled collins glass. Top off with the cola.

Beau's Sister

1½ ounces brandy
1 ounce white crème de menthe
1 ounce heavy cream
1 scoop crushed ice

Combine all the ingredients in a shaker. Mix well and pour into a chilled cocktail glass.

Blackberry Slammer

1 ounce Cognac or other brandy
½ ounce blackberry brandy
1 ounce coffee brandy
½ ounce dry vermouth
½ ounce amaretto
1 ounce lemon juice
1 scoop crushed ice

Mix all the ingredients in a shaker. Pour the mixture into a chilled brandy snifter.

Bombay

1 ounce brandy
1 ounce dry vermouth
½ ounce sweet vermouth
½ teaspoon curaçao
Dash of Pernod
1 scoop crushed ice
Orange slice

Mix all the ingredients, except the orange slice, in a shaker. Pour the mixture into a chilled old-fashioned glass. Garnish with the orange slice.

Bosom Caresser

1½ ounces brandy
½ ounce Triple Sec or curaçao
1 egg yolk
1 teaspoon grenadine
1 scoop crushed ice

Mix all the ingredients in a shaker. Strain the mixture into a chilled cocktail glass.

Bowdoin Appleball

2 ounces apple brandy
Cold ginger ale or club soda
Lemon peel

Pour the apple brandy into a chilled
highball glass with several ice cubes.
Top off the glass with ginger ale or
club soda. Stir gently. Twist the
lemon peel over the drink and drop
it in.

Bracer Highball

1½ ounces brandy
¼ ounce anisette
1 dash of bitters
½ teaspoon sugar
½ ounce lemon juice
1 egg
Cold club soda

In a shaker with crushed ice, mix all
the ingredients, except the club
soda. Strain the mixture into a highball glass. Top off with club soda.

Brandied Apricot

Granulated sugar
1½ ounces brandy
½ ounce apricot brandy
1 ounce lemon juice
Orange peel

Press the moistened rim of a cocktail
glass into sugar. In a shaker with
crushed ice, mix the brandies and
lemon juice. Pour the mixture into
the sugar-rimmed glass and garnish
with the orange peel.

Brandied Apricot Flip

1½ ounces brandy
½ ounce apricot brandy
1 egg
1 teaspoon sugar
1 scoop crushed ice
Freshly grated nutmeg

Mix all the ingredients, except the
nutmeg, in a shaker. Pour the mixture into a cocktail glass and sprinkle
the nutmeg on top.

Brandied Banana Collins

1½ ounces brandy
1 ounce crème de banane
1 ounce lemon juice
Cold club soda
Lemon wedge
Banana slice

Pour the brandy, crème de banane,
and lemon juice into a shaker. Mix
well and strain into a tall glass. Top
off the glass with ice cubes and the
club soda. Garnish with the lemon
wedge and banana slice.

Brandied Cordial Médoc

1½ ounces brandy
½ ounce Cordial Médoc
½ ounce lemon juice
Crushed ice
Orange peel

Mix all the ingredients, except the orange peel, in a shaker. Pour the mixture into a cocktail glass and garnish with the orange peel.

Brandied Ginger

1½ ounces brandy
½ ounce ginger-flavored brandy
¼ ounce lime juice
¼ ounce orange juice

Combine all the ingredients in a shaker with crushed ice. Shake well and strain into a cocktail glass.

Brandied Madeira

1 ounce brandy
1 ounce Madeira
½ ounce dry vermouth
Lemon twist

In a mixing glass, stir the brandy, Madeira, and dry vermouth. Pour the mixture into a cocktail glass and garnish with the lemon twist.

Brandied Peach Fizz

1½ ounces brandy
½ ounce peach-flavored brandy
½ ounce lemon juice
½ teaspoon sugar
¼ ounce banana liqueur
Cold club soda
Peach slice

Combine all the ingredients, except the club soda and peach slice, in a shaker with crushed ice. Mix well and strain into a tall glass. Top off with the soda and several ice cubes. Garnish with the peach slice.

Brandied Peach Sling

1½ ounces brandy
½ ounce peach-flavored brandy
1 ounce lemon juice
1 teaspoon sugar
Chilled club soda
Lemon twist
Peach slice

In a shaker with crushed ice, mix all the ingredients, except the soda and fruit. Strain the mixture into a tall glass with fresh ice cubes. Top off with the soda. Garnish with the lemon twist and peach slice.

Brandied Port

¾ ounce brandy
¾ ounce tawny port
¼ ounce maraschino liqueur
¾ ounce lemon juice
Crushed ice
Orange slice

Mix all the ingredients, except the orange slice, in a shaker. Strain the mixture into a cocktail glass and garnish with the orange slice.

Brandt

2 ounces brandy
½ ounce white crème de menthe
2 dashes of bitters
Lemon twist

In a mixing glass with ice, stir the brandy, crème de menthe, and bitters. Pour the mixture into a cocktail glass and garnish with the lemon twist.

Brandy Apricot Frappe

Finely crushed ice
¾ ounce brandy
¼ ounce crème de noyaux
½ ounce apricot-flavored brandy

Pack a cocktail glass with crushed ice, building the ice into a snow cone. Stir the ingredients in a mixing glass and pour over the crushed ice.

Brandy Berry Fix

1 teaspoon superfine sugar
2 ounces brandy
¼ ounce strawberry liqueur
¾ ounce lemon juice
1 scoop crushed ice
Lemon wedge
Several fresh strawberries

In a highball glass, dissolve the sugar in a splash of water. Pour in the brandy, strawberry liqueur, and lemon juice. Fill the glass with crushed ice and stir well. Garnish with the lemon wedge and the fresh strawberries.

Brandy Blizzard

1½ ounces brandy
¼ ounce white crème de menthe
½ ounce lemon juice
1 scoop crushed ice
Cold ginger ale
Several seedless grapes

Mix all the ingredients, except the ginger ale and grapes, in a shaker. Pour the mixture into a chilled highball glass. Top off the glass with ginger ale and stir gently. Garnish with the seedless grapes.

Brandy Champerelle

½ ounce brandy
½ ounce curaçao
½ ounce yellow Chartreuse
½ ounce anisette

Chill all the ingredients. Carefully pour each ingredient, in the order listed, into a chilled sherry glass. Each layer should float on the one beneath it. To properly layer, slowly pour the liqueurs over the back of a spoon.

Brandy Cooler

2½ ounces brandy
Cold ginger ale
Lemon peel, cut in a spiral

Pour the brandy into a glass filled with ice cubes. Top off with ginger ale and garnish with the lemon spiral.

Brandy Crusta

Lemon wedge
Sugar
1½ ounces brandy
¼ ounce maraschino liqueur
Dash of bitters
¼ ounce lemon juice
½ ounce orange curaçao

Moisten the rim of a glass with the lemon wedge. Press the rim into sugar, then drop the lemon wedge into the glass. In a shaker with crushed ice, mix the rest of the ingredients. Strain the mixture into the prepared glass.

Brandy Fancy

2 ounces brandy
¼ ounce maraschino liqueur
Dash of orange bitters
Dash of bitters

In a mixing glass with ice, stir all the ingredients. Pour the mixture into a fresh cocktail glass.

Brandy Fix

2 to 3 ounces brandy
1 teaspoon sugar syrup
1 teaspoon water
Juice of ½ lemon

Pour all the ingredients into a chilled old-fashioned glass. Fill the glass with ice and stir until frosty.

Brandy Fizz

1½ ounces brandy
1¼ ounces lemon juice
1 teaspoon superfine sugar
Cold club soda
2 dashes of yellow Chartreuse
   (optional)

In a shaker with crushed ice, mix the brandy, lemon juice, and sugar. Strain the mixture into a tall collins glass. Top off with club soda and fresh ice. If desired, float the Chartreuse on top.

Brandy Float

1½ ounces brandy
Cold club soda

Place several ice cubes in an old-fashioned glass. Fill the glass three quarters full with the club soda. Top off with a float of brandy.

Brandy Frappe

1½ ounces brandy
1 ounce dark rum
½ ounce lemon or lime juice
1 teaspoon orgeat
1 egg yolk
1 scoop crushed ice

In a blender, mix all the ingredients until slushy. Spoon the blend into a chilled wineglass.

Brandy Gump Cocktail

1½ ounces brandy
1¼ ounces lemon juice
¼ ounce grenadine
1 scoop of crushed ice

Mix all the ingredients in a shaker. Strain the mixture into a cocktail glass.

Brandy Julep

6 mint leaves
1 teaspoon sugar syrup
1 scoop finely crushed ice
Brandy
Mint sprig
Confectioners' sugar

Place the mint leaves in a chilled double old-fashioned glass. Add syrup and a small amount of cold water. Muddle leaves until bruised, then fill the glass with crushed ice. Top off with brandy and stir until the glass is frosted. Add more ice, if necessary. Garnish with the mint sprig and dust with the sugar.

Brandy Melba

1½ ounces brandy
½ ounce peach schnapps
¼ ounce raspberry liqueur
½ ounce lemon juice
Several dashes of orange bitters
1 scoop crushed ice
Peach slice

Mix all the ingredients, except the peach slice, in a shaker. Strain the mixture into a chilled cocktail glass and garnish with the peach slice.

Brandy Mint Fizz

1½ ounces brandy
¼ ounce white crème de menthe
¼ ounce light crème de cacao
¾ ounce lemon juice
½ teaspoon sugar
1 scoop crushed ice
Cold club soda
Mint sprigs

Mix all the ingredients, except the soda and mint sprigs, in a shaker. Strain the mixture into a tall glass. Top off with the club soda and ice. Garnish with the fresh mint sprigs.

Brandy Puff

1½ ounces brandy
3 ounces milk
Chilled club soda

Pour the brandy into a chilled highball glass with several ice cubes. Add the milk and top off with the club soda.

Brandy Punch

2 ounces brandy
¼ ounce orange curaçao
¼ ounce rum
½ teaspoon superfine sugar
Squirt of club soda

Put all the ingredients, except the club soda, in a highball glass. Fill the glass with ice and top off with the club soda.

Brandy Sangaree

½ teaspoon superfine sugar
Dash of water
2 to 3 ounces brandy
Freshly ground nutmeg

Dissolve the sugar with a little water in a double old-fashioned glass. Add ice cubes and brandy. Stir well and top with a sprinkle of the nutmeg.

Brandy Swizzle

1½ ounces lime juice
1 teaspoon sugar
Cold club soda
1 scoop crushed ice
2 dashes of bitters
2 ounces brandy
Lime peel

In a tall glass, mix the lime juice, the sugar, and 2 ounces of club soda. Fill the glass with crushed ice and stir well. Add the bitters and the brandy. Top off with club soda and stir vigorously. Garnish with the lime peel.

Brandy Zoom

1 teaspoon honey
Hot water
¼ ounce cream
2 ounces brandy

In a mixing glass, dissolve the honey in a splash of hot water. Pour the honey into a shaker with the cream, brandy, and crushed ice. Shake well and pour into a cocktail glass.

Chicago

Lemon wedge
Superfine sugar
1½ ounces brandy
Dash of curaçao
Dash of bitters
Sparkling wine or champagne

Using the lemon wedge, moisten the rim of a chilled wineglass. Roll the rim in sugar until it is evenly coated. Mix the brandy, curaçao, and bitters with crushed ice in a mixing glass. Strain the mixture into the wineglass. Top off with cold champagne.

Coffee Cocktail

1½ ounces brandy
¾ ounce port
Several dashes of curaçao

Several dashes of sugar syrup
1 egg yolk
1 scoop crushed ice
Freshly ground nutmeg

Mix all the ingredients, except the nutmeg, in a shaker. Strain the mixture into a chilled cocktail glass. Sprinkle the nutmeg on top.

Columbia

1½ ounces brandy
½ ounce sweet vermouth
¼ ounce lemon juice
1 teaspoon grenadine
Dash of bitters
1 scoop crushed ice

Combine all the ingredients in a shaker. Mix well and strain into a chilled cocktail glass.

Continental

1½ ounces brandy
1 ounce gin
1 teaspoon dry vermouth
Lemon peel or green olive

Combine the brandy, gin, and vermouth in a mixing glass with ice cubes. Stir well and strain into a chilled cocktail glass. Twist the lemon peel over the drink and drop in, or garnish with the cocktail olive.

Cool Java

1 ounce brandy
1 ounce Triple Sec
1 ounce cold black coffee
1 scoop crushed ice

Mix all the ingredients in a shaker. Pour the mixture into a chilled parfait glass.

Deauville

1 ounce brandy
¾ ounce apple brandy
½ ounce Triple Sec
½ ounce lemon juice
1 scoop crushed ice

Mix all the ingredients in a shaker. Strain the mixture into a chilled cocktail glass.

Fantasio

1 ounce brandy
¾ ounce dry vermouth
1 teaspoon white crème de cacao
1 teaspoon maraschino liqueur
1 scoop crushed ice

Mix all the ingredients in a shaker. Pour the mixture into a chilled cocktail glass.

Foghorn

Makes 2 servings

4 ounces brandy
2 ounces curaçao
1 egg white
2 scoops crushed ice
Freshly ground nutmeg

Mix all the ingredients, except the nutmeg, in a shaker. Pour the mixture into chilled cocktail glasses. Sprinkle the nutmeg on top.

Foxhound

1½ ounces brandy
½ ounce cranberry juice
1 teaspoon kümmel
1 teaspoon lemon juice
1 scoop crushed ice
Lemon slice

Mix all the ingredients, except the lemon slice, in a shaker. Pour the mixture into a chilled old-fashioned glass. Garnish with the lemon slice.

French Green Dragon

1½ ounces brandy
1½ ounces green Chartreuse

In a shaker with crushed ice, mix the brandy and Chartreuse. Strain the mixture into a chilled cocktail glass.

Frozen Fuzzy

1½ ounces brandy
½ ounce peach schnapps
4 ounces orange juice
1 scoop crushed ice

Mix all the ingredients in a shaker. Pour the mixture into a chilled double old-fashioned glass.

Gazette

1½ ounces brandy
1 ounce sweet vermouth
1 teaspoon lemon juice
1 teaspoon sugar syrup
1 scoop crushed ice

Mix all the ingredients in a shaker or blender. Pour the mixture into a chilled cocktail glass.

Georgia Peach Fizz

1½ ounces brandy
½ ounce peach brandy
½ ounce lemon juice
1 teaspoon crème de banane
1 teaspoon sugar syrup
1 scoop crushed ice
Cold club soda
Fresh or brandied peach slice

Mix all the ingredients, except the soda and peach slice, in a shaker or blender. Pour the mixture into a chilled collins glass. Top off with the club soda and stir gently. Garnish with the peach slice.

Gold Dragon

1½ ounces yellow Chartreuse
1½ ounces brandy
1 scoop crushed ice
Lemon peel

In a mixer, shake the Chartreuse, brandy, and ice. Strain the mixture into a chilled cocktail glass. Garnish with the lemon peel.

Goodbye

Makes 2 servings

2 ounces brandy
2 ounces sloe gin
½ ounce lemon juice
1 egg white
2 scoops crushed ice

Mix all the ingredients in a shaker. Strain the mixture into chilled cocktail glasses.

Island Milk

2 ounces brandy
½ ounce dark rum
6 ounces milk
1 teaspoon sugar syrup, or to taste
1 scoop crushed ice
Powdered cinnamon or freshly
    ground nutmeg

Mix all the ingredients, except the cinnamon or nutmeg, in a shaker. Pour the mixture into a chilled highball glass. Sprinkle with cinnamon or nutmeg.

Japan Town

2 ounces brandy
¼ ounce orgeat
¼ ounce lime juice
Dash of bitters
1 scoop crushed ice
Lime peel

Mix all the ingredients, except the lime peel, in a shaker. Strain the mixture into a chilled cocktail glass. Twist the lime peel over the drink and drop it in.

Java Flip

1 ounce brandy
½ ounce port
4 ounces coffee
½ teaspoon sugar syrup
1 egg
1 scoop crushed ice
Freshly ground nutmeg

Mix all the ingredients, except the nutmeg, in a shaker. Pour the mixture into a chilled wineglass and sprinkle with the nutmeg.

Kiss From Heaven

1 ounce brandy
¾ ounce Drambuie
¾ ounce dry vermouth

Stir all the ingredients in a mixing glass with ice. Pour the mixture into a chilled cocktail glass.

La Jolla

1½ ounces brandy
½ ounce crème de banane
¼ ounce lemon juice
1 teaspoon orange juice
1 scoop crushed ice

Combine all the ingredients in a shaker. Mix well and strain into a chilled cocktail glass.

Lifesaver

1½ ounces brandy
¾ ounce cherry brandy or cherry
   liqueur
½ ounce curaçao
½ lemon juice
¼ ounce grenadine
1 teaspoon sugar syrup
1 scoop crushed ice

Mix all the ingredients in a shaker.
Strain the mixture into a chilled
cocktail glass.

Loudspeaker

1 ounce brandy
1 ounce gin
¼ ounce Triple Sec
½ ounce lemon juice
1 scoop crushed ice

Combine all the ingredients in a
shaker. Mix well and strain into a
cocktail glass.

Montecito

1½ ounces brandy
½ ounce Triple Sec
Cold cola
Lemon slice

Pour the brandy and Triple Sec over
ice in a chilled collins glass. Top off
with the cola and garnish with the
lemon slice.

Olympic Lady

1½ ounces brandy
1 ounce apricot brandy
½ ounce amaretto
1 scoop crushed ice

Mix all the ingredients in a shaker.
Strain the mixture into a chilled
cocktail glass.

Santa Barbara Bracer

Makes 2 servings

2 ounces brandy
2 ounces anisette
1 egg white
Crushed ice

Mix all the ingredients in a shaker.
Pour the mixture into 2 chilled cocktail glasses.

Southern Belle

1½ ounces brandy
¾ ounce Southern Comfort
½ ounce lemon juice
Several dashes of orange bitters
1 scoop crushed ice

Combine all the ingredients in a
shaker. Mix well and strain into a
chilled cocktail glass.

SIGNATURE DRINKS

Anatole Coffee

LOEWS ANATOLE HOTEL, DALLAS

½ ounce brandy
½ ounce coffee liqueur
½ ounce hazelnut liqueur
Cold black coffee
Whipped cream
Chocolate shavings

Mix the brandy, liqueurs, and coffee in a blender with ice. Pour the mixture into a chilled wineglass. Top off with the whipped cream and chocolate shavings.

Boss McClure Cocktail

VISTA INTERNATIONAL HOTEL,
WASHINGTON, D.C.

1 ounce brandy
1 ounce gin
½ ounce orange curaçao
½ ounce apricot liqueur
1 scoop crushed ice
Lemon twist

Mix all the ingredients, except the lemon twist, in a shaker. Strain the mixture into a chilled cocktail glass and garnish with the lemon twist.

The Raphael Kiss

RAPHAEL HOTEL, CHICAGO

4 ounces vanilla ice cream
2 ounces chocolate ice cream
½ ounce coffee liqueur
½ ounce brandy
½ ounce cream
Lime wedge
Cinnamon and sugar mixture
½ ounce Sambuca

In a blender, mix the ice creams, coffee liqueur, brandy, and cream. Prepare a wineglass by moistening the rim with a lime wedge and then coating the rim with the cinnamon-sugar mixture. Pour the blended ingredients into the wineglass. Float the Sambuca on top.

TROPICAL DRINKS

Sunshine Colada

¾ ounce brandy
1 ounce coconut cream
1½ ounces orange juice
½ ounce cream
½ ounce orange liqueur
1 cup ice

Combine all the ingredients in a blender and blend until smooth. Pour the blend into a chilled parfait glass.

HOT DRINKS

Alhambra Royale

1 cup hot chocolate
1 orange peel
1½ ounces brandy
1 tablespoon whipped cream

Fill a mug nearly to the brim with hot chocolate. Add the orange peel. Warm the brandy in a ladle over hot water. Ignite the brandy and, as it blazes, pour it into the hot chocolate. Stir well and top with a dollop of the whipped cream.

Café Diablo

Makes 4 servings

2 cinnamon sticks
8 whole cloves
6 whole coffee beans
2 ounces brandy or Cognac
1 ounce Cointreau or Triple Sec
1 ounce hot curaçao
1 pint hot, strong black coffee

Place all the ingredients, except the coffee, in a chafing dish. Warm the contents over low, direct heat. Ignite and allow to blaze for a few seconds. Add the coffee and mix well. Pour into mugs.

Hot Brandy Flip

2 ounces brandy (rum, gin, or
    whiskey may also be used)
1 whole egg
1 teaspoon sugar syrup, or to taste
Freshly ground nutmeg

Mix the brandy, egg, and sugar
syrup in a saucepan. Heat and pour
into a warm mug or glass. Sprinkle
with the nutmeg.

APPLEJACK

Apple Buck

1½ ounces applejack
½ ounce lemon juice
1 teaspoon ginger-flavored brandy
1 scoop crushed ice
Cold ginger ale
Preserved ginger

Mix all the ingredients, except the
ginger ale and ginger, in a shaker.
Pour the mixture into a chilled highball glass. Top off with ginger ale.
Stir gently and garnish with the
ginger.

Apple Sidecar

1½ ounces applejack
½ ounce Triple Sec
½ ounce lime juice
1 scoop crushed ice

Mix all the ingredients in a shaker.
Pour the mixture into a chilled cocktail glass.

Apple Blow Fizz

Makes 2 servings

5½ ounces applejack
½ teaspoon lemon juice
2 teaspoons sugar syrup, or to
    taste
1 egg white
1 scoop crushed ice
Cold club soda

Mix all the ingredients, except the
soda, in a shaker. Pour the mixture
into 2 chilled highball glasses with
ice cubes. Top off the glasses with
the club soda and stir gently.

Apple Fizz

2 ounces applejack
4 ounces apple juice
Dash of lime juice
Club soda
Lime slice

Put all the ingredients, except the lime slice, in a chilled collins glass filled with ice cubes. Stir well and garnish with the lime slice.

Applejack Collins

2 ounces applejack
1 ounce lemon juice
1 teaspoon sugar syrup
Several dashes of orange bitters
1 scoop crushed ice
Cold club soda
Lemon slice

Mix all the ingredients, except the soda and lemon slice, in a shaker or blender. Pour the mixture into a chilled collins glass. Top off with the club soda and stir gently. Garnish with the lemon slice.

Applejack Manhattan

1 3/4 ounces applejack
3/4 ounce sweet vermouth
Dash of orange bitters
1 maraschino cherry

Mix the applejack, vermouth, and bitters in a glass with ice cubes. Stir well and strain into a chilled cocktail glass. Garnish with the cherry.

Big Apple

2 ounces applejack
1/2 ounce amaretto
3 ounces apple juice
1 tablespoon applesauce
Ground cinnamon

Mix all the ingredients, except the cinnamon, in a blender with ice. Blend until smooth. Pour the blend into a chilled parfait glass and sprinkle with the cinnamon before serving.

Central Park

1 ounce applejack
1 ounce apricot brandy
1/2 ounce gin
1/2 ounce orange juice
1 scoop crushed ice
Several dashes of grenadine

Mix all the ingredients, except the grenadine, in a shaker. Strain the mixture into a chilled cocktail glass. Top off with a grenadine float.

Corpse Reviver

1½ ounces applejack
¾ ounce brandy
½ ounce sweet vermouth
1 scoop crushed ice

Mix all the ingredients in a shaker. Strain the mixture into a chilled cocktail glass.

Jack-in-the-Box

1½ ounces applejack
1 ounce pineapple juice
1 ounce lemon juice
Several dashes of bitters
1 scoop crushed ice

Mix all the ingredients in a shaker. Strain the mixture into a chilled cocktail glass.

Jackrose

2 ounces applejack
½ ounce lime or lemon juice
1 teaspoon grenadine
1 scoop crushed ice

Mix all the ingredients in a shaker. Strain the mixture into a chilled cocktail glass.

Marconi Wireless

1½ ounces apple brandy
½ ounce sweet vermouth
Several dashes of orange bitters
1 scoop crushed ice

Combine all the ingredients in a shaker. Mix well and pour into a chilled cocktail glass.

Moonraker

1½ ounces applejack
¾ ounce light rum
½ ounce lime juice
½ ounce orgeat
1 scoop crushed ice
Apple slice

Mix all the ingredients in a shaker. Pour the mixture into a chilled wineglass and garnish with the apple slice.

Mount Fuji

1½ ounces applejack
1½ ounces light rum
1 ounce Southern Comfort
1 ounce sugar
Juice of ½ lime
1 scoop crushed ice
½ lime, scooped out
1 ounce 151-proof rum

Mix all the ingredients, except the lime shell and 151-proof rum, in a blender. Pour the mixture into a sour glass. Place the lime shell on top so that it forms a small bowl. Fill the lime shell with the 151-proof rum and ignite it. The heat will melt the icy drink so you can sip it through a straw.

Red Apple

1½ ounces applejack
1½ ounces grapefruit juice
Several dashes of grenadine
1 scoop crushed ice

Mix all the ingredients in a shaker. Pour the mixture into a chilled cocktail glass.

Snap Apple

3 ounces applejack
½ ounce sweet vermouth
4 ounces orange juice
½ ounce sugar syrup, or to taste

1 teaspoon lemon juice
1 scoop crushed ice

Mix all the ingredients in a shaker. Pour the mixture into a chilled collins glass with additional ice.

Sour Apple

2 ounces applejack
1 ounce lemon juice
1 teaspoon sugar syrup, or to taste
1 scoop crushed ice

Mix all the ingredients in a shaker. Strain the mixture into a chilled cocktail glass.

Sweet Apple

1½ ounces applejack
½ ounce lime juice
1 teaspoon raspberry syrup
1 scoop crushed ice
Cold club soda
1 teaspoon ginger brandy
Lime slice

Mix the applejack, lime juice, syrup, and ice in a shaker. Pour the mixture into a chilled highball glass and top off with the club soda. Stir gently. Carefully pour the ginger brandy over the back of a spoon so that it floats on top. Garnish with the lime slice.

APRICOT BRANDY

Apricot

2 ounces apricot brandy
1 ounce orange juice
1 ounce lemon juice
Several dashes of gin
1 scoop crushed ice

Mix all the ingredients in a shaker. Pour the mixture into a chilled cocktail glass.

Apricot Brandy Fizz

2 ounces apricot brandy
Several dashes of grenadine
Lemon peel
Orange slice
Club soda

Pour the brandy and the grenadine into a chilled old-fashioned glass. Add several ice cubes, the lemon peel, and the orange slice. Top off the glass with the club soda and stir gently.

Big Dipper

1 ounce apricot brandy
3/4 ounce crème de cacao
3/4 teaspoon cream
1 teaspoon grenadine
1 scoop crushed ice

Combine all the ingredients in a shaker. Mix well and pour into a chilled cocktail glass.

Bronx Cheer

2 ounces apricot brandy
6 ounces raspberry soda
Orange peel

In a chilled collins glass, mix the brandy, soda, and several ice cubes. Twist the orange peel over the drink and drop it in.

Golden Gate

1 1/2 ounces apricot brandy
2 ounces orange juice
1 ounce lemon juice
1/2 ounce orgeat, or to taste
1 scoop crushed ice

Mix all the ingredients in a shaker. Pour the mixture into a chilled cocktail glass.

Hotel California

2 ounces apricot brandy
4 ounces orange soda
1 scoop orange sherbet
1 cup ice cubes

Combine all the ingredients in a blender. For a foamier drink, add additional ice cubes. Blend until smooth. Pour the blend into a parfait glass.

Nob Hill Cricket

2 ounces apricot brandy
½ ounce sloe gin
½ ounce lime juice
1 scoop crushed ice

Mix all the ingredients in a shaker. Pour the mixture into a chilled cocktail glass.

Tempter Cocktail

2 ounces apricot brandy
2 ounces port

In a mixing glass with ice, stir the port and brandy. Strain the mixture into a chilled cocktail glass.

BLACKBERRY BRANDY

Black Sheep

2 ounces blackberry brandy
1 ounce blackberry liqueur
½ ounce lime juice
1 scoop crushed ice

Mix all the ingredients in a shaker. Strain the mixture into a chilled cocktail glass.

Yellowfingers

BULL AND BEAR BAR, WALDORF ASTORIA, NEW YORK CITY

1 ounce blackberry brandy
1 ounce crème de banane
½ ounce gin
½ ounce heavy cream
1 scoop crushed ice

Combine all the ingredients in a shaker. Mix well and strain into a chilled old-fashioned glass.

KIRSCH OR CHERRY BRANDY

Cherry Cola

1 ounce cherry brandy
½ ounce maraschino liqueur
4 ounces cold cola
1 maraschino cherry

Pour the cherry brandy, maraschino liqueur, and cola into a highball glass over ice cubes. Stir well and garnish with the cherry.

Spinster

1½ ounces cherry brandy
1 ounce maraschino liqueur
1 scoop crushed ice
1 maraschino cherry

Mix all the ingredients, except the cherry, in a shaker. Strain the mixture into a chilled cocktail glass and garnish with the cherry.

Ostend Fizz

1 ounce cherry brandy
1 ounce crème de cassis
Cold club soda
Lemon peel

In a highball glass, stir the cherry brandy and crème de cassis with ice. Top off with the club soda. Twist the lemon peel over the drink and drop it in.

Villa Bella Fizz

1½ ounces cherry brandy
1 ounce light rum
1 egg white
½ teaspoon granulated sugar
1 tablespoon fresh lime juice
1 scoop crushed ice
Cold club soda
1 maraschino cherry

Combine all the ingredients, except the soda and cherry, in a shaker. Mix well and strain into a highball glass. Top off the glass with the soda and garnish with the cherry.

GRAPPA

Venetian Sunset

FELIDIA, NEW YORK CITY

1 ounce grappa
¼ ounce Campari
2 ounces orange juice
1 teaspoon sugar
½ orange slice
1 mint leaf

In an ice-filled shaker, mix all the ingredients, except the orange slice and mint. Strain the mixture into a large chilled cocktail glass. Garnish with the orange slice and the mint leaf.

PEAR BRANDY

Pear Sour

FOUR SEASONS HOTEL, NEW YORK CITY

2 ounces pear brandy or pear
   schnapps
1 ounce lemon juice
½ ounce sugar syrup
Brandied pear slice

Combine all the ingredients, except the pear slice, in a shaker with crushed ice. Mix well and strain into a chilled cocktail glass. Garnish with the pear slice.

LIQUEURS AND BITTERS

Liqueurs (or cordials; the terms are interchangeable) are luscious sweet drinks that capture the essence of some of the world's unique and beautiful flavors. These potions celebrate oranges from the Orient, herbs from western France, coffee beans from Mexico, and cream from Ireland.

The word "liqueur" comes from the Latin "liquefacere," which means "to melt" or "to dissolve." Liqueurs get their character from herbs, nuts, beans, seeds, fruits, spirits, and recently, cream. These flavoring elements give their essence to the liqueur in one of two basic ways, maceration or distillation.

Maceration is usually used for the production of liqueurs flavored with fruits and grains. This very simple technique consists of soaking the fruits and/or grains in the base alcohol. The flavor of the liqueur is determined by the length of time of the soaking process and by the condition of the fruit.

Distillation is used to concentrate aromatic elements, not to produce alcohol, since the base liquid is an alcohol. The object is to marry the aromatic essences of plants and herbs as they rise with the ascending alcoholic vapors. After a double distillation, the distillate is aged.

Distillates are often blended with the products of maceration in the production of a liqueur, as the flavors of liqueurs are often very complex. After the blending, the mixtures are often aged in oak casks. The blends can be altered by the addition of sugar, honey, water, alcohol, or an aged brandy for more complexity. Color can also be added by the infusion of different plants or fruits. After blending and aging, the liqueur is filtered, then bottled.

Liqueurs, like other spiritous beverages, should always be stored in an upright position so that the cork will not deteriorate from prolonged contact with the alcohol. Liqueurs that have been opened will not deteriorate provided they are kept tightly corked.

There is also a group of odd potions called bitters, which, for want of a better place, are also listed in this chapter.

Nut, Bean, and Seed Liqueurs

ALMOND

• *Amaretto di Saronno* (Italy, 56 proof)   The most popular nut liqueur is not really made from nuts at all, or not from the type of nuts you would expect. It is flavored with the almond-like pits of apricots grown in orchards northwest of Milan. These pits have a nutty but slightly bitter flavor, which explains why the liqueur is called amaretto, "a little bitter," in Italian. The reason many people think this lush liqueur is made from almonds is that the very popular almond cookies made in the region are called amaretti.

There is a lovely story associated with the invention of the Amaretto di Saronno liqueur. It may be just a legend, but it is widely accepted as truth. The year 1525 was a horrendous one for Lombardy, the province in which Milan is located. Famine and war had ravaged the land and the people were destitute. An obscure young artist, Bernardino Luini, a disciple of Leonardo da Vinci, was painting a fresco in the sanctuary of Santa Maria della Grazie in Saronno, a small village north of Milan near Lake Como.

He chose as the model for the Madonna in his painting the proprietress of the small inn in which he was staying. The poor young innkeeper was a beautiful widow raising two small children. She wanted to express her gratitude to the talented artist, but she had no money to spend on a gift. Instead, she invented a special drink made from the apricot pits that her daughter gathered in nearby orchards. She combined the pits with herbs and alcohol and the rest is history. The drink, a true love potion, was the beginning of a ardent romance and Luini went on to become quite a celebrated artist. The painting of his charming blonde lover hangs to this day in the church in Saronno.

The formula for the drink was passed down from innkeeper to innkeeper until 1800 when Carlo Domenico Riena obtained the recipe and began selling it in his apothecary shop. His signature encircles the neck of the product to this day. Since 1939, Amaretto di Saronno has been produced commercially by Illva in Saronno. It is sold in a distinctive square antique bottle with a gold label.

Amaretto di Saronno is now one of the world's best-selling liqueurs. It is deep amber in color and has a unique almond and herb flavor with hints of mint, cinnamon, and vanilla. The liqueur is fairly thick in texture. Its intense sweetness is nicely balanced by the gentle bitterness of the apricot pits.

Amaretto di Saronno has been very successfully marketed in the United States over the last twenty years. It is consumed by itself after dinner, on the rocks, and as part of several mixed drinks. It has joined a precious few other liqueurs—Cointreau, Grand Marnier, Chartreuse—as a frequently used ingredient in pastries and other desserts.

The success of the original amaretto has, of course, brought forth a stream of imitators, some made in Italy and some made domestically. Other Italian amarettos include Lazzaroni (48 proof), Galliano (56 proof), Patrician (48 proof), Trave (54 proof), Stock (56 proof), and Amaretto di Torani (56 proof). Domestic versions include Amaretto di Amore (42 proof), DeKuyper Amaretto di Cupera (56 proof), Gaetano (56 proof), Boston (34 proof), Bols (56 proof), Arrow (56 proof), Hiram Walker (50 proof), and Dubouchett (56 proof). These versions are quite pleasant, if not as complex as the original. Most of them, particularly those made in this country, are considerably less expensive.

• *Crème de Noyaux* Domestic and foreign producers make a cordial flavored with bitter almonds, mace, nutmeg, and other spices. This product is not as strongly almond-flavored as amaretto. It is consumed straight, on the rocks, mixed with vodka, or combined with crème de cacao. Some call this liqueur "crème de noyaux," some call it "crème de noya."

Some American liqueur producers make crème de almond, a clear red cordial usually based on almond oil or, occasionally, apricot pits. Typically it has a snappy cinnamon flavor and is a colorful addition to mixed drinks.

COCOA

• *Crème de cacao*   This liqueur is made from cacao and vanilla beans. It is produced in either white or brown color and there is generally no discernible flavor difference between the two.

COFFEE

The coffee bean has had a long voyage from obscurity to its present position on most of the world's breakfast tables and desks. It was first discovered growing in Abyssinia, which is now Ethiopia. Four thousand years ago, warriors from northern Africa went off to battle with apple-sized balls of ground coffee beans mixed with fat as rations.

By the beginning of the fifth century, coffee had made its way to Arabia and, not too long afterward, to Turkey. Yemeni Arabs actually made wine from coffee beans.

As the trade routes to the mysterious East opened, coffee was gradually introduced into Europe. One story, perhaps apocryphal, tells about how, in 1683, after their defeat near Vienna, the Turks fled, leaving behind sacks of coffee in their deserted tents. The curious Viennese found immediate use for this booty. This and other less dramatic incidents kindled a European passion for coffee that endures to this day.

In the eighteenth century, coffee houses in Vienna, London, and other places became centers of social, political, and literary activities. At about the same time, coffee was introduced into the Americas, where it gained immediate acceptance. Coffee plants were cultivated in the Caribbean and on the mountains of Mexico, where climate and soil were ideal for the proliferation of this tropical crop.

At some point during this process of world proliferation, probably toward the end of the last century, someone got the idea to blend local coffee with distilled spirits to make a drink that combined the unique, toasty flavor of coffee with the smoothness and sweetness of a liqueur. The results of this alchemy included the big two coffee liqueurs, Kahlúa and Tia Maria.

• *Kahlúa* (Mexico, 53 proof)   This smooth and syrupy mahogany-colored liqueur in the distinctive high-neck bottle with the yellow label was being made in Mexico before World War II. Since its introduction into the United States in 1962, Kahlúa has dominated the liqueur market. More than 2.5 million cases are sold worldwide (1.7 million in the U.S. alone).

Kahlúa, the industry standard among coffee liqueurs, has a smoky, toasty coffee flavor with a background of vanilla. It is bright and clean flavored with a snappy finish and an attractive coffee candy sweetness.

• *Tia Maria* (Jamaica, 53 proof)   Although still fairly sweet, Tia Maria is drier and lighter than Kahlúa. It is a product of the Caribbean island of Jamaica and claims to derive from a formula that has been handed down since 1655. In that year, the English stormed this then Spanish island, causing the family that had developed the recipe for the liqueur to flee their plantation. The family's youngest daughter and the recipe were saved by a courageous housekeeper, Tia Maria.

The daughter kept the formula and passed it on to her eldest daughter on her wedding day. In this way, the family tradition continued for nearly 300 years.

In the late 1940s, Dr. Kenneth Lee Evans, a Jamaican physician, was served the liqueur at a friend's home. He immediately got permission to produce the liqueur commercially.

Tia Maria currently sells nearly 200,000 cases each year in the U.S. It is made from Blue Mountain coffee grown north of Kingston, at 6,000 feet above sea level. The amber-colored liqueur has a smoky, roasted aroma and a crisp, tangy coffee and herb flavor with a silky café au lait smoothness.

The success of these two has spawned a bunch of wannabes, some of which compete on the basis of price. There are actually some good ones, too. The best of the lot is Sabra, a delicious, Israeli-made 60-proof version.

Most of the large quantity of coffee liqueur sold in America is not consumed straight up or even on the rocks. The bulk of it goes into mixed drinks, the most popular of which is the Black Russian.

HAZELNUT

• *Frangelico* (Italy, 56 proof)   Frangelico is a relative newcomer from northern Italy that has had a significant recent sales success in the United States. Its main flavoring ingredient is wild hazelnuts. A light amber liqueur, Frangelico is crisp and fairly dry with a lush texture and the taste of toasty hazelnuts. There are hints of vanilla and white chocolate in the complex herbal flavors.

The Frangelico legend concerns a seventeenth-century hermit-monk who created this liqueur out of woodland nuts and herbs. It is made commercially by Barbero in Piedmont, not far from Torino. The bottle is made in the shape of a pious, robed cleric.

Frangelico is a lovely after-dinner drink, straight, in a snifter, and it is also quite good on the rocks. For a refreshing cocktail, blend it half and half with vodka.

There are a few domestic cordials that use a hazelnut base. As with the amaretto reproductions, these are less complex, less expensive, and usually quite pleasant. Gaetano and DeKuyper make widely distributed versions.

Fruit Liqueurs

Americans love fruit, and fruit liqueurs provide an accessible and luscious orchard of captivating natural flavors. Although many of the world's most aromatic fruit liqueurs are made abroad, several domestic companies also offer complete lines. Arrow, Bols, J.W. Dant, DeKuyper, Dubouchett, Garnier, Jacquin, Leroux, Mohawk, Old Mr. Boston, Regnier, and Hiram Walker all provide excellent examples.

Here are some of the fruit liqueurs you might encounter at your favorite spirits merchant.

BANANA

• *Crème de banane* (Foreign and United States, 50 to 60 proof) Many producers make this white or gold liqueur. It is generally very sweet and syrupy. Banana liqueurs are used in desserts and a few mixed drinks.

BLACK CURRANT

• *Crème de cassis* (France and United States, 32 to 40 proof)   A deep red, low-alcohol, syrupy, sweet concoction, this liqueur was of little use until someone mixed it with Aligote, the extremely tart white Burgundy. The resulting apéritif, called kir after the wartime mayor of Dijon, showcases the good qualities of both ingredients, and became a fixture at parties in the 1980s. It can be made with any crisp, dry white wine. The combination of crème de cassis and champagne, called a Kir Royale, is another nice showcase of this liqueur.

BLACK RASPBERRY

• *Chambord* (France, 33 proof)   This thick, sweet, low-alcohol liqueur is flavored mainly by French black raspberries, but other fruits and herbs are used as well, and the mixture is sweetened with honey. It is deep amber tinged with ruby and its appealing flavor suggests candy fruit. Chambord is made by La Maison Delan et Cie in France and packaged in the United States. The bottle is squat and round, with a gold crown. Chambord is particularly delicious poured over vanilla ice cream, and a tablespoon or so in a glass of champagne makes a charming apéritif.

Several domestic producers sell blackberry liqueurs. These are mostly 60 proof and purplish red. They are quite sweet and dense, and are attractive when poured over fruit or ice cream.

CHERRY

• *Cherry Marnier* (France, 48 proof)   Like Grand Marnier, this spirit uses brandy as a base. It is medium sweet and thicker than Peter Heering.

• *Maraschino* (Italy and United States, 50 to 60 proof)   This clear, relatively dry liqueur is made from the spicy Marasca cherries of Italy and Dalmatia (in Yugoslavia). The cherry pits are distilled separately and contribute to a charming bitter-almond nuance. Maraschino is used frequently in mixed drinks.

• *Peter Heering* (Denmark, 49 proof)   This flavorful drink was developed in 1818 using the renowned cherries that grow in southern Denmark. It was popularized in the mid-nineteenth century as cargo transported by the ships of the Heering trading company.

Peter Heering is deep red and light textured. It is medium sweet with luscious wild cherry flavors. Often referred to as Cherry Heering, this fruity liqueur is fine after a meal but light enough to be served as an apéritif.

CITRUS

• *Cointreau* (France, 80 proof)   One of the most popular of all fruit liqueurs, Cointreau sells nearly two million cases in 217 different countries annually. It was formulated in 1879 by Edouard Cointreau, Sr., the head of the successful confectionery and distillery located in the Loire Valley.

Three generations and 142 years later, the same secret formula is still in use by the family at their plant in Angers. Cointreau is bittersweet with a delicate orange flavor derived from the peels of oranges from Europe, the Caribbean, North Africa, and the Middle East. It has a silky texture and, although sweet, leaves a decidedly dry impression on the palate.

Since its American introduction at the 1893 International Exhibition in Chicago, Cointreau has had a devoted following here. To handle the demand, a marketing subsidiary was recently established in New York.

Cointreau can be used in any mixed drinks that call for Triple Sec, but this elegant liqueur is best served on the rocks or on its own.

• *Grand Marnier* (France, 80 proof)   Marnier-Lapostelle was founded by Jean-Baptiste Lapostelle in 1827. At first, the company bottled a number of liqueurs, but by the turn of the century its orange version had taken center stage. Grand Marnier is based on Cognac and the peels of bitter oranges from Haiti. It is amber in color and its dry citrus component combines congenially with the rich toastiness it receives from Cognac. Grand Marnier has become indispensable in dessert making. It is used in many pastries and soufflés. It is also delicious over ice or served neat in a cordial glass or snifter.

• *Curaçao* is a generic name referring to the island that produces some of the Caribbean's best bitter oranges. The peel was brought in the seventeenth century to Holland, where the Dutch created the first orange liqueur.

Today, there are many curaçaos on the market. Most are produced in the United States but are made with imported peels. These liqueurs are usually amber and sweet, with a charming taste of bitterness. Curaçaos are about 60 proof; some use a brandy base. A number of distillers make one that has been tinted blue. There is no significant difference in flavor or proof between this product and the regular variety, or between amber and the few clear curaçaos available.

• *Mandarin Napoleon* (Belgium, 80 proof) This citrus-based liqueur is made by macerating mandarin peel in selected brandies. Folklore says that it is the drink that Napoleon employed to charm the actress, Mademoiselle Mars.

• *Parfait Amour* is a sweet citrus liqueur that is scented and lightly spiced. Although it comes in many colors, it is most often a bright violet.

• *Triple Sec* is an orange liqueur made from both sweet and bitter orange peels. The name means "triple dry," but triple secs are not all dry. The best of them are smooth, sweet, and nicely balanced with fresh fruit flavors and considerable finesse.

Triple Sec can be poured over ice or enjoyed on its own, but it is most frequently used for margaritas.

MELON

• *Midori* (Japan, 46 proof) This bright green liqueur, a recent addition to the bar, is made by the giant Japanese distiller Suntory. Midori is fairly sweet but its muskmelon flavor is delicious and quite charming.

ORANGE-CHOCOLATE

• *Sabra* (Israel, 52 proof) This sweet, dark amber spirit with ruby overtones is made from jaffa oranges and rich chocolate. The combination is quite pleasant, with each flavor retaining its character while blending harmoniously with the other.

PEAR

• *Dettling Williams Pear Liqueur* (Switzerland, 70 proof) Smooth, clear, and quite dry, this is a most elegant drink. It has a fresh, ripe pear flavor and smooth texture.

SLOE

• *Sloe gin* (England and United States, 40 to 60 proof) The sloe is a small wild plum. The liqueur made from it is misnamed, because it is not a gin, although early versions were made by macerating the fruit in gin.

Bright red and medium sweet, it has an intriguing flavor of wild cherry and bitter almond. Sloe gin is almost never consumed on its own; it is used in mixed drinks such as sloe gin fizzes.

Herbal Liqueurs

• *Benedictine* (France, 40 proof) The closely guarded formula for the liqueur Benedictine was first produced in 1510 in the Benedictine Abbey de Fecamp in France. Today, it is still made in the same location. D.O.M. Benedictine is an herbal liqueur made on a Cognac brandy base. After several separate distillations, Benedictine is aged for four years before it is bottled. D.O.M., which is located on every label, stands for the Latin "Dio Optimo Maximo," "To God, Most Good, Most Great." Hundreds of imitations have been tried, but the original formula still stands alone.

• *Chartreuse* (France, 84 proof to 110) Chartreuse dates from the beginning of the seventeenth century when the recipe for an "Elixir de Longue Vie" (elixir of long life) was given to a Carthusian monastery outside Paris by one of Henry IV's captains.

For more than 150 years, the monks tinkered with the formula and, in 1764, at the Carthusian monastery in the Massif de la Chartreuse in southeastern France, they settled on a blend made from 130 different plants and herbs.

Two Chartreuse liqueurs were produced, "Elixir de Santé" and

"Elixir de Table." The latter version was the green drink that is still popular today—the liquid that actually named a color.

Green Chartreuse has a minty, spicy flavor. It is crisp, peppery, and very high in alcohol—55 percent to be exact.

In 1838, a yellow version of Chartreuse was created. It is sweeter and mellower than the green. Honey was added to the mix and the alcoholic content was dropped to 43 percent.

In addition, small lots of both green and yellow Chartreuse are specially aged in oak for twelve years and labeled V.E.P. (Vieillissement Exceptionnellement Prolongé, which means "exceptionally prolonged aging"). These aged liqueurs develop a softer, more complex flavor. The green V.E.P. is 54 percent alcohol and the yellow is 42 percent.

In the early 1920s, the production and marketing of Chartreuse was sold into nonchurch hands. The formula and the direction of production, however, remain under the control of Carthusian monks, who work every day at the present Chartreuse distillery in Voiron, a small city in the foothills of the Alps not far from Grenoble.

• *Crème de menthe* (France and United States, 60 proof)   The flavor of this liqueur can derive from a diverse variety of mint leaves, with the majority of these smooth, sweet cordials being made from peppermint. Crème de menthes are produced in white and green, without any significant flavor difference between the two colors.

• *Liquore Galliano* (Italy, 70 proof)   The most popular of Italian herbal liqueurs, Galliano is lush and moderately syrupy in texture with a smooth herbal-vanilla flavor that finishes with a pleasant twinge of bitterness. This liqueur is less complex than its French cousins but, at the same time, its flavors may be, for many consumers, easier to like.

Liquore Galliano was first made around the turn of this century in Livorno, on the Tuscan coast. It is now produced in a modern plant near Milan. Unlike its French counterparts, this Italian liqueur is given very little age. After several separate distillations, the various lots are blended and then held for three months while their flavors marry. Then, after being adjusted to 40 percent alcohol, Galliano is bottled. In the United States it had a tremendous upsurge in popularity a few years ago when the "Harvey Wallbanger" became a fashionable cocktail.

In Trieste, near the Austrian border, Stock, one of Italy's biggest distillers, makes an attractive Galliano clone called Roiano.

• *Jagermeister* (Germany, 70 proof)   Jagermeister is an herbal concoction made in Wulfenbuttel, Germany, that tastes, at first, like a liqueur, but finishes like bitters with spicy, peppery, and decidedly bittersweet flavors. It is classed here as an herb liqueur, like Benedictine or Chartreuse, but its flavors would also make it welcome in the bitters category.

Made from fifty-six different herbs, Jagermeister has its share of medicinal herbs such as rhubarb roots from the Himalayas, gentian roots from the Alps, valerian roots from Japan, and camomile blossoms from Egypt. In addition, there are plenty of barks, seeds, and resins.

Jagermeister, quite popular in the New Orleans area, has been made since 1878 by the Mast family, which has passed its formula down from generation to generation. It is reddish brown in color. The producers recommend that Jagermeister be served chilled. Some like to follow it with a beer.

• *Pernod* (France, 80 proof)   Pernod is a commercial name that, through the years, has become synonymous with asbinthe. Absinthe is prepared with aromatic plants, balm-mint, hyssop, fennel, star anise, and a high-proof spirit. In fact, absinthe is so powerful, 136 proof, that its sale is prohibited in Switzerland, France, the United States, and other countries. Because of this, the Pernod firm produces an anise-flavored spirit that is 80 proof. It is a light yellow-green color with a strong licorice aroma.

• *Pimm's Cup* (England, 67 proof)   More than one hundred years ago, a bartender in a Pimm's restaurant in London invented the gin sling. This drink became very popular and customers would ask to bring it home for private parties, and weekends away. Eventually, this drink was prepared commercially as Pimm's No. 1. It is produced in England, and sweetened with spices, fruits, and herbs.

• *Sambuca* (Italy, 70 proof)   A licorice-flavored liqueur prepared from the elderbrush.

• *Tuaca* (Italy, 70 proof)   This handsomely packaged Italian liqueur is a relative newcomer to the marketplace. It is light amber in color and has an attractive, moderately sweet herbal-vanilla flavor. Allegedly this liqueur was originally made for Lorenzo the Magnificent, the once powerful ruler of Florence.

Spirit-Based Liqueurs

These liqueurs embellish a standard spirit with added sugars and spices. Many of the blending recipes for these are derived from the eighteenth century and earlier, and often they are carried along by single family producers. The flavor and coloration of the base spirit is maintained in these liqueurs despite the additional sweetening. They can be drunk straight, or used in desserts and mixed drinks

• *Drambuie* (Scotland, 80 proof)   The secret formula for this old Highland malt Scotch whisky–based liqueur was given to the Mackinnon family in 1745 by Bonnie Prince Charles when they helped him escape to France following the battle of Culloden Moor. It was immediately favored by the royalty of the region, who found it a most appealing drink. The name derives from the ancient Gaelic *An dram buidheach,* which translates as "the drink that satisfies." Nowadays, it is enjoyed by a considerably larger segment of the population. Drambuie is one of the most popular liqueurs in the United States.

• *Glayva* (Scotland, 80 proof)   From Edinburgh's ancient port of Leith, this Scotch whisky–based liqueur is produced by the Morrison family. Glayva is a decidedly modern product compared with its neighbor, Drambuie.

• *Irish Mist* (Ireland, 70 proof)   This spicy Irish whiskey–based liqueur is often used as an after-dinner drink. The recipe, which dates back over 1,200 years, disappeared in the seventeenth century and was recovered in Austria and returned to its homeland some years later.

• *Swedish Punsch* (Sweden)   A spicy liqueur based on rum. It dates from the eighteenth century, when Swedish merchants began trading with the East Indies. They brought back Arak, a strong brandylike rum from Java. Swedish Punsch, which is made from Arak, was originally drunk warm, but now it is chilled.

• *Wild Turkey Liqueur* (United States, 80 proof)   Produced by the Austin Nichols Distillery in Lawrenceburg, Kentucky. A special stock of Wild Turkey Straight Bourbon is set aside to make this sweetened liqueur.

Cream Liqueurs

Cream liqueurs are the hottest thing to hit the liquor business in years. It all started in 1979 when a company called International Distillers and Vintners (I.D.V.) brought a totally new product to market. This cream liqueur was the result of a technological breakthrough that allowed fresh cream and alcohol to be combined in such a way that they were completely homogenized—and remained so indefinitely. Made in Ireland, this smooth blend was mixed with sweeteners and flavorings to make something unique. The total effect was reminiscent of the classic brandy Alexander; the big difference was that this drink would never separate.

• *Bailey's Original Irish Cream* (Ireland, 34 proof)   Bailey's, made by the big British conglomerate I.D.V., has been the most dramatic product introduction in the history of the wine and spirits industry. Sales are even greater today and are still growing. It appears that cream liqueurs have a bit more staying power than coolers did.

As might be expected, this impressive success prompted a number of variations from other companies. Some were flavored with rum or coffee, while others were very much like Bailey's, only less expensive. So far, none of them has been able to slow the phenomenal surge in sales of the leader. There was room for other cream liqueurs, however, and a number of them have made modest inroads.

Cream liqueurs are very nice at the end of a meal, served either chilled or at room temperature, neat or on the rocks. They also are delicious poured over ice cream or mixed with brandy to create a less sweet, more potent drink.

Bailey's Irish Cream is a grayish brown color and contains "fresh dairy cream (not more than two hours old), Irish whiskey, and natural flavorings such as vanilla and chocolate. The mixture is then homogenized to ensure uniformity in every bottle, pasteurized to preserve freshness, and then cooled and bottled." Bailey's has medium viscosity and is smooth and creamy without being cloying. It has a fresh and appealing milk chocolate flavor.

Bitters

Bitters are the essences of bark, roots, fruits, plants, stems, seeds, and other botanicals incorporated into an alcohol base. This type of distillate is a relatively modern development—since the nineteenth century—but it is really descended directly from the original medicinal elixirs that were the forerunners of today's liqueurs. Actually, the line of demarcation between bitters and liqueurs is a bit fuzzy. A number of bitters fit the definition of liqueur and vice versa.

The characteristic that sets bitters apart, besides their obvious bitterness, is their original use as a medicine, usually as a stomachic or digestive aid. Within the definition, however, there are two distinct categories of bitters as defined by the Internal Revenue Service: those fit for use as beverages and those not fit for use as beverages. The first group pays a sizable tax, while the second pays practically nothing.

• *Amer Picon* (France, 78 proof)   Amer Picon is a reddish-brown bitter liqueur that has been made in France since 1837. It contains gentian and cinchona bark, which yields quinine, but the most prominent flavor is bitter orange. Aficionados like to drink Amer Picon on the rocks with soda.

• *Angostura* (Trinidad, 90 proof)   The formula for Angostura was developed in 1824 by Dr. Johann Siegert, who was the surgeon-general in the army of the South American hero Simon Bolivar. The introduction of the tonic came after Dr. Siegert spent four years trying to find a potion that would improve the health and appetites of troops. The name derives from the fact that the good doctor was headquartered in the port of Angostura, Venezuela, which is now known as Ciudad Bolivar.

The Angostura formula contains herbs and spices in a formulation that is still kept secret by the Siegert family. The only herb actually named on the label is gentian. Angostura is presently manufactured in Trinidad in the West Indies.

Angostura is a powerful 90 proof, which explains why it is dispensed only in drops and dashes. It does have a unique ability to enhance and intensify the flavors of other ingredients in drinks as well as in foods.

• *Cynar* (Italy, 33 proof)   Artichokes? That's right, this Italian bitter *aperitivo* is made from a maceration of several herbs, but the main flavor comes from artichoke leaves. Cynar (pronounced "chee-nahr") is sipped before dinner in Italy, often on the rocks with a slice of orange. It is also frequently used in mixed drinks.

• *Campari* (Italy, 48 proof)   The world's most popular bitters was created by Gaspare Campari in 1860, the year Italy was united into a single nation. His idea was to offer a new drink to the patrons of his elegant Milan café and it became an immediate success. By the turn of the century, thanks to the marketing savvy of his son Davide, Campari had become a national fixture and, soon after that, it grew into an international triumph. Today, this bright red, spirit-based *aperitivo* is available in 169 countries. More than 5 million cases are sold worldwide.

The Campari company still uses Gaspare's original formula, which contains herbs and fruits from four continents. These ingredients are blended and then aged in oak. Campari's flavor is soft, sweet, and pleasantly bitter.

In Italy Campari is so popular mixed with soda that premixed "Campari-Soda" sells more than 400 million bottles each year. In addition, there are two world famous cocktails made from Campari: the Americano and the Negroni.

• *Fernet Branca* (Italy, 80 proof)   I first tasted this strange brown liquid in Gascony when it was proffered as a certain cure for extreme gastric distress. It worked. This elixir was originally introduced in 1845 by a young Milanese woman named Maria Scala, who subsequently married into the Branca family. The mysterious "bitters liqueur" is made from a secret formula that contains some forty herbs and spices—things like rhubarb, chamomile, anise, cardamom, clove, gentian, and myrrh. Many of these ingredients come from the Alpine foothills not far from Milan, but others are imported from many parts of the world. Each component is carefully tested for quality before being used in production.

The word "fernet" translates as "hot iron," which refers to a poker-like tool that was used to stir the mixture in the early days of Fernet Branca's production. Since the beginning, this popular brand of bitters has been made in Milan exclusively by the Branca family. The secret formula has been carefully passed down from generation to generation, and today the ingredients are put through a computerized measuring program to ensure consistency in the product.

Europe's most popular digestif, Fernet Branca sells more than a million cases a year in Italy alone. Most Italians drink this elixir straight or on the rocks. In Argentina it is often taken as an apéritif, while in Germany it is sometimes followed by beer. Some people like to add it to their coffee after a meal.

• *Gammel Dansk* (Denmark, 76 proof) Forty thousand cases of Gammel Dansk are sold in tiny Denmark every year. This bitters is made from an "age-old" recipe that includes twenty different herbs and fruits. The dark amber drink is peppery, assertively herbal, and completely dry. Its flavor is one of the liveliest and bitterest among bitters.

• *Peychaud's* (United States, 70 proof) Antoine Amedie Peychaud was a New Orleans apothecary who, in 1793, concocted a tonic that was supposed to cure virtually every disease known to man. Although its curative powers may have been somewhat overstated, Peychaud's tonic became a local favorite as a flavoring for mixed drinks.

Peychaud's is usually dispensed a few drops at a time. It is also used in a number of Creole recipes.

CLASSICS

Angel's Tip

1 ounce white crème de cacao
Dash of heavy cream
1 maraschino cherry

Pour the crème de cacao into a liqueur glass. Float the heavy cream on top and garnish with the cherry.

Cape Cod Cooler

2 ounces sloe gin
1 ounce gin
5 ounces cranberry juice
½ ounce lemon juice
½ ounce orgeat
Crushed ice
Lime slice

Combine all the ingredients, except the lime slice, in a shaker or blender. Pour the mixture into a chilled collins glass and garnish with the lime slice.

Grasshopper

1 ounce crème de menthe
1 ounce crème de cacao
1 ounce light cream

Combine all the ingredients in a shaker. Shake vigorously. Strain the mixture into a chilled cocktail glass.

Pousse-Café

Use equal amounts (usually ½ ounce) of each of the following ingredients:

Raspberry syrup (or grenadine)
Crème de cacao
Maraschino liqueur
Curaçao
Crème de menthe (green)
Parfait Amour
Brandy

Layer ingredients one on top of the other in the order given in a large liqueur or parfait glass. This is best accomplished by pouring them slowly over the back of a spoon.

Sloe Gin Fizz

2 to 3 ounces sloe gin
½ ounce lemon juice
1 teaspoon sugar syrup
1 scoop crushed ice
Cold club soda
Lemon slice

In a shaker, mix all the ingredients, except the soda and lemon slice. Pour the mixture into a chilled collins glass. Top off with the club soda and stir gently. Garnish with the lemon slice.

ALMOND LIQUEUR

Coco Amandine

1 ounce almond liqueur
1 ounce coconut cream

Pour both ingredients into a snifter filled with ice. Stir gently.

Toasty Almond Colada

1 ounce almond liqueur
1 ounce coffee liqueur
1 ounce coconut cream
2 ounces cream
1 cup ice

Combine all the ingredients in a blender and blend until smooth. Pour the blend into a chilled parfait glass.

AMARETTO

Amaretto Sour

2 to 3 ounces amaretto
¾ ounce lemon juice
1 scoop crushed ice
1 orange slice

In a shaker, mix the amaretto, lemon juice, and crushed ice. Strain over ice cubes in an old-fashioned glass and garnish with the orange slice.

Amaretto Stinger

2 ounces amaretto
1 ounce white crème de menthe

In a shaker, combine both ingredients with ice. Shake well and strain over fresh ice cubes in an old-fashioned glass.

Café Amaretto

1 ounce amaretto
1 ounce coffee liqueur
1 cup hot coffee
Whipped cream

Pour the liqueurs into a mug of hot coffee. Top generously with the whipped cream.

Café Prego

1½ ounces amaretto
4 ounces hot coffee
½ ounce brandy
2 ounces heavy cream

Pour the amaretto, coffee, and brandy into an Irish coffee glass. Stir well. Hold a spoon just above the surface of the coffee and carefully pour the cream over the back of the spoon. The cream should float on top of the coffee.

Dynasty

1½ ounces amaretto
1½ ounces Southern Comfort

In a shaker or blender, mix both ingredients with ice. Strain the mixture into an old-fashioned glass over fresh ice cubes.

Fairmont Freeze

PYRAMID LOUNGE, FAIRMONT HOTEL,
DALLAS

1½ ounces amaretto
1 scoop vanilla ice cream
Sliced toasted almonds

Blend the amaretto with the ice cream until thoroughly mixed and creamy in texture. Pour the blend into a chilled cocktail glass and sprinkle the almonds on top.

Little Italy

2 ounces amaretto
5 ounces orange juice

Pour both ingredients into a highball glass filled with ice cubes. Stir well before serving.

Radisson Snowball

RADISSON HOTEL, OASIS LOUNGE,
SCOTTSDALE, ARIZONA

1 ounce amaretto
½ ounce white crème de cacao
1 teaspoon coconut cream
1 scoop vanilla ice cream
2 ounces cream
1 scoop crushed ice
½ slice fresh pineapple

Blend all the ingredients, except the pineapple slice, until the mixture reaches a slushy consistency. Pour into a tulip glass and garnish with the pineapple slice.

Secret Love

QUEEN ELIZABETH HOTEL, MONTREAL

1 ounce coconut amaretto liqueur
½ ounce white rum
½ ounce lemon juice
1 ounce orange juice
½ ounce cranberry juice
Maraschino cherry

Combine all the ingredients, except the cherry, in a shaker with ice. Shake well. Strain into a cocktail glass and garnish with the cherry.

Southern Slammer

1½ ounces amaretto
1 ounce Southern Comfort
½ ounce sloe gin
½ ounce lemon juice

In a shaker or blender, shake all the ingredients with ice. Strain the mixture into an old-fashioned glass filled with fresh ice cubes.

BENEDICTINE

Annabelle Special

ANNABELLE'S, LONDON

1½ ounces Benedictine
⅓ ounce dry vermouth
⅓ ounce lime juice
1 scoop crushed ice

Mix all the ingredients in a shaker. Strain the mixture into a chilled cocktail glass.

Quiet Nun

1 ounce Benedictine
½ ounce Triple Sec
1 ounce light cream
1 scoop crushed ice

Combine all the ingredients in a shaker. Shake well and strain into a chilled cocktail glass.

Friar's Coffee

4 ounces hot coffee
½ teaspoon superfine sugar
2 ounces Benedictine
2 ounces heavy cream

Put the coffee and sugar in an Irish coffee glass. Stir until the sugar dissolves. Add the Benedictine and stir again. To layer the cream on top, hold a spoon just above the surface of the coffee and carefully pour the cream over the back of the spoon.

BLACK RASPBERRY LIQUEUR

Di Nuovo

YELLOWFINGER'S, NEW YORK CITY

1 ounce black raspberry liqueur
¾ ounce hazelnut liqueur
¼ cup puréed raspberries
½ cup heavy cream
Whipped cream
Chopped nuts
Fresh berries

In a blender, combine the liqueurs, raspberries, and cream with approximately ½ cup ice. Blend well. The blend should have a smooth consistency and be light pink. Pour the mixture into an 8-ounce tulip glass.

Add a dollop of whipped cream and a light sprinkling of chopped nuts. Garnish with a large strawberry or a few fresh raspberries.

Cadiz

¾ ounce black raspberry liqueur
¾ ounce amontillado sherry
½ ounce Triple Sec
½ ounce heavy cream
1 scoop crushed ice

Mix all the ingredients in a shaker. Pour the mixture into a chilled old-fashioned glass.

CHOCOLATE LIQUEUR

Café Diana

OLD LYME INN, OLD LYME, CONNECTICUT

1¼ ounces chocolate liqueur
1¼ ounces Chambord
Hot coffee
Whipped cream
Fresh raspberry

Pour the liqueur and Chambord into a warm coffee mug. Top off with hot coffee and a dollop of whipped cream. In season, garnish with the fresh raspberry.

Treasure Chest

1 ounce chocolate almond liqueur
¼ ounce gold rum
½ ounce amaretto
1 ounce cream
1 scoop crushed ice

Mix all the ingredients thoroughly in a blender. Pour the mixture into a chilled cocktail glass.

COFFEE LIQUEUR

Coco Java

1 ounce coffee liqueur
1 ounce coconut cream

Pour both ingredients into a snifter filled with ice. Gently stir.

Cool Irish Coffee Colada

1 ounce coffee liqueur
1 ounce Irish whiskey
1½ ounces coconut cream
1 ounce cream
1 cup ice

Combine all the ingredients in a blender and blend until smooth. Pour the blend into a chilled parfait glass.

Keoke Coffee

THE REDWOOD ROOM, CLIFT HOTEL, SAN FRANCISCO

¾ ounce coffee liqueur
½ ounce brandy
Hot coffee
Freshly whipped cream

Pour the liqueur and brandy into an Irish coffee glass. Add fresh hot coffee to within 1 inch of the rim. Spoon ¾ inch whipped cream on top of the coffee.

Kona Gold

1½ ounces crème de cacao
1 ounce peach brandy
Large scoop of vanilla ice cream
½ ripe banana, peeled and sliced
Pinch of ground nutmeg
1 maraschino cherry

Combine all the ingredients, except the nutmeg and cherry, in a blender. Blend until smooth. Pour the blend into a wineglass. Top with a sprinkle of the nutmeg and the cherry.

Margi's Mocha Mint

¾ ounce coffee liqueur
¾ ounce crème de menthe
¾ ounce crème de cacao
1 scoop crushed ice

Combine all the ingredients in a shaker. Mix well and strain into a chilled cocktail glass.

Root Beer

1 ounce coffee liqueur
1 ounce Galliano
1 ounce lemon juice
½ teaspoon superfine sugar
3 ounces cola

Combine all the ingredients, except the cola, in a shaker with ice cubes. Shake well. Strain the mixture into a highball glass over fresh ice cubes. Top off with cola. Stir well.

Sombrero

1½ ounces coffee liqueur
1 ounce cream

Pour the liqueur over ice cubes in a chilled old-fashioned glass. Float the cream on top of the coffee liqueur by slowly pouring it over the back of a spoon.

Toasted Almond

WINDOWS ON THE WORLD,
NEW YORK CITY

1½ ounces coffee liqueur
1 ounce amaretto
1½ ounces cream
Pinch of ground nutmeg or
   cinnamon

Mix all the ingredients, except the nutmeg, in a shaker with ice. Strain into a chilled cocktail glass and sprinkle a little nutmeg or cinnamon on top.

Velvet Dress

1 ounce coffee liqueur
¾ ounce brandy
¾ ounce Triple Sec
1½ ounces heavy cream

In a shaker, mix all the ingredients with ice. Strain the mixture into a cocktail glass.

CRÈME DE CACAO

Angel's Tit

¼ ounce crème de cacao
¼ ounce maraschino liqueur
¼ ounce heavy cream
1 maraschino cherry

Layer the ingredients, except the cherry, in a pony glass. Chill for a half hour before serving. Garnish with the cherry.

Angel's Wings

1 ounce white crème de cacao
Dash of heavy cream
½ ounce brandy
1 maraschino cherry

Pour the crème de cacao into a liqueur glass. Float the heavy cream on top. Gently pour the brandy over the cream. Garnish with the cherry.

Beetlejuice

1 ounce white crème de cacao
1 ounce dark crème de cacao
½ ounce coffee liqueur
2 teaspoons peppermint schnapps
1 ounce light cream

Combine all the ingredients in a shaker with ice cubes. Shake and strain into a cocktail glass.

Caribbean Grasshopper

1 ounce white crème de cacao
½ ounce green crème de menthe
1½ ounces coconut cream
Mint sprig

Pour all the ingredients, except the mint, into a large snifter filled with ice cubes. Stir gently and garnish with the sprig of mint.

Morton's Coffee

MORTON'S OF CHICAGO, BOSTON

Ground cinnamon
Granulated sugar
1 ounce dark crème de cacao
1 ounce amaretto
1 ounce Irish cream
Hot coffee
Unsweetened fresh whipped cream

Press the moistened rim of a coffee mug into a mixture of equal parts cinnamon and sugar. Pour the crème de cacao, amaretto, and Irish cream into the mug. Top off with hot coffee and a generous dollop of the whipped cream.

Pink Squirrel

1 ounce crème de cacao
1 ounce crème de noyaux
1 ounce heavy cream
1 scoop crushed ice

Combine all the ingredients in a shaker. Mix well and strain into a chilled cocktail glass.

Sea Cow

FOUR SEASONS HOTEL, TORONTO

¾ ounce dark crème de cacao
½ ounce rye whiskey
½ ounce anisette
1½ ounces cream
Sugar
Green crème de menthe
Grated nutmeg

Shake the crème de cacao, whiskey, anisette, and cream with ice. Strain the mixture into a wineglass rimmed with sugar and green crème de menthe. Sprinkle the top with the nutmeg.

Snow Cap Colada

1 ounce white crème de cacao
1 ounce almond liqueur
½ ounce brandy
2 ounces coconut cream
1 ounce cream
1 cup ice

Combine all the ingredients in a blender and blend until smooth. Pour the blend into a chilled parfait glass.

CRÈME DE MENTHE

Diana

2 ounces white crème de menthe
½ ounce brandy

Pour the crème de menthe into a pony glass. Float the brandy on top.

Note: This drink can also be served with crushed ice, using an extra ounce of crème de menthe and 3 teaspoons of brandy.

Green Orchid

¾ ounce green crème de menthe
½ ounce Pernod
1 egg white
Cold club soda

Mix all the ingredients, except the club soda, in a shaker with crushed ice. Strain the mixture into a highball glass. Top off with the club soda and ice.

London Fog

½ ounce white crème de menthe
1 ounce anisette
1 scoop vanilla ice cream
1 scoop crushed ice

Put all the ingredients in a blender and blend briefly. Pour the blend into a chilled parfait glass.

Mint Twist

1 teaspoon white crème de menthe or peppermint schnapps
1 teaspoon green crème de menthe
1 scoop vanilla ice cream

Combine all the ingredients in a blender and blend until smooth. Pour the blend into a chilled parfait glass.

Pacifier

1 scoop crushed ice
1½ ounces white crème de menthe
Several dashes of Fernet Branca

Pack a sherry glass with the crushed ice. Pour in the crème de menthe and top off with a float of the Fernet Branca.

Shirley McLake

1½ ounces crème de banane
1½ ounces white crème de menthe

Pour both the ingredients into a chilled old-fashioned glass. Add several ice cubes and stir well.

Mocha Mint

Makes 4 servings

1 cup cold coffee
1 pint chocolate ice cream
¼ cup crème de menthe
4 very thin chocolate mint wafers

In a blender, combine the coffee, ice cream, and crème de menthe. Spoon the blend into sherbet or wine glasses. Garnish each serving with a chocolate mint wafer.

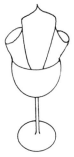

CURAÇAO

Fog City Blues

1½ ounces blue curaçao
½ ounce white crème de cacao
½ ounce light cream
1 scoop crushed ice

Mix all the ingredients in a shaker. Pour the mixture into a chilled cocktail glass.

Gloom Chaser

1 ounce curaçao
1 ounce orange liqueur
½ ounce lemon juice
¼ ounce grenadine
1 scoop crushed ice

Mix all the ingredients in a shaker. Pour the mixture into a chilled cocktail glass.

Ice Cream Flip

1 ounce orange curaçao
1 ounce maraschino liqueur
1 egg
1 scoop vanilla ice cream
Freshly grated nutmeg

Combine all the ingredients, except the nutmeg, in a blender. Blend and pour into a cocktail glass. Sprinkle the nutmeg on top.

Paradise

1 ounce curaçao
1 ounce hazelnut liqueur
1 ounce cream

In a shaker, mix the liqueurs, the cream, and a few ice cubes. Strain the mixture into a chilled cocktail glass over crushed ice.

GALLIANO

Golden Dream

1½ ounces Galliano
1 ounce Triple Sec
1 ounce orange juice
1 teaspoon cream

Mix all the ingredients in a shaker
with ice cubes. Strain the mixture
into a chilled cocktail glass.

Harvey Wallbanger

1½ ounces vodka
4 ounces orange juice
½ ounce Galliano

Pour the vodka and orange juice
into a chilled collins glass with several ice cubes. Stir well. Top off the
glass with the Galliano so that it
floats on top. Do not stir before
serving.

Jaguar

2 ounces Galliano
1 ounce white crème de cacao
1 ounce heavy cream
1 scoop crushed ice

Combine all the ingredients in a
blender. Blend for about 10 seconds. Strain the blend into a chilled
cocktail glass.

Tyrol

1 ounce Galliano
½ ounce brandy
½ ounce green Chartreuse
½ ounce cream
Freshly grated nutmeg

Mix all the ingredients, except the
nutmeg, in a shaker filled with
crushed ice. Pour the mixture into a
cocktail glass and sprinkle the nutmeg on top.

GRAND MARNIER

The Palace Café Royale

THE PALACE CAFE, SANTA BARBARA, CALIFORNIA

Makes 4 servings

2 teaspoons Grand Marnier
1 teaspoon Cognac
¼ cup sugar
½ cup heavy cream
½ teaspoon vanilla extract
2 teaspoons sour cream
Granulated sugar
Hot coffee
Grated chocolate

Combine all the ingredients, except the sugar, coffee, and chocolate, in a mixer or blender. Mix well, until the cream holds a stiff peak. Coat the rim of a clear mug or champagne glass with the sugar. Pour the hot coffee into a prepared glass. Put a dollop of whipped cream mixture on top of the coffee. Sprinkle the chocolate on top.

HAZELNUT LIQUEUR

Nutcracker

1½ ounces hazelnut liqueur
1½ ounces coconut amaretto
1½ ounces cream
Crushed ice

Combine all the ingredients in a shaker or blender. Shake well and strain into a chilled cocktail glass.

Robin Hood

1½ ounces hazelnut liqueur
2 teaspoons brandy
1 ounce lemon juice
1 teaspoon grenadine
1 maraschino cherry

Combine all the ingredients, except the cherry, in a shaker with ice. Shake well. Strain into a cocktail glass and garnish with the cherry.

Snickers Bar

FOUR SEASONS HOTEL, BOSTON

1½ ounces hazelnut liqueur
1 ounce coffee liqueur
Handful of cocktail peanuts
Large scoop of vanilla ice cream
Cold milk
Whipped cream

Combine all the ingredients, except the milk and whipped cream, in a blender. Add the milk while blending on low speed until a medium thickness is reached. Pour the blend into a cocktail glass and top off with a dollop of the whipped cream.

IRISH CREAM LIQUEUR

Chip Shot

THE BALBOA CAFE, SAN FRANCISCO

¾ ounce Irish cream
¾ ounce Tuaca
1½ ounces hot coffee

Pour all the ingredients directly into an old-fashioned glass.

Irish Berry

1 ounce Irish cream
½ ounce vodka
1 ounce coconut cream
1½ ounces strawberries
Dash of grenadine
½ cup ice

Combine all the ingredients in a blender. Blend until smooth and pour the blend into a saucer-shaped champagne glass.

Slippery Nipple

THE BALBOA CAFE, SAN FRANCISCO

¾ ounce Irish cream
¾ ounce Sambuca

Combine both ingredients in a shaker with ice. Mix and strain into a shot glass.

JAGERMEISTER

Bee Sting

THE BALBOA CAFE, SAN FRANCISCO

¾ ounce Jagermeister
¾ ounce Bearenjaeger

Chill both ingredients. Pour both
ingredients into a shot glass.

Poison Milk

AARON RAMSEY, PARAGON,
SAN FRANCISCO

¾ ounce Jagermeister
¾ ounce Irish cream

Chill the Jagermeister. Pour both ingredients into a shot glass.

Dead Nazi

THE BALBOA CAFE, SAN FRANCISCO

¾ ounce Jagermeister
¾ ounce Rumplemintz

Chill both ingredients and pour into
a shot glass.

MELON LIQUEUR

Midori Sour

2 ounces melon liqueur
1 ounce light rum
1 ounce cream

Mix all the ingredients in a shaker
with ice. Strain the mixture into a
chilled whiskey sour glass.

Sniapin Verde

FELIDIA, NEW YORK CITY

2 ounces melon liqueur
1 ounce grappa
1 scoop crushed ice
1 orange slice

Combine all the ingredients, except
the orange slice, in a shaker. Mix
well. Pour the mixture into an old-
fashioned glass and garnish with the
orange slice.

St. Patrick's Irish Breeze

GRISWOLD INN, ESSEX, CONNECTICUT

1½ ounces melon liqueur
Grapefruit juice
Cranberry juice

Pour the liqueur into a large glass filled with ice. Top off the glass with equal parts of grapefruit and cranberry juice.

PERNOD

Pernod Cocktail

½ ounce water
Several dashes of sugar syrup
Several dashes of bitters
1 scoop crushed ice
2 ounces Pernod

In an old-fashioned glass, combine all the ingredients, except the Pernod, and stir well. Add the Pernod and stir again before serving.

Suissesse

Makes 2 servings

3 ounces Pernod
1 ounce anisette
1 egg white
Several dashes of cream (optional)
1 scoop crushed ice

Combine all the ingredients in a shaker. Mix well and strain into chilled cocktail glasses.

PIMM'S CUP

Pimm's Cup

1 ounce Pimm's Cup No. 1
Lemon-lime soda
1 cucumber slice or spear

Pour the Pimm's into a highball or a double old-fashioned glass. Add ice and fill the glass with lemon-lime soda. Garnish with the cucumber. (This is a traditional accompaniment to Indian food.)

RASPBERRY LIQUEUR

Raspberry Rickey

AUREOLE, NEW YORK CITY

1 to 2 tablespoons raspberry
  liqueur
Cold club soda
2 lime wedges
4 to 6 raspberries (red, yellow,
  or black)

Pour the liqueur into a large wine-glass. Fill the glass with ice and top it off with club soda. Squeeze 1 lime wedge into the drink. Garnish with raspberries and the second lime wedge. Serve with a straw.

RUM CREAM LIQUEUR

Aloha

KAHALA HILTON HOTEL,
HONOLULU

1½ ounces rum cream liqueur
1 ounce dark rum
½ ounce lime juice
2 ounces pineapple juice
2 ounces orange juice
1 ounce coconut syrup, or to taste
Small scoop of vanilla ice cream
1 scoop crushed ice
1 fresh pineapple strip

Mix all the ingredients, except the pineapple strip, in a blender until smooth. Do not overmix. Pour the blend into a chilled hurricane or collins glass. Garnish with the pineapple strip.

SAMBUCA

Fox Tail

1 ounce Sambuca
½ ounce heavy cream
Pinch of instant coffee powder

Pour the Sambuca into a pony glass. Using the back of a spoon, slowly pour the cream in so that it floats on top. Finally, dust the drink with the coffee powder.

Hot Shot

THE BALBOA CAFE, SAN FRANCISCO

½ ounce Sambuca
½ ounce hot coffee
Whipped cream

Pour the Sambuca and coffee into a pony glass. Layer the freshly whipped cream on top.

Roman Snowball

1 scoop crushed ice
2 to 3 ounces Sambuca
5 coffee beans

Fill a tulip glass with the ice, then pour in the Sambuca. Drop the coffee beans into the glass and serve this drink with a straw. You can chew the coffee beans after they have soaked in the Sambuca.

SLOE GIN

Love

Makes 2 servings

4 ounces sloe gin
1 egg white
1 ounce lemon juice
Several dashes of grenadine
2 scoops crushed ice

Combine all the ingredients in a shaker. Mix well and pour into chilled cocktail glasses.

Moulin Rouge

1½ ounces sloe gin
½ ounce sweet vermouth
Several dashes of bitters
1 scoop crushed ice

Mix all the ingredients in a shaker. Strain the mixture into a chilled cocktail glass.

Sloe Gin Cocktail

1½ ounces sloe gin
½ ounce dry vermouth

Combine both ingredients in a shaker with ice. Shake well. Strain the mixture into a chilled cocktail glass.

Sloe Screw

1½ ounces sloe gin
Orange juice

Pour the sloe gin over ice cubes in an old-fashioned glass. Top off the glass with orange juice and stir.

Stoplight

2 ounces sloe gin
1 ounce gin
1 ounce lemon juice
1 scoop crushed ice
1 maraschino cherry

Mix the sloe gin, gin, and lemon juice in a shaker with crushed ice. Strain the mixture into a chilled cocktail glass. Garnish with the cherry.

TRIPLE SEC

Alfonso Special

1½ ounces Triple Sec
¾ ounce gin
1 teaspoon dry vermouth
1 teaspoon sweet vermouth
Several dashes of bitters
Crushed ice

Combine all the ingredients in a shaker. Mix well and strain into a chilled cocktail glass.

Beverly's Hills

1½ ounces Triple Sec
½ ounce Cognac
¼ ounce coffee liqueur
Crushed ice

Mix all the ingredients in a shaker. Strain the mixture into a chilled cocktail glass.

Café du Franc

GORDON RESTAURANT, CHICAGO

Burnt sugar
Cinnamon
½ ounce Triple Sec
½ ounce hazelnut liqueur
½ ounce Irish cream
Hot coffee
Whipped cream

Coat the rim of a coffee mug with the sugar and cinnamon. Pour all three liqueurs into the coffee mug. Top off with hot coffee and a dollop of the whipped cream.

Lollipop

1 ounce Triple Sec
1 ounce green Chartreuse
1 ounce kirsch
Dash of maraschino liqueur

In a shaker, mix all the ingredients with ice. Strain the mixture into a cocktail glass without ice.

Stewart Plaid

1 ounce Triple Sec
¾ ounce coffee liqueur
½ ounce Irish cream

Combine all the ingredients in a shaker with ice. Shake well and strain into a cocktail glass.

Two-Wheeler

2 ounces Triple Sec
3 ounces orange juice
2 ounces cream

Mix all the ingredients in a shaker with ice. Strain the mixture into a chilled cocktail glass or a wineglass.

Velvet Hammer

1 ounce Triple Sec
1 ounce white crème de cacao
1 ounce heavy cream
1 scoop crushed ice

Combine all the ingredients in a shaker. Mix well. Strain the mixture into a chilled cocktail glass.

TUACA

Griswold Inn Hot Apple Cider

GRISWOLD INN, ESSEX, CONNECTICUT

1½ ounces Tuaca
Hot apple cider
Whipped cream

Pour the Tuaca into a glass coffee mug. Top off the mug with hot apple cider and a dollop of the whipped cream.

Hot Apple Pie

THE BALBOA CAFE, SAN FRANCISCO

1½ ounces Tuaca
Apple juice or cider
Whipped cream
Freshly grated nutmeg
Cinnamon stick

Add the Tuaca to a mug of hot apple juice or cider. Layer fresh whipped cream on top and sprinkle on the nutmeg. Garnish with the cinnamon stick.

WINE DRINKS

A great cocktail doesn't necessarily have to include spirits. Certain wines and fortified wines add style and complexity to mixed drinks. In fact, over the last decade with the trend toward lighter drinks, wine drinks have become more and more important.

Drinks using champagne or sparkling wines have been particularly successful. The elegance of these drinks makes them popular as apéritifs before formal dinners. In addition, still wine is wonderful in punches and some mixed drinks.

A whole other group of drinks uses fortified wines—sherry, port, and Madeira. These rich, intense wines have had brandy blended into them to stabilize their flavors and increase ("fortify") their alcohol content.

MADEIRA

Most people have heard of Madeira but have never tasted it. Some have used this great wine only for cooking.

Madeira is a fortified wine made in a group of islands located 350 miles off the coast of Morocco. During colonial times, it was extremely popular in America. Legend has it that the signing of the Declaration of Independence was celebrated with a toast of Madeira. The wine was reputedly George Washington's favorite.

Madeira's popularity hit its peak in the mid-nineteenth century, but then the vineyards suffered a double tragedy. First they fell victim to oidium, a damaging mildew, and then, a few years later, phylloxera, the vine louse that destroyed most of the vineyards of Europe. By the time the Madeira vineyards had recovered enough to produce adequate commercial quantities, Madeira's popularity had disappeared.

What a shame, because Madeira may very well be one of the best of all. It surely is the most interesting of all fortified wines.

Madeira uses varietal grape names to label its wines. Although some of the great varieties have been replaced with others since the phylloxera blight, the wines are still labeled "Sercial," the driest type; "Verdelho," off-dry to medium; "Boal" (also called "Bual"), sweet; and "Malmsey," sweetest of all. There is also a sweet blend called "Rainwater."

PORT

Port is a wine that was designed for export by the exporters. The wine, as we know it today, was created to please wine drinkers in England, not Portugal. English wine merchants were looking for a wine to replace popular French varieties, the supply of which was frequently being cut off because of hostilities between Britain and France. In the late 1600s they discovered the wines of the Douro in Portugal.

The Douro River winds through the green hills of northern Portugal and empties into the Atlantic at Oporto, a handsome city whose name translates as "the port." The wine that was being grown on the slopes along the river was harsh, strong, and lacking in finesse.

English merchants, recognizing the basic soundness of the wines, suggested winemaking improvements to the peasant farmers who produced them. They even brought coopers from England to teach the Portuguese how to make barrels. Eventually they were able to reconstruct the wine in a style that they knew would sell back home.

The wine did get better and did become popular in England. But it changed again, this time dramatically. In the mid-eighteenth century, many growers began adding brandy to the wine in the fermenting tank. The effect of this was to stop the fermentation process while there was still some natural grape sweetness in the wine.

Port became a fixture in England and its popularity has spread to every part of the world. The current annual production in the port region is 12 million cases. The grapes are grown in 85,000 vineyards, many of which climb up steep slopes that are carved into narrow terraces. This vast number of properties is distributed among 25,000 owners.

Forty-eight different grape varieties are grown in the delimited region—twenty white and twenty-eight red. Fifteen of the varieties are considered particularly desirable, while the others are acceptable or merely tolerated. Among the best reds is Pinot Noir, known in Portugal as Tinta Francisca. White port is often made from Malvasia grapes, a variety that is also grown in Madeira, South Africa, and California.

There are two basic types of port: wood port and bottle port. Wood port is wine that ages in wood until it is ready to drink. After bottling, wood ports do not need further aging, although some of them will improve when kept for a year or two.

Wood ports are made in three types: ruby, tawny, and white. Ruby, the most popular of all ports, is deep and full-bodied. Ruby port, a blend of wines from three or four vintages, is usually sweet and fruity in flavor.

Tawny ports can be made by blending red and white ports, or by using older ruby ports that have developed an amber hue. Inexpensive tawnies are made the first way, while the more expensive versions are always blends of only well-aged red wines—ruby ports that have been aged twenty years or more. Tawny differs from ruby in that it is subtler, deeper, less sweet, with a nutlike flavor.

White ports are made the same way red ports are made; the only difference is that white grapes are used. The wine is generally drier than either ruby or tawny, but it has the same rich, nutty flavor.

Bottle ports are wines that are meant to age and improve in the bottle rather than in the barrel. The finest bottle port is vintage port, the greatest of all fortified wines. These wines come from the best vineyards in the best years and are vinified in the painstaking traditional manner, which includes crushing by treading.

A classic vintage will approach its peak between fifteen and twenty-five years after the harvest. It maintains its character for another fifteen years or more and then slowly loses depth and color. However, a good vintage port almost never becomes undrinkable because its high alcohol content acts as a preservative. Wines more than 100 years old can be very attractive.

The most important vintages declared since 1960 were: 1960, 1962, 1963, 1966, 1967, 1970, 1972, 1975, 1977, 1979, 1980, 1983, 1985, and 1991.

The most reliable port shippers are: Calem, Cockburn, Croft, Delaforce, Dow, Ferreira, Fonseca, Graham, Offley Forrester, Sandeman, Taylor, and Warre.

Port is usually consumed after dinner in small stemmed glasses. It is exquisite sipped alone, without accompaniment, but it also can be quite delicious with cheese (Stilton is the preferred type), fruit, or nuts. Port is also an interesting addition to mixed drinks.

SHERRY

Sherry is produced in the town of Jerez de la Frontera in Spain's sunny province of Andalusia. (In fact, the name "sherry" is an anglicization of Jerez, known as Xeres in France.) This region, north of Cadiz and Gibraltar on the Atlantic coast, has a climate that is ideal for growing wine grapes. The vineyards surround the town (the "Frontera" is a result of Jerez being a frontier outpost in the defense against the Moors) and two neighboring villages, Sanlucar de Barameda and Puerto de Santa Maria.

The Palomino grape, the major variety used in sherry, is grown on vines that have a life span of twenty to thirty years. At that age, when the vines' productivity begins to decline, they are pulled out and the soil is allowed to rest for five years or more. Every year land is rotated, some being retired, some coming into service anew.

Palomino vines are planted only in albariza soil, which is almost white because of its 40 percent chalk content. This earth, although troublesome to cultivate and low in yield, soaks up water in the rainy season.

Because of the unusual properties of the soil, approximately two dozen distinct operations are needed throughout the year to assure a successful vintage. Besides such time-consuming jobs as fertilizing, pruning, staking, and tying, vineyard workers must make bowl-shaped hollows around each vine to collect water during the rainy season. This procedure is begun only when there are sure signs of approaching rain; otherwise the delicate exposed roots can be scorched. At the end of the rainy period, the water holes have to be filled and the soil leveled.

This leveling goes on all during the spring, and the earth is also tamped to minimize the evaporation of moisture. Eventually, this difficult work leads to the harvest in September, when the tight bunches of plump, tough-skinned greenish grapes are picked. The harvest lasts until all the vines have been picked over several times.

Although there are more than six thousand growers in the region, most of whom have been making sherry for more than a century, the industry is dominated by about a dozen enormous companies. Several of these operations are family owned and have British, rather than

Spanish, names. This is one of the indications of the 400-year-old English passion for sherry. Another is the fact that nearly 40 percent of all the sherry production is shipped to the British Isles, while only 6 percent finds its way to buyers in the United States.

It took several centuries for the sherry we drink now to evolve. The wine that Falstaff referred to as "sack" was a product of Jerez, but it was very different from the wine produced there today. In the early 1700s, large above-ground warehouses (called *bodegas*) were erected in and around Jerez and, after almost a century of experimentation, the *solera* system, the method that sets sherry apart from all other wines, was perfected.

Sherry lives its first seven or eight years in 132-gallon butts (casks) made of fine-grained American oak. After the crush, which in some locations is still accomplished by stomping, the new wine is left to ferment slowly for two to three months in these casks until all its sugar content has been converted to alcohol. By New Year's Day, the young wine "falls bright"—all the impurities drop to the bottom of the cask, clarifying the wine.

At this point, the wine is given its first tentative classification. Like the men who make it, sherry is ruggedly individualistic, and actually decides by itself whether it is to be a pale fino or a heavier, more darkly colored oloroso. The process by which the wine does this is still a mystery. Two butts harvested and crushed at the same time from grapes grown side by side in one vineyard often develop differently.

And how very different they are. Fino is completely dry and very light in color. It has a light to medium body and a flavor that is elegant and crisp. Oloroso, on the other hand, is a deeply golden-amber wine with a nutty aroma and a flavor that is somewhat sweet.

It is possible to distinguish between a fino and an oloroso at this early stage because a fino develops a thick coating of yeast on its surface, while an oloroso does not. This yeast cap is called the *flor*.

Some fino becomes amontillado, a wine that acquires the burnished character of an oloroso, with a full body, a crisp nutty taste, and, depending on the shipper, a dry to slightly sweet taste.

After this period of declaration and maturation, called the *anadas* stage, fino and amontillado wines are fortified with grape brandy to 15½ percent alcohol, while olorosos are raised to 18 percent alcohol. Then the sherry is introduced to the solera, where young wines are blended with older ones to produce a wine of consistent taste and quality. The solera system is made up of row upon row of identical butts, each row containing wine one year older than that in the row above it. Soleras are often ten rows high.

Wine for shipment is always drawn from the oldest (bottom) row of casks, but never more than half the wine in this tier is withdrawn in one single year. The bottom butts are replenished by wine drawn from the row above, topped off with wine from the row above it, which is, in turn, refilled from the row above it, and so on. This complex method of fractional blending eliminates the effect of any differences in vintages and creates a wine of extraordinary depth and complexity.

Prior to shipping, the wines are fined (clarified) with beaten egg whites, which settle slowly through the wine, removing impurities as they go. Then the alcoholic content of the wines is adjusted through the addition of neutrally flavored grape brandy. Finally, dryness and paleness are regulated by the addition of sweet solera wine made from the Pedro Ximenez (or PX) grape. All of these options give each individual shipper a personal and distinctive style.

Several of the big Jerez shippers maintain bodegas in the town of Sanlucar de Barrameda, where the salt air from the Atlantic Ocean adds a definite fragrance and lightness, tinged with a slight bitterness. The fino made there, called manzanilla, is a marvelously delicate wine that ranges from pale green to gold in color. Unfortunately, manzanilla is the ultimate example of a wine that doesn't travel well, and if moved from Sanlucar, it loses some of its special characteristics.

Cream sherries are dark olorosos that have been sweetened. They are rich, luscious, and very creamy in texture.

VERMOUTH

There are two basic types of vermouth—dry and sweet. Dry vermouth is the pale French style that is herbal and soft with a nutty, sherry-like finish. This is the type of vermouth that is used in the martini. Noilly Prat (a French firm), Martini & Rossi, and Cinzano (two Italian firms) are the primary producers. There are also domestic versions made.

Sweet vermouth—the Italian style—is ruby to dark amber in color. It has a sweet, lush, smooth, and spicy flavor. It is the type of vermouth used in such mixed drinks as manhattans and negronis. Punt e Mes is the richest and most flavorful version, but there are also excellent sweet vermouths made in northern Italy by Cinzano and Martini & Rossi. There are domestic versions as well.

There are a few interesting new vermouths on the market that are intended to be consumed on their own, as apéritifs. Martini & Rossi makes a sweet, lush, and spicy white vermouth called "Bianco." Cinzano has released two "Riservas," departures that emphasize varietal grape varieties instead of the usual neutral base wine. The white is mostly Chardonnay, while the red is predominantly Cabernet. All vermouths range from 16 to 19 percent in alcohol. In addition, many apértif wines are made with a mostly vermouth base. These wines are usually spiced, slightly sweet, and can be either red or white.

Madeira

Boston Eggnog

1 egg yolk
¾ teaspoon sugar
4 ounces Madeira
½ ounce brandy
¼ ounce rum
Cold milk
Freshly grated nutmeg

Beat the egg and sugar in a shaker. Add crushed ice, Madeira, brandy, and rum to the shaker. Shake well and strain into a tall glass. Top off with cold milk and fresh ice. Sprinkle nutmeg on top.

Port

Broken Spur

1½ ounces white port
1 ounce gin
1 ounce sweet vermouth
1 teaspoon anisette
1 egg yolk
1 scoop crushed ice

Combine all the ingredients in a shaker. Mix well and pour into a chilled old-fashioned glass.

Chocolate Cocktail

3 ounces ruby port
1 ounce yellow Chartreuse
1 egg yolk
1 teaspoon grated chocolate

Mix the port, Chartreuse, and egg yolk in a shaker with ice. Strain the mixture into a chilled cocktail glass and sprinkle with a bit of the grated chocolate.

Red Wine

Appetizer

2 to 3 ounces red apéritif wine
Juice of 1 orange
1 scoop crushed ice

Combine all the ingredients in a blender. Mix well and strain into a cocktail glass.

The Locomotive

6 ounces dry red wine
½ ounce curaçao
½ ounce maraschino liqueur
½ ounce honey
1 egg
Lemon slice
Ground cinnamon

In a saucepan, mix red wine, curaçao, maraschino, and honey. Stir well until the honey is dissolved. Gradually warm the mixture over direct heat, but do not boil. Beat the egg lightly and stir it into the wine. Bring the mixture to a simmer. Pour into a warmed mug. Top with the lemon slice and a bit of the ground cinnamon.

Portland Cocktail

1½ ounces red apéritif wine
1½ ounces light rum
4 dashes of orange bitters
Twist of ripe lime peel

Stir the wine, rum, and bitters with ice until well chilled. Strain the mixture into a chilled cocktail glass and garnish with the lime peel.

Trump's Sangria

TRUMPS, WEST HOLLYWOOD, CALIFORNIA

Orange slice
Lemon slice
8 ounces red wine
Dash of anisette
1½ ounces Triple Sec
1 ounce orange juice
Cold club soda

Squeeze the orange and lemon slices into a 16-ounce balloon glass. Add ice and the remaining ingredients, except the soda. Top off with soda.

T Street Punch

Makes 48 (4-ounce) servings

2 pounds confectioners' sugar
Juice of 2 dozen lemons
1 pint strong tea
3 (750 ml) bottles dry red wine
1 (750 ml) bottle brandy
1 (750 ml) bottle chilled
    champagne or sparkling wine
Lemon slices

In a large punch bowl, dissolve the sugar in the lemon juice. Add the tea and large chunks of ice. Pour in the wine and the brandy and chill for 2 hours. Before serving, pour in the champagne. Serve the punch in wine goblets and decorate with the lemon slices.

Sherry

Adonis Cocktail

3 ounces fino sherry
1 ounce sweet vermouth
Dash of orange bitters
Twist of orange peel

Mix all the ingredients, except the orange peel, in a small pitcher with ice. Strain the mixture into a cocktail glass. Drop the orange peel into the glass.

Brandy Bonanza

1½ ounces sherry
1 ounce brandy
Chilled riesling or other crisp
    white wine

Pour the brandy and sherry into a highball glass. Top off with the chilled wine.

Sherry Cobbler

1 scoop crushed ice
Several dashes of curaçao
Several dashes of pineapple syrup
4 ounces amontillado sherry
Twist of lemon peel
Mint sprig
Pineapple stick

Fill a large wine goblet with crushed ice. Add the curaçao and syrup. Add the sherry and churn until the outside of the glass appears frosty. Drop the lemon peel into the drink. Garnish with the mint and the pineapple.

Straight Law Cocktail

2 ounces fino sherry
1 ounce gin
Twist of lemon

Mix the sherry and the gin with ice. Strain the mixture into a chilled cocktail glass. Twist the lemon peel over the drink and drop it in.

Sparkling Wine and Champagne

American Flyer

1½ ounces light rum
¼ ounce lime juice
½ teaspoon sugar syrup,
  or to taste
1 scoop crushed ice
Champagne or sparkling wine

Combine all the ingredients, except the champagne, in a shaker and mix thoroughly. Strain the mixture into a chilled wineglass. Top off with chilled champagne.

Black Velvet

½ pint champagne or sparkling wine
½ pint Guinness stout or other dark porter

Chill both ingredients and pour them into a chilled highball glass. Stir minimally in order to preserve the fizz.

Breakers' French 75

1 ounce gin
½ ounce lemon juice
Champagne or sparkling wine

Mix the gin and lemon juice in a highball glass. Add ice cubes and top off with champagne.

Caribbean Champagne

4 ounces dry champagne
½ teaspoon white rum
½ teaspoon banana liquer
2 dashes of orange bitters
½ scoop crushed ice
1 banana slice

In a saucer-shaped champagne glass, stir all the ingredients, except the banana. Garnish with the banana slice.

Champagne Cooler

1 ounce brandy
1 ounce Triple Sec
Champagne or sparkling wine
Mint sprigs

Pour the brandy and Triple Sec into a chilled wine goblet. Top off with champagne and stir gently. Garnish with the mint sprigs.

Champagne Julep

Mint leaves
1 teaspoon sugar syrup
1 scoop crushed ice
3 ounces bourbon
Brut champagne or dry sparkling wine

Muddle about a half-dozen mint leaves in a tall collins glass with the syrup. Fill the glass two thirds full with crushed ice. Pour in the bourbon and stir briskly. Add additional ice, if necessary. Top off with cold champagne or sparkling wine. Stir gently and garnish with a large mint sprig.

Earthquake Cooler

1 ounce vodka
1 ounce orange liqueur
Dash of lime juice
Dash of orange bitters
Champagne or dry sparkling wine

Mix all the ingredients, except the champagne, in a shaker with crushed ice. Strain the mixture into a large chilled wineglass. Top off with some chilled champagne and stir gently.

French 75

1 ounce lemon juice
$\frac{1}{2}$ ounce sugar syrup, or to taste
$1\frac{1}{2}$ ounces Cognac or other good brandy
Brut champagne or sparkling wine

In a collins glass, mix the lemon juice and sugar syrup with several ice cubes. Stir until the sugar is dissolved. Add the Cognac and top off with cold champagne.

Imperial Kir

2 ounces crème de cassis
1 ounce kirsch
Crushed ice
Champagne, sparkling wine, or white wine

Mix the cassis and kirsch in a shaker with crushed ice. Pour the mixture into a large wineglass. Top off with cold champagne or wine and stir gently.

Luscious Lisa

1 ounce brandy
1/2 ounce raspberry liqueur
4 ounces brut champagne or
   sparkling wine
1/2 teaspoon framboise

Stir the brandy and raspberry liquer in a mixing glass with ice cubes. Pour the mixture into a chilled tulip glass. Top off the glass with cold champagne and a framboise float.

Mimosa

6 ounces brut champagne or
   sparkling wine
3 ounces orange juice, preferably
   freshly squeezed

Chill both ingredients, then mix in a chilled wine goblet.

Soyer au Champagne

2 tablespoons vanilla ice cream
Several dashes of curaçao
Several dashes of maraschino
   liqueur
Several dashes of brandy
4 ounces champagne or sparkling
   wine
Orange slice
1 maraschino cherry

Put the vanilla ice cream into a large champagne flute. Add the curaçao, maraschino, and brandy. Mix well. Top off the glass with cold champagne and stir. Garnish with the orange slice and maraschino cherry.

SIGNATURE DRINKS

Aureole Cocktail

AUREOLE, NEW YORK CITY

1/2 teaspoon raspberry wine
5 ounces champagne or sparkling
   wine

Pour the raspberry wine into a champagne flute. Top off the flute with chilled champagne.

Ballroom Derby

THE BALLROOM, NEW YORK CITY

5 ounces champagne or sparkling
   wine
Dash of dry sherry
Twist of lemon

Combine all the ingredients in a fluted champagne glass and serve.

Beau Nash Splash

HOTEL CRESCENT COURT, DALLAS

1 tablespoon Mandarin Napoleon
   liqueur
4½ ounces brut champagne or
   sparkling wine
Twist of orange peel

Pour the liqueur into a champagne
flute. Add the champagne to the
flute. Garnish with the orange twist.

Bellini

BELLINI BY CIPRIANI, NEW YORK CITY

3 ounces champagne or sparkling
   wine
1 ounce white peach juice

Mix both ingredients in a mixing
glass or bowl. Pour the mixture into
a champagne flute.

Note: In Venice, at Harry's Bar, bel-
linis are invariably made with Prosecco, a sparkling white wine from
the Veneto.

Champagne Cocktail

THE SIGN OF THE DOVE,
NEW YORK CITY

1 small sugar cube
2 to 3 drops of Angostura bitters
Splash of brandy
Splash of Grand Marnier
4½ ounces champagne or
   sparkling wine

Place the sugar cube in a glass. Add
the bitters, then a touch each of
brandy and Grand Marnier. Top off
with the champagne or sparkling
wine. (This drink has an attractive
amber color but only a hint of bitterness, and the sugar cube causes bubbles to rise furiously and steadily.)

Champagne Royal

THE PUMP ROOM, CHICAGO

½ ounce black raspberry liqueur
½ ounce pear brandy
1 fresh strawberry
4 ounces champagne or sparkling
   wine

Place the liqueur, brandy, and strawberry in a champagne glass and
freeze. After frozen, top off with
champagne.

Jade

DORCHESTER HOTEL, LONDON

Dash of melon liqueur
Dash of blue curaçao
Dash of lime juice
Dash of bitters
4 ounces champagne or sparkling
  wine
Lime slice
1 green cherry

Mix the melon liqueur, curaçao, juice, and bitters in a shaker with crushed ice. Strain the mixture into a tall champagne glass and top off with the champagne. Garnish with the lime and green cherry.

Strawberry Mimosa

NEW YORK HILTON, NEW YORK CITY

3½ ounces orange juice
3 to 4 large strawberries
3½ ounces brut champagne or
  sparkling wine

In a blender, mix the orange juice and strawberries with a little crushed ice. Pour the blend into a chilled wineglass. Top off with cold champagne or sparkling wine and stir gently.

Rose

THE WESTIN ST. FRANCIS,
SAN FRANCISCO

¼ ounce black raspberry liqueur
5 ounces brut champagne or
  sparkling wine
Twist of lemon

Pour the liqueur into a champagne flute. Fill the glass with the champagne. Garnish with the lemon twist.

CHAMPAGNE PUNCHES

Champagne Cup

Makes 10 servings

1 quart champagne or sparkling
   wine
1½ ounces Grand Marnier
1½ ounces maraschino liqueur
3 ounces curaçao
6 ounces brandy
1 tablespoon confectioners' sugar
Orange slices
Pineapple slices
Cucumber peel
4 mint sprigs

Combine all the ingredients, except
the fruit, cucumber, and mint, in a
large pitcher with several ice cubes.
Stir well and garnish with the orange, pineapple, cucumber, and
mint sprigs.

Roman Punch

Makes 30 (5-ounce) servings

2 pounds sugar
Juice of 10 lemons
Juice of 3 oranges
10 egg whites
1 quart champagne or sparkling
   wine
1 quart gold rum
½ ounce orange bitters

In a large punch bowl, dissolve the
sugar in the fruit juices. Add the rind
of 1 orange to the punch bowl. Separately beat the egg whites, then add
them to the punch. Pour in the
champagne, rum, and bitters and stir
well. Keep the punch cold by sur-
rounding the bowl with crushed ice.

Vermouth

Achampanado

3 to 4 ounces dry vermouth
½ teaspoon sugar syrup
Juice of ¼ lime
Cold club soda

Pour the vermouth into a chilled collins glass with ice. Add the syrup and lime juice. Stir until the sugar syrup is dissolved. Top off with club soda.

Addington

2 ounces dry vermouth
2 ounces sweet vermouth
Cold club soda
Twist of orange peel

Pour both vermouths into a chilled collins glass over ice. Top off with club soda and stir. Twist the orange peel over the glass and drop it in.

Americano

⅔ ounce sweet vermouth
⅓ ounce Campari
Splash of Perrier
Orange slice
Lime slice

Pour all the liquid ingredients into an ice-filled cocktail glass. Stir well and garnish with the orange and lime slices.

Chrysanthemum Cocktail

2 ounces dry vermouth
1½ ounces Benedictine
Several dashes of Pernod
Twist of orange peel

Stir the vermouth and Benedictine in a mixing glass with ice. Strain the mixture into a chilled cocktail glass. Add the Pernod and stir. Drop the orange twist into the drink.

Duchess Cocktail

⅓ ounce dry vermouth
⅓ ounce sweet vermouth
⅓ ounce Pernod

Combine all the ingredients in a shaker with crushed ice. Mix well and strain into a chilled cocktail glass.

Harvard Wine

1 ounce dry vermouth
¾ ounce brandy
Dash of orange bitters
Cold club soda

In a mixing glass with ice, stir the vermouth, brandy, and bitters. Pour the mixture into a chilled cocktail glass and top off with club soda.

Hong Kong

1 ounce dry vermouth
1 ounce gin
¼ ounce lime juice
Dash of bitters
¼ teaspoon sugar

Mix all the ingredients in a shaker with crushed ice. Pour the mixture into a chilled cocktail glass.

Lamb's Club

¾ ounce dry vermouth
¾ ounce sweet vermouth
¾ ounce gin
¼ ounce Benedictine

Stir all the ingredients in a mixing glass with ice. Pour the mixture into a chilled cocktail glass.

Lone Tree

¾ ounce dry vermouth
¾ ounce sweet vermouth
¾ ounce gin
Several dashes of orange bitters
1 scoop crushed ice
1 olive

Mix all the ingredients, except the olive, in a shaker. Strain the mixture into a chilled cocktail glass and garnish with the olive.

Picon

1 ounce sweet vermouth
1 ounce Amer Picon
1 scoop crushed ice

Mix all the ingredients in a shaker. Pour the mixture into a chilled cocktail glass.

San Francisco

1 ounce dry vermouth
1 ounce sweet vermouth
1 ounce sloe gin
Several dashes of bitters
Several dashes of orange bitters
1 scoop crushed ice

Mix all the ingredients in a shaker. Pour the mixture into a chilled cocktail glass.

Serpent's Tooth

1½ ounces sweet vermouth
¾ ounce Irish whiskey
½ ounce kümmel
¾ ounce lemon juice
Several dashes of bitters
1 scoop crushed ice
Lemon peel

Mix all the ingredients, except the lemon peel, in a shaker. Pour the mixture into a chilled old-fashioned glass. Twist the lemon peel over the drink and drop it in.

Third Edition

1 ounce sweet vermouth
1 ounce dry vermouth
1 ounce gin
1 teaspoon white crème de menthe
Several dashes of orange bitters

Pour all the ingredients into a mixing glass with several ice cubes. Strain the mixture into a chilled cocktail glass.

Third Rail

2 to 3 ounces dry vermouth
Several dashes of curaçao
Several dashes of peppermint
    schnapps
Lemon or orange peel

Stir the vermouth, curaçao, and schnapps with ice cubes in a mixing glass. Strain into a chilled cocktail glass. Twist the lemon or orange peel over the drink and drop it in.

Vermouth Cassis

3 ounces dry vermouth
1 ounce crème de cassis
Cold club soda

Mix the vermouth and cassis in a chilled highball glass with ice. Top off the glass with club soda.

White Wine

Kir

5 ounces dry white wine
½ ounce crème de cassis

Chill both ingredients. Mix them in
a chilled wineglass.

SIGNATURE DRINKS

Dorchester Coupe aux Fraises

DORCHESTER HOTEL, LONDON

3 or 4 strawberries
½ ounce brandy
½ ounce orange liqueur
2½ ounces white wine
2½ ounces sparkling wine
Fresh mint sprig

In a small bowl, marinate the strawberries in the brandy and orange liqueur. After several hours, place the
strawberries in a champagne glass
and top with the white and sparkling
wines. Garnish with the fresh mint
sprig.

Occidental White Sangria

OCCIDENTAL GRILL, WASHINGTON, D.C.

Makes 4 servings

18 ounces dry but fruity wine
  (Chenin Blanc)
1½ ounces gin
1½ ounces brandy
¾ ounce liquid sour mix
2 ounces 7-Up
2 ounces ginger ale
½ ounce diced apple
1½ ounces diced lemon
1½ ounces diced orange

Fill a 44-ounce pitcher with ice. Add
all the ingredients and stir well. You
may also add other diced summer
fruits such as pears, apricots, and
peaches.

NONALCOHOLIC DRINKS

Nowadays, nonalcoholic drinks have assumed an increasingly important role. We have become more and more aware of the problem of alcohol abuse, especially as it relates to driving. Everyone, at one time or another, is confronted with circumstances that require the avoidance of alcohol, if only temporarily.

As a permanent or a temporary teetotaler, one needn't always opt for boring bottled water or dreary soft drinks. Some of the same creative energy that went into many of the mixed drinks that precede this chapter, have also had a role in concocting the following interesting combinations of nonalcoholic ingredients.

CLASSICS

Almost Cape Cod

3 ounces cranberry juice
3 ounces white grape juice
Orange peel, cut into a long spiral

Pour the juices into a chilled cocktail glass over ice cubes. Twist the orange peel over the drink, then drape it over the glass.

Black Cow

10 ounces cold root beer
1 scoop vanilla ice cream

Pour 3½ ounces of the root beer into a 14-ounce chilled tall glass. Add 2 teaspoons of the ice cream and stir. When creamy, add the remaining ice cream and pour in the rest of the root beer.

Bloody Mary—Not!

Makes 4 (8-ounce) servings

1 quart tomato juice
¼ cup bottled horseradish,
    or 2 tablespoons freshly grated
    horseradish
¼ cup chopped green bell pepper
¼ cup chopped celery
¼ cup chopped scallions
2 teaspoons hot pepper sauce,
    or to taste
4 celery ribs

In a blender, blend half the tomato juice with the horseradish, green pepper, celery, and scallions. Add the hot pepper sauce. Pour the blend into an ice cube tray and freeze until the blend is solid. Place 4 wineglasses in the freezer to frost. When the blend is frozen solid, empty the cubes into the blender and add the rest of the tomato juice. Blend until smooth. Pour the blend into the frosted wineglasses and garnish with the celery ribs.

Lemonade

Juice of 1 lemon
2 tablespoons sugar
1 scoop crushed ice
6 ounces water
1 lemon peel spiral
1 lemon slice

In a shaker, mix together the lemon juice, sugar, and crushed ice. Strain the mixture into a tall, chilled collins glass. Fill the glass with the water and stir well. Garnish with the lemon peel and the lemon slice.

Shirley Temple

1½ ounces grenadine
5½ ounces lemon-lime soda
4 or 5 ice cubes
1 maraschino cherry

Pour the grenadine and soda into a chilled cocktail glass with the ice cubes. Stir well and garnish with the maraschino cherry.

Virgin Eggnog

10 ounces milk
1 egg
1 scoop crushed ice
1 teaspoon grated nutmeg or
    ground cinnamon

Combine the milk, egg, and crushed
ice in a shaker. Shake well and strain
into a chilled tall collins glass. Sprinkle the nutmeg or cinnamon on top.

Virgin Mary

3 ounces tomato juice or V-8 juice
3 ounces clam juice
3 dashes of Tabasco
3 dashes of Worcestershire sauce
½ teaspoon lemon juice
1 scoop crushed ice
1 teaspoon finely chopped fresh
    dill

Mix all the ingredients, except the
dill, in a shaker. Shake well and pour
into a chilled old-fashioned glass.
Top off with the chopped dill.

Wassail

Makes 14 (4-ounce) servings

3 cups apple cider
1 cup unsweetened pineapple juice
1½ cups orange juice
½ cup grapefruit juice
½ cup lemon juice
2 cinnamon sticks
1½ teaspoons allspice
½ teaspoon ground cloves
½ cup superfine sugar, or to taste
1 orange
14 whole cloves

Put the cider, the juices, and the
cinnamon sticks in a large saucepan.
Tie the allspice and ground cloves in
a cheesecloth and drop it into the
saucepan. Bring the mixture to a
boil, then reduce the heat and simmer for 5 minutes. Taste the wassail
and add the sugar to taste. Slice the
orange into 7 cross-sectional slices.
Cut each orange slice in half and
pierce each half with a clove. Pour
½ cup of the hot wassail into each
punch cup and garnish with the
clove-studded orange section.

CREATIVE CONCOCTIONS

Big Banana

½ ripe banana, peeled and sliced
4 ounces cold milk
1 ounce pineapple juice
1 teaspoon coconut extract
4 ounces crushed ice

Combine all the ingredients in a blender and blend until smooth. Pour the blend into a chilled tall collins glass.

Corona Punch

Makes 46 servings

2 quarts fresh orange juice
1 quart fresh grapefruit juice
1 quart ginger ale
1 cup fresh lime juice
1 cup orgeat or sugar syrup, to taste
½ cup grenadine
1 large cake of ice

Chill all the ingredients and pour them into a chilled punch bowl. Add the ice to the bowl.

Goddaughter

½ cup cranberry juice
½ cup grapefruit juice
4 or 5 ice cubes

Mix the cranberry and grapefruit juices in a blender until foamy. Pour the mixture into a large cocktail glass with the ice cubes.

Long Boat

THE SAVOY HOTEL, LONDON

2 ounces lime juice cordial
2 ice cubes
5 ounces ginger beer or ginger ale
1 fresh mint sprig

Pour the lime juice cordial into a tall collins glass over the ice cubes. Top off with the ginger beer or ginger ale and garnish with the mint sprig.

Mendacious Mimosa

2 ounces freshly squeezed orange juice
6 ounces nonalcoholic sparkling wine
Freshly squeezed lemon juice (optional)

Pour the orange juice into a champagne flute and top with nonalcoholic sparkling wine. For a crisp, balanced drink, add lemon juice to taste.

Note: Other champagne and wine drinks can be made using nonalcoholic wines. A dash of lemon juice is often a good idea to add zip to these soft and often flabby wines.

Mickey Mouse

5 ounces cola
4 ice cubes
1 scoop vanilla ice cream
2 tablespoons whipped cream
2 maraschino cherries

Pour the cola into a tall collins glass over the ice cubes. Add the ice cream. Top off with the whipped cream and garnish with the cherries.

Orange Fizz

3 ounces orange juice
3 ounces ginger ale
4 ice cubes
1 orange slice
1 maraschino cherry

Put the orange juice, ginger ale, and ice in a large wineglass and stir gently. Garnish with the orange slice and cherry.

Orange Glow

Makes 6 (8-ounce) servings

4 cups fresh orange juice
1½ cups unsweetened pineapple juice
½ cup fresh lemon juice
2 tablespoons grenadine
4 ice cubes per serving

In a large pitcher, combine the juices and the grenadine. Stir well and pour into chilled cocktail glasses over the ice cubes.

Orange-Strawberry Smoothie

Makes 4 servings

1 quart freshly squeezed orange juice
1 cup frozen sliced strawberries

Combine the juice and strawberries in a blender and blend until smooth. Chill the blend in the refrigerator until ready to serve. When ready, pour the blend into chilled tall collins glasses.

Party Punch

Makes 8 (8-ounce) servings

1 cup fresh orange juice
Juice of 2 lemons
2 cups cranberry juice cocktail
1 cup superfine sugar
2 cups ice cubes
1 quart chilled club soda
1 orange, sliced for garnish
1 lemon, sliced for garnish

In a large pitcher, mix the juices and the sugar. Stir well to dissolve the sugar. Add the ice and pour in the club soda. Float the orange and lemon slices on top of the punch for garnish.

Pippi Longstocking

4 ounces cold apple juice
1 teaspoon grenadine
1 teaspoon lemon juice
4 ounces cold ginger ale
1 apple slice

Pour the apple juice, grenadine, and lemon juice into a champagne flute and stir well. Top off the glass with the ginger ale and garnish with the apple slice.

Pussy Foot

THE SAVOY HOTEL, LONDON

2 ounces fresh orange juice
2 ounces fresh lemon juice
2 ounces fresh lime juice
Dash of grenadine
1 egg yolk
Splash of soda water
1 maraschino cherry
1 orange slice

Combine all the ingredients, except the soda water, cherry, and orange, in a shaker. Shake well and strain into a chilled cocktail glass. Top off with a splash of the soda water and garnish with the cherry and the orange slice.

Santa Claus Cider

2 ounces half-and-half
1 egg
½ teaspoon superfine sugar
3 ounces crushed ice
6 ounces apple cider
Freshly grated nutmeg

Combine all the ingredients, except the cider and nutmeg, in a shaker. Shake well and strain into a chilled tall collins glass. Pour the cider into the glass and top with the grated nutmeg.

Strawberry-Banana-Pineapple Smoothie

Makes 4 (6-ounce) servings

1½ cups sliced stemmed
    strawberries
1 ripe banana, peeled and sliced
Juice of 1 lemon
2 tablespoons sugar
1 cup pineapple juice

Blend the strawberries, banana, lemon juice, and sugar in a blender or food processor. Slowly add the pineapple juice. Blend until smooth, then pour the blend into a mixing bowl and freeze for 1 hour. When ready to serve, fold into chilled tall collins glasses.

Tropical Treat

Makes 3 (8-ounce) servings

1 ripe mango, skinned, pitted, and
    sliced
1 banana, peeled and sliced
1 cup plain nonfat or low-fat
    yogurt
1 cup low-fat milk
2 ice cubes

Put all the ingredients in a blender. Blend until thick and creamy. Pour the blend into chilled tall collins glasses.

HOT DRINKS

Café au Lait

4 ounces hot coffee
2 ounces hot milk
2 teaspoons superfine sugar,
    or to taste

Pour the hot coffee and the hot milk into a coffee mug. Add sugar and stir to dissolve.

Café Toulouse

Makes 6 (8-ounce) servings

8 ounces heavy cream
2 tablespoons superfine sugar
1 teaspoon vanilla extract
2 egg whites
4¼ cups hot French-roast coffee

In a mixing bowl, beat the heavy cream until it is almost stiff. Add the sugar and the vanilla extract and beat until the cream holds its shape. In a separate bowl, beat the egg whites so that they are in peaks. Fold the egg whites into the whipped cream mixture. Divide the mixture into 6 warm coffee cups. Finally, pour the coffee into the cups.

Mocha Coffee

½ cup hot coffee
½ cup hot chocolate
1 tablespoon whipped cream
Dash of powdered cinnamon
Dash of grated nutmeg
Dash of grated orange peel

Pour the hot coffee and hot chocolate into a warm mug. Stir well. Top off the drink with the whipped cream, then sprinkle on the cinnamon, nutmeg, and orange peel.

Orange Flame

Makes 4 (6-ounce) servings

18 ounces cold orange juice
⅓ cup superfine sugar
6 mint sprigs
2 ounces lemon juice
20 ice cubes
4 strips orange peel

In an enamel pan over low heat, bring 8 ounces of the orange juice, the sugar, and the mint sprigs to a boil, stirring constantly. Pour the remaining orange juice and the lemon juice into the pan. Put 5 ice cubes in each chilled highball glass and pour in the drink mixture. Light a match and twist an orange peel over each drink, next to the flame. Drop a peel into each glass.

Index